thought and experience, Ayokunle offers a fresh and compelling perspective on the nature and mission of the church. *Omolúàbí*-shaped ecclesiology serves as a powerful framework for understanding how African diaspora communities can navigate the challenges of a new cultural environment while preserving their spiritual heritage.

This book offers invaluable insights into the experiences of African Christians in the UK and provides a blueprint for building vibrant, inclusive, and missional congregations. It stands as a testament to the power of rigorous academic research to illuminate the lived experiences of communities at the margins and to offer transformative theological perspectives. Having known the author to be an *omolúàbí* himself, I heartily commend the book as essential reading for those interested in the intersection of culture, theology, and church leadership.

Joseph Ola
Lecturer in African Christianity,
Church Mission Society

There are influential forces militating against church growth, especially in the diasporic context. In this book, Dr. Paul Araoluwa Ayokunle critically investigates contemporary realities influencing church growth among African diaspora congregations in Liverpool. The book is well-grounded in theoretical and practical discussions of issues relating to church growth in this context, and develops pertinent responses to the issues identified in it. This volume is essential material for researchers and practitioners in the fields of Black diasporic studies, migration studies, church growth and planting, and missiology, as well as those who are interested in knowing more about the potential of diaspora congregations for growth and reactions. This book, without any reservation whatsoever, is hereby recommended.

Deji Ayegboyin, PhD
Professor of Church History, Doctrinal Theology, and African Christianity,
University of Ibadan, Nigeria

For too long, African diaspora Christianity in western Europe has been analysed using interpretative discourses that embrace reverse mission to contrast their effectiveness with those of indigenous churches in host communities. What Paul Araoluwa Ayokunle has done in this book is employ a church growth perspective that argues that Liverpool's African diaspora congregations (ADCs) are missional communities whose growth embraces an African-shaped ecclesiology to thrive amidst Christian contraction and secularity. By using this missiological theme, the book contributes new research impetus that embellishes our understanding of ADCs beyond what currently exists in the literature.

Bosco Bangura, PhD
Assistant Professor of Missiology, World Christianity, and Intercultural Theology,
Evangelical Theological Faculty, Belgium

Once in a while, a book appears that opens up new avenues of discussing a subject in exciting ways that can potentially reshape the discipline for future generations. This book is one of those. It takes us beyond previously charted territories in the study of the church in Africa to propose an African-shaped ecclesiology (grounded on the Yoruba concept of *omolúàbí* that emphasizes the need for community and wisdom in social relations) to help African Christians follow Christ in worshipping communities shaped by African cultural sensibilities. Paul Araoluwa Ayokunle suggests that such an ecclesiology is what African Christians in the diaspora need when they seek to grow their churches beyond their own fellow African communities. This book will be helpful to teachers of theology and missions as well as leaders of diaspora congregations around the world. It comes with my recommendation.

Harvey Kwiyani, PhD
Executive Director, Missio Africanus
Lead, African Christianity Programme and Diaspora Centre,
Church Mission Society

This is a well-written and thoroughly researched book focusing on African diaspora congregations in Liverpool, but it also has findings that resonate more widely, both for the African diaspora and white British churches. Here readers will journey through the history and current state of the church growth movement, the role of contextualization as a necessary practice for church planting and leadership issues as they emerge from the research. I particularly find the chapters on ecclesiology very interesting and original, where Dr. Ayokunle develops a contextualized African ecclesiology from his Yoruba context. I think it is this very specificity that will help the research to resonate with readers and cause them to ask what an ecclesiology might look like for their own context. The chapter on church growth and dynamics of race is a key contribution to this discourse and one that deserves a wider readership, especially in the UK context.

Cathy Ross, PhD
Lead, Pioneer Mission Leadership Training Centre,
Church Mission Society
Canon Theologian, Leicester Cathedral, UK

Dr. Ayokunle's groundbreaking book offers a profound exploration of the complex dynamics shaping the growth of African diaspora congregations in a UK context. It fills a critical gap in the literature by examining the church growth phenomenon within this specific – and marginalized – context.

Ayokunle's development of the concept of *omolúàbí*-shaped ecclesiology is a significant contribution to theological discourse. Within the Yoruba tradition, to be an *omolúàbí* is to embody the virtues and values that reflect the best of humanity! By grounding ecclesiology in the rich tapestry of African

Church Growth in African Diaspora Communities

Yoruba Shaped Ecclesiology and Mission

Paul Araoluwa Ayokunle

ACADEMIC

© 2025 Paul Araoluwa Ayokunle

Published 2025 by Langham Academic
An imprint of Langham Publishing
www.langhampublishing.org

Langham Publishing and its imprints are a ministry of Langham Partnership

Langham Partnership
PO Box 296, Carlisle, Cumbria, CA3 9WZ, UK
www.langham.org

ISBNs:
978-1-83973-971-2 Print
978-1-78641-154-9 ePub
978-1-78641-155-6 PDF

Paul Araoluwa Ayokunle has asserted his right under the Copyright, Designs and Patents Act, 1988 to be identified as the Author of this work.

All rights reserved. No part of this publication may be reproduced, stored in a retrieval system or transmitted, in any form or by any means, electronic, mechanical, photocopying, recording or otherwise, without the prior written permission of the publisher or the Copyright Licensing Agency.

Requests to reuse content from Langham Publishing are processed through PLSclear. Please visit www.plsclear.com to complete your request.

Unless otherwise indicated Scripture quotations are from the Holy Bible, New International Version®, NIV®. Copyright © 1973, 1978, 1984, 2011 by Biblica, Inc.™ Used by permission of Zondervan.

Scripture quotations marked (NRSV) are from the New Revised Standard Version Bible, copyright © 1989 National Council of the Churches of Christ in the United States of America. Used by permission. All rights reserved.

Scripture quotations marked (ESV) are from The Holy Bible, English Standard Version®(ESV®), copyright © 2001 by Crossway, a publishing ministry of Good News Publishers. Used by permission. All rights reserved.

British Library Cataloguing-in-Publication Data
A catalogue record for this book is available from the British Library

ISBN: 978-1-83973-971-2

Cover & Book Design: projectluz.com

Langham Partnership actively supports theological dialogue and an author's right to publish but does not necessarily endorse the views and opinions set forth here or in works referenced within this publication, nor can we guarantee technical and grammatical correctness. Langham Partnership does not accept any responsibility or liability to persons or property as a consequence of the reading, use or interpretation of its published content.

Contents

Abstract xv
Acknowledgments xvii
List of Abbreviations xix

Chapter 1 1
   Introduction
     1.1 Research Questions and Aims 3
     1.2 Nature of the Study 4
     1.3 Background of the Study 4
     1.4 Originality and Contributions of the Study 7
     1.5 Limitations of the Study 9
     1.6 Discussion of Key Terms 10
         1.6.1 Diaspora 10
         1.6.2 African Congregation 13
         1.6.3 Church Growth 15
     1.7 Structure of the Study 19
     1.8 Conclusion 21

Chapter 2 23
   Literature Review
     2.1 Introduction 23
     2.2 Voices Attending African Diaspora Christianity in Europe
         (Britain) 23
         2.2.1 Early Explorers 24
         2.2.2 More Recent Contributors 31
         2.2.3 Present State of the Discourse 37
     2.3 On Church Growth: Pervasive Ideas 38
         2.3.1 Core Teachings of McGavran and the Church
              Growth Movement 40
     2.4 Conclusion 44

Chapter 3 45
   Methodology
     3.1 Introduction 45
     3.2 Theoretical Framework 45
         3.2.1 Qualitative Research Strategy 47
         3.2.2 Rationale for a Qualitative Research Approach 48

  3.2.3 The Relevance of Ethnography to the Study 49
3.3 Data Collection Methods 50
  3.3.1 Interviews 51
3.4 Data Collection Process..54
  3.4.1 Choice of Congregations and Participants.........................54
  3.4.2 Interview Process..56
3.5 Data Analysis and Synthesis 60
  3.5.1 Rationale for Grounded Theory Approach for Data
     Analysis..61
  3.5.2 Data Analysis Process 63
3.6 The Reflexive Researcher..65
  3.6.1 My Role as a Researcher 66
  3.6.2 Dynamics of Power and Gender 69
3.7 Ethical Considerations..71
  3.7.1 Informed Consent 71
  3.7.2 Confidentiality and Anonymity 72
  3.7.3 Non-Invasive Interaction with Participants.......................73
3.8 Conclusion 74

Chapter 4 75
Theories of Church Growth
4.1 Introduction...75
4.2 The Strictness Thesis 75
4.3 Modernization Theory..78
4.4 Types of Church Growth 79
  4.4.1 Numerical Growth 79
  4.4.2 Organic Growth..81
  4.4.3 Influence Growth..81
  4.4.4 Google Growth 82
  4.4.5 Other Typologies 83
4.5 The Holy Spirit and Church Growth...83
4.6 Prayer and Church Growth..85
4.7 Common Church Growth Models..86
  4.7.1 Megachurch Model 86
  4.7.2 Multiplication Model 87
  4.7.3 Cell Church Model...87
  4.7.4 Natural Church Development Model 88
  4.7.5 ICGK Model..88
4.8 Brief Critique of the Popular Church Growth Models.................89
4.9 Multi-Ethic Church...91
  4.9.1 In Search of a Name and Description.................................91

  4.9.2 Why Multi-Ethnic Congregations?..93
 4.10 Contextualization 95
  4.10.1 What is It?..96
  4.10.2 The Breadth of Contextualization 99
  4.10.3 Functions of Contextualization 100
 4.11 Conclusion 103

Chapter 5 105
Church Growth and Development of African Diaspora Congregations in Liverpool
 5.1 Introduction..105
 5.2 The Element of Migration 105
  5.2.1 Convergence of Migration and *Missio Dei*:
   Biblical Witness 106
  5.2.2 European Migration and the Renewal of African
   Christianity...109
 5.3 How Christianity Is Looking in Britain and the Wider West.....112
 5.4 Streams of African Christianity in Britain and the Rise of
  African Diaspora Congregations...113
 5.5 African Diaspora Congregations in Liverpool 115
  5.5.1 Daniels Ekarte and the African Churches Mission
   (ACM)...116
  5.5.2 From ACM to Present Time 118
 5.6 Conclusion 120

Chapter 6 121
Research Findings and Implications
 6.1 Introduction..121
 6.2 NVivo Coding..121
 6.3 Dominant Themes..122
  6.3.1 Ecclesiological Dispositions and Praxis 123
  6.3.2 Contextual Realities of the UK..129
  6.3.3 Leadership 133
 6.4 Other Ideas That Emerged 141
  6.4.1 2GMs' Allegiance to ADCs 141
  6.4.2 Spiritual Enablement..142
  6.4.3 Membership Benefits 143
  6.4.4 Congregation's Demographics...144
  6.4.5 Finances 145
  6.4.6 The Church's Poor Image...146

  6.5 Mulling over the Research Questions 147
    6.5.1 What Are the Overarching Church Growth Factors? 147
    6.5.2 What Solutions Are Emerging? 149
  6.6 Conclusion 150

Chapter 7 151
 Omolúàbí-*Shaped Ecclesiology*
  7.1 Introduction 151
  7.2 The Need for a Contextualized African Ecclesiology 152
  7.3 Personhood in African (Yoruba) Thoughtform 154
    7.3.1 *Omolúàbí* Concept 155
    7.3.2 Fundamental Attributes of *Omolúàbí* 157
  7.4 What *Omolúàbí*-shaped Ecclesiology Would Look Like 165
    7.4.1 Recognition of and Harmony with the Spirit 165
    7.4.2 Building Relationships 166
    7.4.3 Stress on Social Ministry 167
    7.4.4 Excellent Leadership 168
    7.4.5 Holistic Salvation 169
  7.5 OSE as a Useful Tool for ADCs' Growth in Liverpool 172
    7.5.1 Responding to Issues of Race and Homogeneity 172
    7.5.2 Leveraging the Goodwill of *Omolúàbí* 173
    7.5.3 Paying Attention to Training 174
    7.5.4 Dealing with Secularism 175
    7.5.5 Addressing Accountability Concerns 175
    7.5.6 Managing Conflicts 176
  7.6 Conclusion 177

Chapter 8 179
 Church Growth and the Dynamics of Race
  8.1 Introduction 179
  8.2 How Racism Hampers ADCs' Growth in Liverpool 179
    8.2.1 The Mindset Barrier 180
    8.2.2 Attitudes and Actions Speak Louder 183
  8.3 Reflecting on the Awkward Idea of Race 193
    8.3.1 Race as a Social Creation 194
    8.3.2 Differentiating Race and Ethnicity 197
    8.3.3 Racism and Slavery 198
    8.3.4 Remembering the Epochal Racial Riots of 1919 200
  8.4 Conclusion 202

Chapter 9 203
   Church Growth and Adaptive Leadership
       9.1 Introduction 203
       9.2 Defining Adaptive Leadership 204
       9.3 The Need for Adaptive Leadership Style 205
       9.4 Adaptive Leadership Structure 207
           9.4.1 Adaptive Leadership Foundational Orientations..............207
           9.4.2 Key Concepts in Adaptive Leadership..........................208
           9.4.3 Adaptive Leader Behaviours: A Model for
                 ADC Leaders..211
       9.5 Conclusion 220

Chapter 10 221
   Summary and Conclusions
       10.1 Leadership in ADCs..222
       10.2 Beyond Homogenous Congregations.....................223
       10.3 Engaging *Omolúàbí*-shaped Ecclesiology 224
       10.4 What More?...225

Bibliography 231

Appendix I..267
   Expanded Code List

Appendix II 269
   *Religious Affiliation Among Adults in Great Britain NATCEN's
   British Social Attitudes Survey*

Appendix III...273
   List of Some ADCs in Liverpool

Appendix IV...275
   Interview Questions

Appendix V 277
   Research Information Sheet

Appendix VI...281
   Sample Interview Transcript

List of Tables

Table 1. Key Characteristics of Population Samples 56
Table 2. NVivo Codes 122

List of Figures

Figure 1. Illustrating Open and Axial Coding Phases in Generating a
        Theme (Right to Left) 64

Abstract

This thesis explores church growth phenomenon among African diaspora congregations (ADCs) in Liverpool, United Kingdom (UK). Thus, it lies in the field of African diaspora studies. While significant volumes of work in this knowledge area have focused on various aspects of African diaspora Christianity, the church growth dimension, in connection with Liverpool ADCs, remains unexamined. Yet these churches are springing up and multiplying within an interesting context and conditions that dictate their varying growth experiences. Indeed, ADCs must confront adaptive challenges that impact their sustenance and expansion as they *do church* in an unfamiliar land like the UK.

The aim of this study is to explore the elements influencing the church growth phenomenon amidst ADCs in Liverpool and to develop appropriate responses to the identified issues. The research seeks to answer the central question of what primary factors impact church growth among ADCs in Liverpool. It takes a qualitative research approach, borrowing from ethnography. Hence the inquiry, which investigates three ADCs, is an ethnographically informed fieldwork and not a full-fledged ethnography. It employs semi-structured interviews as the chief data collection tool and a grounded theory strategy for data analysis.

The key findings of this study include the overwhelming imprints of ecclesiology, contextual realities of the UK, and leadership on the church growth experience of the research population. In response to these factors, the contextualized African way of being church, *omolúàbí*-shaped ecclesiology (OSE), emerges, nesting the Adaptive Leadership strategy (AL). While AL promotes a more effective leadership approach for Liverpool ADCs in tackling adaptive challenges, OSE, an extensive concept, touches on all three identified principal church growth elements. The African-shaped ecclesiology reflects the contribution that every culture can bring to global theological conversations and the attempts to know more about God. Indeed, it provides a contextualized, relatable, and attractive way of being the church, building bridges between ADCs and their Western hosts. OSE ultimately aids church growth by promoting multi-ethnic congregations, making the task of *missio Dei* more easily realized.

Acknowledgments

Writing this thesis has taken me through an interesting trajectory with multiple high and low moments. Various people have been instrumental in navigating these different seasons. I consider these individuals collaborators whose contributions I cannot overlook. Indeed, in whatever form, every input has been of great help. I, therefore, relish this opportunity to express my immense gratitude to all my *destiny helpers* on this mission. Of course, I am aware that any attempt to record every name here may be impossible due to the volume.

First, I would like to tender a deep appreciation to my supervisory team, Prof. Peter McGrail, my Director of Studies (DOS), and Dr. Harvey Kwiyani, my immediate guide. Both were extraordinarily down-to-heart and supportive all the way. I value every moment I shared with my DOS, who doubled as the head of the Theology Department at the university throughout most of this investigation. Despite his tight schedule, his oversight and thorough fine-tuning of my methodology set the proper roadmap for this study. The opportunity he created for close work with him as a research assistant was also rare and sharpened my research skills. During this research, Dr. Kwiyani gradually grew beyond an academic supervisor into a mentor and friend. I marvelled at the patience and meticulousness he brought to reviewing all my writings. His optimism for the African continent and the invaluable contributions he believes it can offer to the world are extremely contagious.

Second, I do not take the timely and invaluable contributions of colleagues like Rev. Damilola Abraham and Rev. Joseph Ola lightly. They assisted in editing and reviewing different aspects of the thesis. I cherish their constructive criticism, comments, and suggestions, which have served only to beautify this writing. I equally appreciate Dr. Philip Oyewale, a senior colleague and spiritual father, who provided me with valuable materials and tips in navigating this journey at its inception. Pursuing a doctoral degree would have been undoubtedly more stressful and lonelier without all of them.

I am similarly indebted to all who volunteered to be part of this research. I particularly appreciate the gatekeepers of each congregation, the pastors who granted unusual access to their church members. I was amazed and humbled by the way these leaders engaged with me and facilitated a quick completion of my fieldwork. Indeed, their reputations were on the line when they gave unfettered access to an outsider to investigate their local assemblies. This gesture, I do not trivialize. The success of this project would have been impossible without the ministers and other participants.

Finally, I profoundly appreciate my family's invaluable contributions. I celebrate my always-supportive wife, Abimbola Ayokunle, for her understanding and endurance, even when thesis writing took over family times. She made balancing fatherhood, ministry, work, studies, and life less demanding. The joy that our precious daughter, Ruby Ayokunle, exudes since her arrival during this study is also an excellent medicine in down moments. The consistent and timely financial contribution, alongside other forms of support, from my parents, Rev. Dr. Samson and Pastor Mrs. Toyin Ayokunle, is also laudable. Indeed, the contributions minimized possible distractions and difficulties on the research journey. Lastly, I acknowledge Rev. Olajide and Mrs. Olayemi Olutunde, my adorable in-laws, who were always concerned about my wellbeing and the success of this study. They were great cheerleaders all the way.

List of Abbreviations

1GM	First Generation Migrant
2GM	Second Generation Migrant
ACM	African Churches Mission
ADC	African Diaspora Congregation
AL	Adaptive Leadership
BMC	Black Majority Church
CAN	Christian Association of Nigeria
CGM	Church Growth Movement
GT	Grounded Theory
HUP	Homogenous Unit Principle
NBC	The Nigerian Baptist Convention
NBTS	The Nigerian Baptist Theological Seminary
OSE	*Omolúàbí*-shaped Ecclesiology
RCCG	The Redeemed Christian Church of God
SSI	Semi-Structured Interview
TOP	Temple of Praise
UK	United Kingdom
USA	United States of America

CHAPTER 1

Introduction

This preliminary chapter introduces the study, an examination of the church growth experience of African diaspora congregations (ADCs) in Liverpool. The dissertation essentially seeks to answer the question of what prime elements impress upon the sustenance and expansion of Liverpool ADCs. I find this research question highly important and fascinating for two reasons. First, with the growth of Christianity on the African continent, it is safe to think of many of the African migrants spreading around the world as Christians.[1] In fact, Latin American theologian and Professor of Missions, Samuel Escobar, highlights that "On almost every continent, migration movements have brought to cities, and industrial or commercial centres, legions of mission minded lay people from Third World churches."[2] In other words, African migrants "bring their faith along"[3] as they move, perhaps in the fulfilment of the *blessed reflex*,[4] and establish their own congregations (ADCs) everywhere they go. However, as they do church and missions the same way they have known from home, they soon discover that "what worked in Africa does not work here [in Britain]."[5] This predicament presents a multifaceted

---

1. Kugbeadjor and Kwiyani, "Exploring Adaptive Challenges," 6.
2. Escobar, "Mission from Everywhere," 194.
3. Kwiyani, *Sent Forth*, 12.
4. *Blessed reflex* is a term used in the nineteenth century by Western missionary champions to describe a future where Christians from the then unevangelized lands in the global South would return to challenge and renew the West. See more in Kwiyani, *Sent Forth*, 70–76; Also see Ross, "'Blessed Reflex.'"
5. Kugbeadjor and Kwiyani, "Exploring Adaptive Challenges," 7.

adaptive challenge[6] in church growth, which this research aims to identify and propose ways of handling.

Second, religion did not often seem to take centre stage in migration research historically. In fact, professor of history of religions Klaus Hock, observes that:

> traditionally, for a long time migration research has not taken into account the significance of religion both for specifically, migrant communities, and generally, for migration as a global phenomenon – not even in view of the transatlantic African migration . . . the phenomenon of "religion on the move" has only recently attracted the attention of scholars of Religious Studies who have finally started to acknowledge the significance of migrant religions for Religious Studies and the History of Religions.[7]

Hock's viewpoint is perhaps even more valid for the African Christian diaspora in Britain, with literature on the community still in its infancy. A search, for instance, via the Endnote software on 19 April 2019 of the Library of Congress and the University College London (UCL) catalogues returned the respective figures of 457 and 1,554 works published on African diaspora studies. Constraining the search criteria to the literature available on African Christian diaspora came back with one and ten results, respectively.[8] By further limiting the search parameters to Europe, only UCL produced a result – the work of Roswith Gerloff.[9] It is, of course, concerning that writings

---

6. Adaptive challenges generally develop when an organization's survival strategies, its sustaining ideals, and practices, are no longer sufficient or able to overcome its current realities. It can occur because of varying circumstance such as the emergence of a competitor, unexpected life happenings that necessitate a lifestyle change, or, as with the research population, relocation to a new environment. For more, see Kugbeadjor and Kwiyani, "Exploring Adaptive Challenges," 7–8. I have also expanded on adaptive challenges within the wider discourse of the Adaptive Leadership concept in chapter 9 of this thesis.

7. For further details, see Hock, "Catching the Wing," 329–339.

8. The single result from the Library of Congress catalogue was Afeosemime U. Adogame, *The African Christian Diaspora*. Eight of ten results generated from the UCL catalogue were either writings of the same author (Afeosemime Adogame) or reviews of his publications; The remaining two returns were the works of another scholar, Roswith Gerloff. They are *The Significance of the African Christian Diaspora in Europe* and *Open Space: The African Christian Diaspora in Europe and the Quest for Human Community*.

9. Gerloff, *African Christian Diaspora*.

on ADCs, especially in Liverpool, remain invisible, unpublished, or too few, despite the community constituting a sizable number of new and emerging religious gatherings in the city.[10] Therefore, the essence of this study is to attempt to close the gap by investigating a significant religious experience (church growth) of the African diaspora in Liverpool.

In this chapter, I expand the research question while also presenting the study's aims. Then I discuss the nature of the investigation before situating the study within its context by explaining the background. Deliberation of the research's originality and contributions to knowledge follow. I also found it pertinent to account for the study's limitations to clarify its scope. Afterwards, I discuss some important terms in the thesis before highlighting the structure of the study. A brief conclusion ends the chapter.

1.1 Research Questions and Aims

Carefully developed research questions are fundamental to all research, as they provide focus for an inquiry and streamline the research objectives to specific aspects the study is intended to address.[11] Moreover, innovative questions result in fascinating and significant theories.[12] In contrast, poorly formulated questions can and likely will cause problems that eventually affect the entire research process.[13] With this understanding, I present the research questions and aims of this study.

The primary research question this investigation sets out to answer is: what principal factors impact church growth among African diaspora congregations (ADCs) in Liverpool, England? In addressing this query, the following sub-questions develop:

1. What are the catalytic or inhibiting elements conditioning church growth in these congregations?

---

10. Samson Ayokunle estimated the number of African diaspora congregations in Liverpool at eleven or twelve in 2004 and between fifteen and twenty by 2007. However, no specific figures seem to exist to date in literature, especially as pockets of these congregations continue to mushroom in the city and country at large. Ayokunle, "Elements Sustaining Public Worship," 5–6.

11. Burke and Christensen, *Educational Research*, 164.

12. Sandberg and Alvesson, "Ways of Constructing Research," 24.

13. Agee, "Developing Qualitative Research," 431.

2. What are the possible responses to the growth challenges faced by the congregations?

The overarching aims of this study are to (a) explore the key elements influencing growth among ADCs in Liverpool, and (b) formulate a grounded theory to address the identified challenges to growth.

1.2 Nature of the Study

This inquiry is an addition to the body of knowledge regarding African Christian diaspora studies. It illuminates a crucial dimension of the multifaceted experiences of the African diaspora in the UK: church growth. The study follows an ethnographically informed fieldwork approach. By implication, it is not a full-fledged ethnography but employs ethnographic methods for data collection and analysis. The investigation similarly proceeds within the qualitative research framework and culminates in the development of a grounded theory response to the church growth challenges identified.

1.3 Background of the Study

Jesus Christ, the founder and head of the church, is alive forever. In the same vein, the church, his body, is a living organism and by implication, must grow.[14] David Smith, a former pastor of Eden Baptist Chapel, Cambridge, and missionary with the Qua Iboe Fellowship in Nigeria, explains the heart of Donald McGavran's missiology as follows: "the growth of the church is always and everywhere God's purpose . . . God desires a harvest . . . [In fact] . . . a stagnant and declining church is never the will of God."[15] Moreover, church growth is a "chief and irreplaceable purpose of mission."[16] It is then understandable that church leaders long for the flourishing of their ministries and congregations. However, growing an organization is not a simple task. In fact, business administrator and scholar Carter McNamara observes that for both non-profit and remunerative establishments, certain considerations and decisions

---

14. Akin-John, *Impact-Driven Church*, 13.
15. Smith, "Church Growth Principles," 25.
16. McGavran, *Understanding Church Growth*, 32.

are necessary for the intentional growth or expansion of the organization.[17] McNamara's comment aligns perfectly with the research population's situation, whose struggle to set up, sustain, and expand their congregations in the diaspora is real and further complicated by the generic adaptive challenges of immigrants in a strange land.[18]

Moreover, the displacement and rapid disappearance of religion (especially Christianity) from the public life of many Western nations is increasingly glaring and hard to dispute. For instance, a 2016 social attitudes survey conducted by Britain's largest independent social research agency, NatCen, indicates that fifty-three percent (53%) of all adults in the UK have no religious affiliation.[19] Not long after this research started, on 5 April 2019, the Office for National Statistics (ONS), UK, released a report that indicated that the population of non-religious people in Britain had surged by forty-six percent (46%) in the seven years between 2011 and 2018. The data also showed that the number of Christian adherents had declined by fifteen percent (15%) over the same timeline.[20] These figures are perhaps not surprising against the backdrop of a study piloted by Professor of Religious History John Wolffe in the twentieth century. The survey examined the statistics of church participation in Britain between 1851 and 1951 and suggested an unabating trend of Christianity dwindling and disappearing from British life during that period. For instance, the research showed how Protestant denominations were already losing ground in England by the 1920s.[21]

More recently, in the UK, the closing down of churches and their abandonment and adaptation for other purposes has equally been gaining in popularity. Of course, the research context, Liverpool, is not spared. While before the completion of St. Peter's Church in 1704, the city had only St.

---

17. McNamara, "Business Development."
18. See Kugbeadjor and Kwiyani, "Exploring Adaptive Challenges," 7–8.
19. NatCen, *British Social Attitudes Survey*; See appendix II for comprehensive survey report or visit NatCen, *British Social Attitudes: Record Number of Brits with no Religion*, http://www.natcen.ac.uk/news-media/press-releases/2017/september/british-social-attitudes-record-number-of-brits-with-no-religion/.
20. For the ONS report from the national annual population survey see Office for National Statistics, "Religion by Local Authority."
21. Scotland and Wales maintained approximately the same level of adherence but only until the Second World War. See Wolffe, *God and Greater Britain*, 71; See also Heyck, "Decline of Christianity," 437–453.

Nicholas church serving it, by 1877 its worship buildings multiplied to a total of 251.[22] Nevertheless, this positive momentum has reversed in recent years. Charitable trust GENUKI, in 2015, advanced that there were one 187 churches in Liverpool at the time. There were forty Anglican, ten Baptist, seventeen Congregational/Independent, forty-nine Methodist, twenty-six Presbyterian/Unitarian, twenty-five Roman Catholic, five Jewish synagogues, and fifteen other uncategorized churches.[23]

In *The Churches of Liverpool*,[24] a book documenting the history of church buildings in that city, author Colin Wilkinson's lament indicates how concerning the disappearance of historic churches in Liverpool is. Wilkinson bemoans:

> The demise of key churches invokes a deep sense of loss, and the reasons for their often unnecessary destruction raise the question of how fragile is our surviving heritage? The recent pronouncement by Cardinal Murphy-O'Connor, the head of the Catholic Church in England, that Christianity had almost been vanquished in Britain coincided with the planned closure of three further Catholic churches in Liverpool to add to three others recently closed.[25]

Beyond the reality of diminishing church buildings in Liverpool, another challenge consolidates the background of this inquiry: the bane of secularism, liberalism, and the rationalization philosophy of the Western world. Eddie Gibbs, Anglican minister and professor of church growth, mentions how the secularization of Western societies has created "moral confusion and spiritual wasteland."[26] Indeed, these sociological phenomena, put together, are reflected partly in the continuous disappearance of religious institutions, fall in church attendance, and decline in popularity and impact of religious beliefs.[27] Besides the purview of religion, though, the influence of

---

22. Wilkinson, "Introduction," 6.

23. GENUKI, "List of Churches For: Liverpool." This list does not account for African congregations in the city.

24. Lewis, *Churches of Liverpool*.

25. Wilkinson, "Introduction," 6.

26. Gibbs, *Leadership Next*, 12.

27. Bruce, *Religion in the Modern*, 26. While the trio (secularization, liberalism, and rationalization) often show up in discourses as interconnected or synonymous terms, they generally refer to the place of religion in modern societies.

secularization also permeates all of life, with the British political, social, economic, and educational systems bearing witness.[28]

Consequently, it is not uncommon to contemplate secularization as occurring at different degrees in society: its individual, institutional, and societal dimensions, as did the late British professor of sociology, Bryan Wilson.[29] He explicates that secularization occurs when "religion – seen as a way of thinking, as the performance of particular practices, and as the institutionalization and organization of these patterns of thought and actions – has lost influence at the societal, individual level and institutional/organizational levels."[30] With its multisided penetrating influence in Britain, secularism cannot but shape the entire Christian experience of ADCs (including church growth). Scholar David Hawkins rightly observes that "the liberalising tendency of British Society and Christianity has affected the way African Christians encounter God, Jesus, the Bible and Salvation."[31]

1.4 Originality and Contributions of the Study

While most undergraduate research projects aim to test students' competence in doing research, postgraduate investigations, whether at the master's or doctoral level, explore opportunities to make original contributions to knowledge in specific disciplines.[32] The concern, however, comes from the ambiguity that surrounds what original research really is. There is no

---

28. Bruce, "Secularization and Church Growth," 294. The influence of secularization in Britain underlines many developments like the embrace of Deism, Darwinism, and alternative relationships – an endorsement of the sexual lifestyle of the 1960s – among others. See more in Olofinjana, *Reverse in Ministry*, 47.

29. See for example Wilson, *Religion in Secular Society*. See also Shiner, "Concept of Secularization."

30. Wilson, *Religion in Secular Society*, 10–11. Secularization theory is rooted in twentieth century sociological reasoning and became prominent in influencing popular opinion in the 1960s. Generally, the thesis propounded that scientific rationality and modernization will lead to an inescapable decline in religious belief, ideals, and practice worldwide. While this is not true for all places, it is sadly the case for Britain. For further details, see Olofinjana, *Reverse in Ministry*, 47; for classical and more recent arguments on secularization, see Luckmann, *Invisible Religion*; Jenkins, "Review of The Religious and the Secular"; Berger, *Desecularization of the World*; Bruce, "Demise of Christianity."

31. Hawkins, "Foreword," xi.

32. White, *Developing Research Questions*, 13.

consensus on the meaning of the concept.[33] Nonetheless, common threads in the various descriptions available include the dimensions of novelty, uniqueness, and innovation.[34] Researcher John Finn provides further guidelines to evaluate the originality of a research. According to the scholar, one must check if the study meets any of the following criteria: *new facts + new ideas*, *new facts + old ideas, old facts + new ideas,* and the fourth, which does not constitute original research, *old facts + old ideas*.[35] Originality, then, is a process of probing, analysing, and scrutinising existing knowledge to be part of its improvement and development.[36]

By the above standards, this research demonstrates the quality of originality in multiple ways. First and fundamentally, the church growth situation of Liverpool ADCs is a subject that has not attracted and sustained deliberate attention from scholars. The few published writings on the UK's African diaspora Christians[37] have not explicitly focused on Liverpool. Moreover, the available unpublished works have also considered other matters, including marital issues, worship, and others.[38] So, by the phenomenon it investigates among the research population (church growth), this inquiry fits the *old facts + new ideas* expression of originality. It expands the current knowledge on African diaspora Christians in the UK with ADCs' growth experience.

Second, this study formulates a grounded theory solution to the church growth challenges identified from the investigation. The emerging, authentic African-shaped ecclesiology, for instance, is another interplay of old facts and fresh ideas. It presents a new ecclesiological framework for the research population by exploring and drawing from the *omolúàbí* identity construct of the Yoruba ethnic group in Nigeria. The *omolúàbí*-shaped ecclesiology is an extensive concept whose applicability transcends ADCs to the church in Africa and the globe.

---

33. Alajami, "Beyond Originality," 1.

34. Alajami, 1.

35. Finn, *Getting a PHD*, 20.

36. Alajami, "Beyond Originality," 2.

37. See for instance Haar, *Halfway to Paradise*; Adogame, *African Christian Diaspora*; Gerloff, *African Christian Diaspora*; Sturge, *Look What the Lord*.

38. A couple are Oyewale, "Critical Analysis"; Ayokunle, "Elements Sustaining Public Worship."

1.5 Limitations of the Study

Regardless of researcher experience, suitability of research method, or nature of the study, inquiries are rarely free of limitations. There are usually downsides to a research design that potentially impact data interpretation and conclusions.[39] Therefore, in this brief section, I have pondered the drawbacks of this study. The first limitation concerns the nature of the theorized solution proposed by the research. The theory is rooted in the field data. As such, the proposed response to church growth challenges mainly correlates to the research population and the UK context. Thus, its application cannot be generalized or extended to settings where the theory has not originated. In other words, while the inquiry is reliable and valid, able to yield the same result if carried out under the same conditions by other researchers,[40] its findings and recommendations are constrained to the UK climate.

The second limitation of the research is the challenge of scanty or unavailable records on ADCs in Liverpool, which created some challenges in the initial selection of population samples. In most cases, the available databases of churches in the UK do not account for the presence or existence of these communities. Even on the government's online register for charitable organizations in the country, the records of these assemblies are largely omitted.[41] Nonetheless, ADCs continue to proliferate in Liverpool, springing up in homes, pubs, and temporary apartments.

The third is the drawback of the COVID-19 infection, the viral attack that became a pandemic in the first quarter of 2020 while fieldwork was underway. The pandemic saw governments introduce lockdowns and restrictions on physical interactions and engagements globally. Many places of worship shut down, and most only continued functioning online – at least for those who could adapt quickly enough. This situation immediately challenged the research methodology. It required rethinking the research method. The data-gathering exercise eventually happened mostly through telephone interviews, whose downsides include the lack of opportunity to observe the interviewees' facial cues, body language, and other forms of potentially relevant data.

---

39. Ross and Zaidi, "Limited by Our Limitations," 261.

40. Walliman, *Research Methods*.

41. See Charity Commission for England and Wales, https://register-of-charities.charitycommission.gov.uk/.

1.6 Discussion of Key Terms

In this part, I present some critical concepts in the thesis that require special attention and definition for clarity and better engagement. The key terms are diaspora, African congregation, and church growth.

1.6.1 Diaspora

Resolving the term *diaspora* is not easy,[42] considering the porousness and variations that come with it.[43] For instance, in humanities, a broad application of diaspora describes migrant communities' conditions abroad as they experience life in a marginalized situation. Yet the term also has a strong religious sense, which derives from Jewish and early Christian religious history. Hence, when applied to contemporary experiences, *diaspora* appears more as variations of religious usage.[44] Due to the complexity of the terminology, arriving at a definition of the concept becomes challenging. However, it may be helpful to consider the etymology of the word.

Diaspora originates from the Greek word *diaspeirein*, which breaks down into *dia*, meaning "across," and *speirein*, implying "scatter." Literally, the term means "scatter across," transliterated as "dispersion." Diaspora finds usage with reference to the Jewish dispersion beyond Israel, the major diaspora beginning in the eighth to sixth centuries BC.[45] However, technically, diaspora originally and largely applies to the community of the Jews outside Palestine from about 100 BC to AD 100.[46] Hock observes that in traditional theological usage, as a verb, *diaspora* initially had a negative sense, describing the breakdown or disconnection of elements, or those headed towards destruction.[47] He added that as a noun, the term evolved semantically later in the third century BC with the translation of the Hebrew Scriptures into Greek (the Septuagint).[48] The concept subsequently grew into a notion with three

---

42. Hock, "Religion on the Move," 235.
43. Sundiata, "Africanity, Identity and Culture," 13.
44. Hock, "Religion on the Move," 235–236.
45. Oxford University Press, "Diaspora."
46. "Diaspora," in *New International Dictionary*, 296.
47. Hock, "Religion on the Move," 236.
48. Hock, 236. As the historical theologian Ryan Reeves notes, although the term Septuagint is commonly thought of as the Greek translation of the Hebrew Bible, technically, no such thing as "the Septuagint" exists. The Septuagint is rather a collection of the most reliable Greek manuscripts reconstructed to approximate a translation of the original Old

aspects – the land of dispersion of the Jews, the situation of being dispersed, and the scattered people.[49]

Simultaneously, *diaspora* also became infused into a soteriological concept to describe a "punishment for disobedience against the Law with the prospect of repentance, renewed obedience and subsequent gathering and return to the Promised Land."[50] Even though it flowed through into the New Testament and early Christianity, this thought gradually made way for geographic and sociological notions. However, since the Reformation, *diaspora* has referred to confessional minorities (Catholic or Protestant diaspora); or, in relatively recent times, the condition of faithful Christians in secularized societies.[51]

The application of the term *diaspora* to people of African descent is fundamentally an adaptation of the Jewish experience to the circumstances of Africans scattered beyond the shores of Africa.[52] Of course, diaspora Africans have some commonalities with the Jewish situation in that their dispersion also includes elements of initial and substantial forced migration or spread. However, the difference lies in historical circumstances and comprehensiveness.[53] Indeed, the massive African dispersion beyond the African continent occurred in five phases, with the first three dating back more than 100,000 years to about 500 BC. Historian Colin Palmer argues that while the earliest stream's boundaries are still debatable, the significant movement within and beyond Africa, stretching back over 100,000 years, constitutes the launchpad for any historical study of the dispersion and peopling of Africans, including early human history.[54]

Palmer adds that the second stream of African diaspora took place around 3000 BC when Bantu speakers migrated from the region currently known as

---

Testament from Hebrew to Greek. The origin of the Septuagint is linked to the reign of Ptolemy Philadelphus, an Egyptian king, who commissioned seventy-two translators from Jerusalem to translate the Hebrew Bible (Torah) into Greek for his library in Alexandria. Today, the term generally refers to various Greek translations of the Hebrew Bible and such additional books as Tobit, Maccabees, Sirach, and others. For further details, see Ryan, "What is the Septuagint?"

49. For more see Hock, "Religion on the Move," 236. See also Haar, *Halfway to Paradise*, 77; "Diaspora," in *Merriam-Webster Dictionary*, 198–199.
50. Hock, "Religion on the Move," 236.
51. Hock, 236.
52. Haar, *Halfway to Paradise*, 79.
53. Ayokunle, "Elements Sustaining Public Worship," 11.
54. Palmer, "Defining and Studying," 28.

Nigeria and Cameroon to other parts of Africa and the Indian Ocean. The third wave saw merchants, enslaved people, soldiers, and traders move to Europe, Asia, and the Middle East around 500 BC. This extended stream of dispersion makes the slave trade to the Mediterranean and Middle Eastern world after 700 BC by Muslims familiar. The fourth phase is the famous transatlantic slave trade of the fifteenth century to the nineteenth century that saw Africans trafficked to Europe and America. The fifth stream began in the nineteenth century, especially as slavery faded.[55] Sadly, "awareness of the slave past continues to live among people of African descent, many of whom, over a period of a century or more, came from Africa to Britain via slave colonies in the West Indies."[56]

As with the broader term *diaspora*, the concept of *African diaspora* also poses some challenges. For instance, American scholar and historian Ibrahim Sundiata speaks of several diasporas represented by "the Black Diaspora" in Latin America, with the "Hispanic" race increasingly reconstituting the community rather than Africans. In fact, this scholar avoids defining the term *diaspora* altogether.[57] Gerrie ter Haar, Emeritus Professor of Religion, also opines that the American experience of people of African ancestry, who have a shared memory of the transatlantic slave trade relocating them to North and South America, overwhelmingly shapes the African diaspora idea.[58]

Yet, for Europe, the circumstances of the displacement of Africans are somewhat different. The alignment shared with the North American diaspora is mostly regarding "the historical phenomenon of the dispersion and settlement of Africans abroad."[59] Bearing in mind that "understandings attached to the diasporic condition may vary both within and between diasporas,"[60] ter Haar identifies three elements of the African diaspora experience in Europe, which, in turn, shape a working definition of the concept for this thesis. These elements of *dispersion*, *identity*, and *return*[61] find expression in the description of African diaspora put forward by the First African Diaspora Studies

---

55. Palmer, "Defining and Studying," 28–29.
56. Haar, *Halfway to Paradise*, 82.
57. Sundiata, "Africanity, Identity and Culture," 13.
58. Haar, *Halfway to Paradise*, 77.
59. Harris, *Global Dimensions*, 4–5.
60. Ben-Rafael, "Diaspora."
61. For further details see Haar, *Halfway to Paradise*, 80–88.

Institute of Howard University. I have adopted the definition for this writing. The African diaspora is:

> the voluntary and forced dispersion of Africans at different periods in history and in several directions; the emergence of a cultural identity abroad without losing the African base, whether spiritually or physically; the psychological or physical return to the homeland, Africa.[62]

Again, the above definition projects the element of *dispersion* – either voluntarily (like the nineteenth-century migration) or involuntarily (similar to the earlier waves of displacement), as identified by ter Haar. Moreover, the scattering is related to different periods in history. Hence it accommodates, in some way, the multiple phases of major African movements previously enumerated. The definition also implicitly suggests the second element, *identity*, by mentioning the struggle to assimilate culturally without losing African consciousness. Lastly, the description speaks of *return* as it paints a picture of a physical or psychological journey to the African continent.

1.6.2 African Congregation

In early times, the term *Africa* applied to the headland known today as Tunisia, but it gradually evolved to encapsulate the entirety of Mediterranean Africa west of Egypt. *Africa* has further metamorphosed in modern times to capture the whole continent and its diverse cultures.[63] Therefore, it is imaginable that an African originates from the African mainland. However, this thought does not appear to be a shared understanding within the African community in Britain, where distinction often occurs between *African* and *Afro-Caribbean*. While the former refers to immigrants from Africa, Afro-Caribbean describes people of African descent whose ancestry is in the Caribbean.

Notwithstanding, this dissertation applies the term *African* broadly, including the two categories above, to remove the needless classification and unnecessary gap. Hence, in this study, *Africans* connote people from Africa who have migrated to the UK, including African descendants whose ancestry is traceable to the Caribbean. Similarly, for ease of interaction with

---

62. Shepperson, "African Diaspora Concept."
63. Oden, *How Africa Shaped*, 80–82.

some materials, the appellation *Black* generally describes the same category of people, including any dark-skinned person, while *White* applies to Western people.

The challenge here is not just defining the term *African*. There is also complexity as to what African *congregations* in the West really are. While these assemblies are diverse, they share common threads that distinguish them from mainline churches in the West.[64] Therefore, it would be awkward to squeeze them into existing Western categories in an attempt to capture them. In fact, Allan Anderson, professor of mission and pentecostal studies, cautions against "evaluating African movements according to Western criteria,"[65] a convenient practice considering Western dominance in literature.[66] Of course, the problem of an appropriate label or identity is not exclusive to African congregations in the West. It is inherited from their parents, the African Indigenous Churches (AICs) in Africa,[67] who have expanded in contemporary Africa and to the modern African diaspora.[68]

To correctly capture an understanding of African congregations in the West, Arlington Trotman, former director of the Churches' Commission for Racial Justice (a 1990s replacement of the Community and Race Relations Unit of the British Council of Churches established in 1971), suggests that a non-racial or nationalistic description is required.[69] Therefore, in this dissertation,

---

64. Many scholars agree about the significant similarities of the African assemblies in the diaspora. See, for instance, O'Donovan, *Biblical Christianity*, 4; Parratt, *Reinventing Christianity*, 59.

65. Anderson, *African Reformation*, 210.

66. Jehu Hanciles explores this idea of extending Western thoughts and experiences as the norm for other societies in his work. Hanciles, *Beyond Christendom*.

67. African Indigenous Churches, also referred to as AICs in its different nuances (such as African Instituted/Initiated Churches), denote congregations that descended from mission-founded churches in Africa beginning from the 1890s. This time represents the first developmental level of AICs among South Africans as "Ethiopian churches," and in West Africa as "African Churches." The second level occurred in the 1920s and 1930s, which include the Zionists in South Africa, Aladura Churches (Nigeria), Spirit churches (Ghana), and others. Third is the proliferation of the so-called Pentecostal/charismatic churches, especially from the 1950s and 60s onwards. AICs were established by Africans in reaction to the lethargic Christianity introduced by the mission churches in Africa. They are self-supporting, self-financing, and self-governing. For more details, see Spickard and Adogame, "Africa, the New African Diaspora," 3; Olofinjana, *Reverse in Ministry*, 21; Ayegboyin and Ishola, *African Indigenous Churches*, 9.

68. Spickard and Adogame, "Africa, the New African Diaspora," 3.

69. Trotman, "Black, Black-led or What?," 35.

I have not preferred such common tags as "African-led churches,"[70] "African Independent Churches (AICs),"[71] "African and African Caribbean churches,"[72] "African Churches,"[73] "African Immigrant Churches,"[74] and "Black Majority Churches (BMCs)."[75] In fact, the term African Pioneered Churches (APCs), as employed by theologian, Joseph Ola,[76] would have been more appropriate. It suggests that though Africans initiate the congregations, they do not have to remain African in leadership or even membership. Additionally, as this scholar notes, APC also silently illuminates "the pioneering endeavour that planting a church as an African in a contextually different and complex multicultural setting as Britain entails."[77]

Nevertheless, APC still tends to imply an ideal in leadership or membership make-up of the African congregations whose reality is different. Indeed, many of the local churches remain African-led and constituted. So alternatively, I have preferred the label African diaspora congregations (ADCs) in this dissertation. While this description may also portray some elements of nationalism or race, the emphasis it seeks is the context or location of the congregations where the experience of church growth is unfolding.

1.6.3 Church Growth

Defining church growth may not be as straightforward as one may imagine. Yes, *"church growth is complex."*[78] In fact, grasping the concept of church alone has resulted in various models and images of the church over the years.[79] Hence, while the essence of the church remains unchanged, its form

---

70. Haar, *African Christians in Europe*, 14; Olofinjana, *Reverse in Ministry*, 47.
71. The acronym AIC often differs in meaning where the "I" could imply a range of words such as "Indigenous," "Independent," "Initiated," "Instituted," or "International." See Gornik, *Word Made Global*, 28; Olofinjana, *Reverse in Ministry*, 36.
72. Daneel and Robert, *African Christian Outreach*, 165–185.
73. Kalu, *African Christianity*, 494–515.
74. Kwiyani, *Sent Forth*, 105.
75. Sturge, *Look What the Lord*, 53.
76. Refer to Ola, "African Pioneered Churches."
77. Ola, 56.
78. Emphasis in the original text. Wagner, *Your Church Can Grow*, 31.
79. One popular work that extensively explores the images and models of the Church is Dulles, *Models of the Church*.

is dynamic in response to different historical situations.[80] Moreover, with transforming images comes an evolving ecclesiology, a theological expression of the image of the church, a way of perceiving, relating to, and being the church, and an adaptive response to a constantly changing historical development.[81] Of course, the adaptive nature of ecclesiology to various situations is an important truth for African Christians in the UK, who *do* church in a *strange* environment that requires adjustments. Indeed, these migrant Christians, as with some Church of Pentecost (CoP) pastors in Britain,[82] "have to adapt their ministries [including ecclesiology] to their new contexts, but that is the most difficult thing to do."[83]

The complexity in defining church growth also emanates from the emergence of popular church growth ideas. The concepts have come almost solely from an American perspective, applied to the same context – perhaps to a fault – and propagated as universal principles, crystalising into unavoidable terminology and a body of knowledge in contemporary mission scholarship and praxis.[84] An example is the church growth theories of Donald McGavran, twentieth century American missiologist and premier leader of the Church Growth Movement (CGM).[85] Scholar George Martin observes that McGavran

---

80. The essence of the church refers to the permanent, continuing elements of the church. It is a constant factor in the various changing historical images of the church, which survives irrespective of the changing history of mankind, the church, and of theology. The forms are the transient and changing historical images of the church in every age. For more details, see Küng, *Church*, 3–6. Craig van Gelder also writes extensively on the essence of the church in his book. See Van Gelder, *Essence of the Church*.

81. Küng, *Church*, 6. Although I have used the term loosely in this dissertation to simply refer to a way of doing or being church, I am aware that ecclesiology has a more comprehensive meaning in theological discourse. For further details on ecclesiology, see also Cegielka, *Handbook of Ecclesiology*; Boff, *Ecclesiogenesis: The Base Communities*; Ward, *Perspectives on Ecclesiology*.

82. The CoP is the largest Protestant church originating from Ghana with no less than three million members scattered around the world and registered in at least ninety-two countries, including the UK.

83. Kugbeadjor and Kwiyani, "Exploring Adaptive Challenges," 7.

84. Stetzer, " Evolution of Church Growth," 1, 12.

85. Donald Anderson McGavran was born to American, missionary parents in Damoh, India on December 15, 1897. He received his higher education in the United States. McGavran spent his first career as an educator, evangelist, church planter, field executive, and evangelist in India. He became obsessed with why some churches reached people and grew while others declined. He would later dedicate twenty years of his life to this cause as he examined the phenomenon in India, the Philippines, Mexico, Jamaica, Thailand, Puerto Rico, West Africa, North America, and other places. His first publication in 1955, titled *The Bridges of God* announced his name in the field of Christian missions, but his ideas only had great impact in

introduced "concepts that remain components of missions vocabulary and practice" to date. Martin further credits the wide use of such terms as "church growth," "harvest fields," "people groups," and other common missiological jargon to McGavran.[86] Many of McGavran's American students and colleagues, such as Peter Wagner, Win Arn, Eddie Gibbs, Lyle Schaller, Elmer Towns, Thom Rainer, and Robert Schuller, also built upon and promoted church growth concepts.[87]

The challenge with the widespread church growth thoughts of McGavran and others goes beyond their overwhelming American influence and includes their relative success across regions. Indeed, while it appears that significant effectiveness has attended many of these voguish theories in the global South (Africa, Asia, and Latin America – the current heartland of Christianity),[88] the experience of the North, especially the UK, where the principles did not originally emanate, seems different. This is despite McGavran's efforts to apply his church growth ideas to Europe and North America as far back as the early 1980s, as evident in the 1983 revised edition of his ground breaking classic work, *Understanding Church Growth*.[89] The identities distinguishing the British people from Americans[90] may have magnified the poor outcome of McGavran's church growth theories in Britain. Kate Fox, social anthropologist and co-director of the Social Issues Research Centre, illuminates British peculiarities as she examines conversational and behavioural codes,

---

missions as founding dean of Fuller Theological Seminary's School of World Missions in 1965. There, his understanding deepened and widened through the research works of his students and collaboration with colleagues such as Alan Tippett, Ralph Winter, Arthur Glasser, and Peter Wagner. His subsequent publication, titled *Understanding Church Growth* (1970, 1980, 1990 editions) have changed the course of contemplating missions to date, pioneering the Church Growth Movement. The methodology, objectives, and further details on CGM can be found in such publications as Wagner, *Your Church Can Grow*; and Wagner, *Our Kind of People*.

86. Martin, "Editorial: Why Another Look," 5–7.

87. See classical works such as Rainer, *Book of Church Growth*; Wagner, *Our Kind of People*; Staylor, *Dimensions of Church Growth*; McGavran and Wagner, *Understanding Church Growth*; Inskeep, "Short History."

88. For statistics and more on how the global South is becoming the face of world Christianity, see Hanciles, *Beyond Christendom*, 121–123.

89. See McGavran, *Understanding Church Growth*.

90. By distinctive identities, I refer to the means by which a people make meaning of their social world as it has evolved historically. For more, see Miller, "Reflections on British National"; see also Levy, "Citizenship and National Identity."

those "hidden rules of English behaviour," in her work entitled *Watching the English*.[91]

From the above discussion, contemplating church growth in the UK based on popular, American parameters is awkward. Hence the need for a definition that considers the UK context and has a generally applicable framework. An examination of the multiple developmental facets of Jesus, the head of the church (Col 1:18), as recorded in Luke 2:52, is helpful. The passage suggests some elements that could serve as indicators of the growth of the church, the body of Christ. Luke writes: "And Jesus increased in wisdom and in years, and in divine and human favour." (NRSV) Practical theologian Charles Erdman suggests that the text affirms Jesus's growth, which proceeded as bodily and mental development and an increase in charm and spiritual power.[92] A holistic growth, indeed. professor of Bible interpretation Bob Utley additionally notes how the passage re-echoes a preceding text (Luke 2:40),[93] which also attests to the humanity and compound aspects of Jesus's growth.[94] Theologian and writer Gene Getz identifies four dimensions of Jesus's development from Luke 2:52 as follows: mental (increase in wisdom), physical (increase in years), spiritual (increase in divine favour), and social growth (increase in human favour).[95] Scholar Kevin Madigan agrees and points out that Jesus's advancement in age is essentially a numerical increase.[96]

Since the head and the rest of the body connect to form one entity, it is ideal for the body to enjoy the same order of nourishment and growth as the head. By implication, the same developmental pattern of Jesus should characterize the church such that Jesus's growth dimensions present appropriate parameters for defining church growth. This dissertation proposes the following definition of church growth: *the proportional development of the church in leadership, numerical size, spirituality, and social engagement*. Here, Jesus's growth in wisdom corresponds to leadership maturity, with leaders often needing to demonstrate sound judgement in administering the

---

91. Fox, *Watching the English*, 33–546.

92. Erdman, *Gospel of Luke*.

93. "The child grew and became strong, filled with wisdom; and the favor of God was upon him" (Luke 2:40).

94. Utley, "Luke the Historian," 55.

95. Getz, " Christian Home Part II," 157–160.

96. Kevin Madigan, "Did Jesus 'Progress in Wisdom'?," 179.

material and immaterial resources of the church. Christ's increase in years, as a numerical dimension of growth, translates to growth in the membership size of the church. Jesus's growth in divine favour implies a qualitative spiritual growth – growth in faith and grace – of the church. Progression in human favour means that the church improves on its social involvements, both internally and externally.

1.7 Structure of the Study

In this first chapter of a ten-part dissertation, I introduced the research. I highlighted the research question the study pursues and why it is important to me. Then I presented the aims of the inquiry, the chief being to discover the prime factors impacting church growth among African diaspora congregations in Liverpool. A discussion of the nature of the study followed before considering the backdrop against which the inquiry emerges. Prior to the concluding thought, other issues of concern in the chapter were originality, contribution to knowledge, limitations of the study, and the discussion of key terms in the dissertation.

To establish the inquiry within context, in chapter 2, I survey important voices in the field of African diaspora Christianity in Europe, with a special focus on Britain. The exploration unfolds in two parts. The first part examines the research of earlier contributors to the field, while the second part looks into what recent scholars are saying. After the two-part discourse, I explore some widely embraced church growth ideas, a dialogue that precedes a brief conclusion of the chapter.

I dedicate the third chapter to the research methodology. Here, I present the theoretical framework for the research orientation of this inquiry – qualitative research. I also contemplate the rationale behind the inquiry's approach before describing the process of data collection and analysis. In expanding the data collection and analysis procedure, I show how I selected the most appropriate tools for gathering the field data and the process of systematic data analysis. I also consider a reflexive account of my role as a researcher in the investigation while not overlooking some ethical considerations for the study. I then wrap up all discourses with a concise conclusion.

Chapter 4 covers the theories of church growth. While these are numerous, the chapter only contemplates some common concepts underlining and shaping church growth understanding and activities. Themes in the chapter range from theories about church growth types to popular church growth models, and other church growth principles. This exploration of church growth theories equally engenders discussions on multi-ethnic congregations and contextualization, both being essential concepts in the field of missions. A concise conclusion ties up all conversations at the end of the chapter.

Chapter 5 is an account of the development of African diaspora congregations in Liverpool. While the context of conversations here is sometimes Britain, and even Europe as a whole, Liverpool remains the primary focus. The examination of migration's role in the mission of God, and indeed church growth, begins the chapter. After that, I consider the movement of Christianity (as it were) from Europe to Africa and then back to Europe. The phases of the migration of African Christianity to Europe, which have produced African diaspora congregations in Britain, also receive attention. The final conversation preceding the conclusion focuses more narrowly on Liverpool. It accounts for the development of African diaspora congregations in the city.

The sixth chapter reports the research findings and the outcome of the study in relation to existing literature. Here, the focus is on analysing the field data, identifying interconnections and relationships between different aspects of the data. Dominant themes emerge along with other categories. These broad themes help us ponder the research questions in connection with the synthesized data. A summary of ideas ends the chapter.

In chapter 7, I formulate the *omolúàbí*-shaped ecclesiology to address the issues arising from the research findings. The contextualized African ecclesiology aims to provide a framework for ADCs to "be and do church" in ways that promote fruitful missions and church growth in the UK. The OSE is extensive and beneficial not only to ADCs and the church in Africa, but also to the global church. After considering how OSE challenges the church growth hindrances the study identifies, I converge all arguments and bring the chapter to a close.

Chapter 8 investigates one of the critical issues arising from the research findings: the dynamics of race and how it affects ADCs' growth in Liverpool. As a sequel to this reflection, to understand the depth of racialization in the research context, I remark on the needless creation of race and the ideology of European racism. Then, I critique the notion of a biological basis for racial stratification. I also differentiate between ethnicity and race, since the former is common in literature discussing human diversity. Before concluding the chapter, I highlight the two critical events of slavery and race riots in the history of race relations in the UK, focusing on Liverpool.

Chapter 9 unfolds the adaptive leadership (AL) strategy as a nested response within OSE to the leadership-oriented issues arising from the investigation. The need for AL becomes critical following the huge reference to leadership as a primary factor influencing church growth among the research population. Moreover, AL's design is appropriate for handling unfamiliar situations and challenges that require new learnings for solutions, as with the church growth endeavour of ADCs in the UK. Therefore, this chapter unpacks the structure and process of adaptive leadership as a productive leadership approach for ADCs in Liverpool and the UK. It particularly highlights how ADCs can benefit practically from the AL technique before wrapping up with concluding thoughts.

The tenth chapter summarizes the ideas I have presented and developed in the dissertation and the conclusions of the discussions. I point out some positives and aspirations arising from the investigation. In other words, I resolve arguments and propositions advanced in the study after highlighting the central thoughts of the thesis. I also share some perspectives on how the research findings can positively shape mission practice for the global church.

1.8 Conclusion

This introductory chapter has presented the main questions pursued by the study. To further set the stage for the investigation, other relevant discussions concerned the nature of the study, its background and aim, and the need for the inquiry. The chapter also highlighted the research's originality and contribution to knowledge, including its limitations. It was also important to define some critical terminology used in the thesis. All these provided an overall opening and general insight into the research project. The subsequent chapter presents a review of literature relevant to the inquiry.

CHAPTER 2

Literature Review

2.1 Introduction

This chapter looks at some crucial literature pertinent to this inquiry. It starts by exploring the early and leading contributors in the field of African diaspora Christianity in Britain and, extensively, Europe. This step was critical in tracing the current state of conversations on African diaspora Christianity in Britain. The implication is that this research can build upon existing knowledge in the field as it processes new ideas. Subsequent to the review of scholarly voices on African diaspora Christianity, the second part of the chapter examines some popular church growth notions both in theory and practice. Here, notably, I survey the Church Growth Movement (CGM) concepts that have been widely embraced and thus have shaped general church growth thoughts and praxis. The chapter wraps up with a conclusion.

2.2 Voices Attending African Diaspora Christianity in Europe (Britain)

The conversation about African Christianity in the diaspora has continued to gain popularity among scholars. Of course, with the oldest African congregations in Europe found on the turf of former colonial powers (Britain in particular), Britain often forms a common context for exploring African diaspora congregations in Europe.[1] In discussing the voices commenting on

---

1. Haar, *Halfway to Paradise*, i.

African congregations in Europe, the British situation is presented extensively, which is helpful for this study.

2.2.1 Early Explorers

Some scholars came on the scene of African diaspora Christianity dialogue as early as the 1970s to form the foremost voices on the subject in Europe today. Though these front-liners are from Germany, Holland, and Nigeria, the geographical context of their work cuts across all of Europe and extends to Africa. As I look at the various contributors in the following conversations, I first highlight the European scholars mainly because their voices sounded long before their counterparts.

2.2.1.1 Roswith Gerloff

Born and educated in Germany, Roswith Gerloff (1933–2013) was a renowned scholar who brought much attention to the impact of Black churches in Britain from the angle of theology, research, and partnership.[2] This Lutheran pastor, ordained as a United Evangelical Church minister, worked in England for many years and founded (in 1978) and directed (until 1985) the Centre for Black and White Christian Partnership in Selly Oak, Birmingham.[3] Her comprehensive doctoral dissertation, titled "A Plea for British Black Theologies: The Black Church Movement in Britain in its Transatlantic Cultural and Theological Interaction with Special Reference to the Pentecostal Oneness (Apostolic) and Sabbatarian Movements,"[4] firmly established her voice in the field of African diaspora Christianity. Indeed, she had been interested in African diaspora Christianity in Britain since the 1970s, when her first article on the Black Christian experience in Birmingham, entitled "Black Christian Communities in Birmingham: The Problem of Basic Recognition,"[5] was published in 1975.[6] The article itself was a product of her decision in the summer of 1973 to investigate the contemporary but largely unknown Black Pentecostalism in Britain and its link to migration and perennial racism.

---

2. The National Church Leaders' Forum, "NCLF Update News."
3. Hocken, "Review of *A Plea*," 117.
4. Gerloff, "Plea for British Black Theologies."
5. Gerloff, "Black Christian Communities."
6. Kwiyani, *Sent Forth*, 88.

Consequently, Gerloff began a long spell of engagement with African diaspora Christianity across Europe and has published widely on Black Pentecostalism, intercultural learning, and Black religion.[7]

Gerloff must, indeed, be commended for her boldness and outstanding efforts in the studies of Black Christianity in Britain, for at the time of her first publication, the missional implications of the African presence in Britain had not begun to attract scholarly attention. It was not until the mid-1990s that sociologists of religion, such as Grace Davie, started to ponder the changes in British Christianity during the second half of the twentieth century.[8] Some publications earlier in the 1980s and 1990s centred on Afro-Caribbean immigrants, West African immigrants, and the interactions between the two groups.[9] However, the writings did not deliberately inquire into these communities' missional experiences and implications for British Christianity.

Gerloff's dissertation examined various issues around Black Christianity in Britain and metamorphosed into a two-volume book capturing much of her thinking and findings on the topic.[10] In the book, Gerloff alludes to the exponential growth of independent Black congregations in Britain since the Second World War. She explains that immigration engendered and has aided the development of Black congregations in Britain. Plus, while the inherent sociological factors of British society, such as racial discrimination and social deprivation, are realities that impact these communities, their proliferation is greatly facilitated by strong cultural and theological forces that have shaped their spiritual experiences. In fact, Gerloff believes that their faith, theologies, and organization could serve as a model for other ethnic minorities. In his foreword to the book, Swiss theologian Walter Hollenweger,, with a special interest in global Pentecostalism, also writes about the "original theological contribution" that Black Pentecostal Christianity brings, which challenges "western Filioque pneumatology."[11] In the pneumatology of Black Christianity, Hollenweger explains that the Spirit is not just the third person of the Trinity who can then be easily dismissed or confined, but "a cosmological

---

7. Gerloff, "My Pilgrimage in Mission."

8. Kwiyani, *Sent Forth*, 88. One important work of Grace Davie at this time was Davie, *Religion in Britain*.

9. Ludwig and Asamoah-Gyadu, *African Christian Presence*, 7.

10. See Gerloff, *Plea for British Black*.

11. Hollenweger, "Foreword," x.

reality for life and liturgy, for politics and prayer, for healing and wholeness, for unity and diversity."[12]

2.2.1.2 Gerrie ter Haar

Gerrie ter Haar is a scholar of religion interested in religious expressions and the experiences of Africa and the African diaspora. The Dutch emeritus Professor of Religion and Development at the International Institute of Social Studies (ISS) of Erasmus University, Rotterdam, has done immense work on African diaspora Christianity.[13] Ter Haar has authored or edited over twenty books (translated into Spanish, French, Italian, and Japanese) and has published in a wide range of journals on African diaspora Christianity and other issues such as "development, human rights, conflict and peace, religion and politics, and religion and migration."[14] Her third book on religious traditions in Africa, a ground-breaking piece on African diaspora Christianity, *Halfway to Paradise: African Christians in Europe*,[15] came out in 1998.

Halfway to Paradise details African diaspora Christianity, particularly that of the Ghanaians in the Netherlands. Most of the research occurred between 1992 and 1996. Hence, the book mostly chronicles developments during the early 1990s.[16] The trailblazing status of *Halfway to Paradise* among European discourses on African diaspora Christianity is thus understandable. Mission theologian Harvey Kwiyani states that many of the issues evolving from the book have yet to be addressed nearly two decades after its publication.[17] There is, for instance, the persistent issue of race and ethnicity, along with the unwaning yearning for recognition by political agencies of African Christian communities in Europe. Suffice it to say that the book methodically takes African Christianity seriously.

Of great significance is another writing of ter Haar, *Strangers and Sojourners: Religious Communities in Diaspora*, which was a collection of essays from a conference organized in 1995 by the author at Leiden University.[18] Arguing

---

12. Hollenweger, x.
13. African Studies Centre Leiden, "Gerrie ter Haar."
14. African Studies Centre Leiden.
15. Haar, *Halfway to Paradise*.
16. Haar, i–ii.
17. Kwiyani, *Sent Forth*, 90.
18. Haar, *Strangers and Sojourners*.

that the modern world is full of diasporas, the book explores the past and present applications of the term *diaspora* in relation to religious communities in different settings. Specific chapters discuss various diaspora groups, such as Africans in modern Europe, Hindus in Britain, and Jews in ancient Egypt. The author also indicated that the study of African Initiated Churches in Europe was at its nascent stage at the time of writing, an observation that is still mostly valid today.[19] Therefore, it is helpful to have this collection of articles giving attention to the presence of the religious communities of African migrants to Europe, as opposed to the more popular scholarly focus on Afro-Caribbeans. Since her publication, ter Haar has established herself as one of the foremost researchers and commentators on African diaspora Christianity. She continues to write on African Christianity both in Africa and the diaspora. Her works include *How God became African: African Spirituality and Western Secular Thought*[20] and "The Role of Religion in Development: Towards a New Relationship between the European Union and Africa."[21]

2.2.1.3 David Goodhew

The Anglican priest and scholar, David Goodhew, is the vicar of St. Barnabas Church, Middlesborough, and the Co-Director of the Centre for Church Growth Research at Durham University.[22] He has published widely (including edited volumes) on the subject of church growth in Britain including *The Desecularisation of the City: London's Churches, 1980 to the Present*,[23] *Growth and Decline in the Anglican Communion, 1980 to the Present*,[24] *Towards a Theology of Church Growth*,[25] and *Church Growth in Britain, 1980 to the Present Day*.[26] In his writings, Goodhew revaluates the common literary portrayal of Christianity in Britain as receding due to the secularising culture of the society. For instance, his notable edited volume, *Church Growth in Britain, 1980*

---

19. Haar, *Strangers and Sojourners*, 3.
20. Haar, *How God Became African*.
21. Ellis and Haar, " Role of Religion."
22. Centre for the Study of Modern Christianity, "Centre for Church Growth."
23. Goodhew and Cooper, *Desecularisation of the City*.
24. Goodhew, *Growth and Decline*.
25. Goodhew, *Towards a Theology*.
26. Goodhew, *Church Growth in Britain*.

to the Present Day,[27] brings together contributions from assorted researchers and commentators on the dynamics of church growth in Britain. The compendium explores the varied expressions of church growth among mainstream churches and the proliferation of Black Majority Churches in England while also assessing the forms of church growth happening in Scotland, Wales, and Northern Ireland. In this four-part work, the authors demonstrate that despite the unabating secularization leading to decline in the British church, in the thirty-year period since 1980, substantial growth has also been occurring in the life of the church over a wide geographical area. Although this growth is mostly beyond mainstream churches and multicultural in nature, it has not been getting as much attention from researchers or scholars as has the church decline argument and secularization.

2.2.1.4 Jehu Hanciles

Sierra Leonean Jehu J. Hanciles is the D.W. and Ruth Brooks Professor of World Christianity and Director of the World Christianity Program at Candler School of Theology, Emory University (USA). He has lived and worked across several continents in countries such as Sierra Leone, Scotland, Zimbabwe, and the United States. He was also a visiting professor at various schools before joining the Candler School of Theology faculty in 2012.[28] His interest in global Christianity, primarily through the prism of migration, is then understandable. As a highly sought-after scholar, Hanciles not only holds membership with different academic bodies – including the American Academy of Religion, American Society of Church History, and American Society of Missiology – but has also worked within various ecclesiological traditions. These include "Presbyterian church (Scotland), a Pentecostal church (Zimbabwe), a Baptist church, and the Vineyard (United States)," despite growing up in an Anglican tradition.[29]

Since completing his PhD in 1995 at the University of Edinburgh, Scotland,[30] Hanciles has produced publications on World Christianity from an African perspective, but drawing significantly from his experience and learning in

---

27. Goodhew, ed. *Church Growth in Britain*.
28. Candler School of Theology, "Jehu J. Hanciles."
29. Candler School of Theology.
30. His master's degree in 1991 is also from the University of Edinburgh.

Britain.³¹ He has consciously accentuated African immigrants' contributions and potential impacts on the sustenance and future of Christianity in Britain, the West, and around the globe, despite the experience of marginalization and socio-economic difficulties attending these immigrant communities in the diaspora. Hence, in his renowned 2008 publication, *Beyond Christendom*,³² Hanciles examines global trends, such as globalization and migration (South-to-North most prominently), and how these events are coming together to impact the West and the future of global Christianity. Of course, as he shows with statistical figures and in agreement with other scholars, the heartland of Christianity has now shifted from the global North to the global South (Africa, Asia, Latin America), which is currently home to two-thirds of all Christians in the world. Thus, it may be fair to imagine that the majority of the immigrant groups showing up in the West are Christians. This trend, indeed, is not without potential implications for the religious life of Britain and the West in general, where rapid erosion of the Christian faith from the public scene is taking place. Hanciles has developed these thoughts further in one of his latest books, titled *Migration and the Making of Global Christianity*.³³

2.2.1.5 Afeosemime Adogame

Nigerian scholar Afeosemime (Afe) Adogame is the Maxwell M. Upson Professor of Religion and Society, doubling as Chair of the History and Ecumenics Department, Princeton Theological Seminary, New Jersey (US). His PhD was in the history of religions from the University of Bayreuth in Germany. At Bayreuth, Adogame served as a teaching and senior research fellow before moving in 2005 to the University of Edinburgh.³⁴ While he has a wide range of research and teaching interests, he tends to focus on investigating new ways religions present themselves in Africa and the African diaspora, especially African Christianity and fresh indigenous religious movements.

---

31. Some of his works include *World Christianity: History, Methodologies, Horizons*; "Keeping the Faith: Immigration, Religion, and the Unmaking of Global Culture"; "'Africa is our Fatherland': The Black Atlantic, Globalization, and Modern African Christianity"; *Euthanasia of a Mission: African Church Autonomy in a Colonial Context*; "'Singing the Song of the Lord on Foreign Soil': What the Early Centuries Tell Us about the Migrant Factor in the Making of Global Christianity."
32. Hanciles, *Beyond Christendom*.
33. Hanciles, *Migration and the Making*.
34. The Religious Studies Project, "Afe Adogame."

Adogame's special interests also include the link between migration and religion, politics, globalization, the economy, media, and civil society.[35]

In 1998, Adogame studied the Celestial Church of Christ, an African Initiated Church from Nigeria with many branches in Germany, for his PhD project. His publication in 1998, "A Home Away from Home: The Proliferation of the Celestial Church of Christ (CCC) in Diaspora-Europe,"[36] and "Celestial Church of Christ: The Politics of Cultural Identity in a West African Prophetic Charismatic Movement"[37] in 1999 perhaps derive from this doctoral thesis. Adogame's dissertation certainly raised issues that would generate much curiosity in the following years. For instance, just five years later, in February 2003, Bayreuth University put together the "Religion in the Context of African Migration" conference, which attracted assorted scholars from Europe, Africa, and North America. This conference produced a book jointly edited by Adogame and Cordula Weissköeppel, *Religion in the Context of African Migration*.[38]

Adogame has written extensively in journals, books, papers, and other literature, and the majority of his works have centred on Europe. In fact, he has teamed up with most of the European voices on issues connected with African Christianity in Africa and abroad.[39] Some of his collaborative works are *Christianity in Africa and the African Diaspora: The Appropriation of a Scattered Heritage*[40] and *Fighting in God's Name: Religion and Conflict in Local-Global Perspectives*.[41] Other writings by Adogame include *Who is Afraid of the Holy Ghost? Pentecostalism and Globalization in Africa and Beyond*[42] and *Indigeneity in African Religions: Oza Worldviews, Cosmologies and Religious Cultures*.[43]

---

35. Princeton Theological Seminary, "Afe Adogame."
36. Adogame, "Home Away from Home."
37. Adogame, "Celestial Church of Christ."
38. Adogame and Weissköppel, *Religion in the Context*.
39. Kwiyani, *Sent Forth*, 91–92.
40. Adogame, Gerloff, and Hock, *Christianity in Africa*.
41. Adogame, Adeboye, and Williams, *Fighting in God's Name*.
42. Adogame, *Who Is Afraid*.
43. Adogame, *Indigeneity in African Religions*.

2.2.2 More Recent Contributors

The last two decades have witnessed more conversations on African Christianity in the diaspora. In other words, interest in African Christianity on the European continent and in the diaspora is increasing. Of the growing number of voices in this field of discourse, I find the following particularly important as they have been consistently on the scene and are significantly visible.

2.2.2.1 Babatunde Adedibu

Babatunde Aderemi Adedibu is the provost of Redeemed Christian Bible College, an affiliate of the University of Ibadan, Nigeria. This scholar holds a PhD in Missiology from North-West University, South Africa. He is a professor in the Department of Christian Religious Studies, Redeemer's University, Ede, Nigeria. Adedibu is motivated by issues surrounding religious expressions and experiences in Africa and the African diaspora. He is particularly interested in non-Western Christianity and how this intersects with mission, migration, and theology.[44]

Adedibu has published significantly on African diaspora Christianity in Britain due to his research interest.[45] Indeed, his doctoral thesis titled "The Urban Explosion of Black Majority Churches: Their Origin, Growth, Distinctives and Contribution to British Christianity"[46] has formed the bedrock of his subsequent writings, such as *A Coat of Many Colours: The Origin, Growth, Distinctives and Contribution of Black Majority Churches to British Christianity*,[47] which elaborate on ideas expressed in his dissertation. In the book and his thesis, Adedibu compares British Christianity to a "coat of many colours" because of the growing presence of Black Majority Churches (BMCs) in the region. Of course, the multiplication of these churches also affects the theological landscape of the land.

---

44. Religious Communities and Sustainable Development, "Adedibu, Babatunde Aderemi."
45. See for instance, "Origin, Migration, Globalisation and the Missionary Encounter of Britain's Black Majority Churches"; "Mission from Africa: A Call to Re-imagine Mission within African-Led Pentecostal Churches in Britain"; *Coat of Many Colours: The Origin, Growth, Distinctives and Contribution to Black Majority Churches to British Christianity*; "The Changing Faces of African Independent Churches as Development Actors across Borders."
46. Adedibu, "Urban Explosion of Black."
47. Adedibu, *Coat of Many Colours*.

The professor insists that, unlike the widespread belief among some Black British theologians, the *Windrush* migration was only an impetus for the spread of BMCs in Britain and not the beginning of the movement. Even though he identifies the theology of these BMCs as resembling that of American Pentecostalism, especially in pneumatic and experiential approaches, Adedibu highlights how instead the African worldview shapes the Pentecostal theology of BMCs. In fact, in one of his relatively recent articles, "Faith without Borders: Maximising the Missionary Potential of Britain's Black-Majority Churches,"[48] Adedibu maintains that the majority of BMCs in England, Germany, and North America are "repositories of migrant cultures, where inherent cultural ideologies are expressed through the worship and liturgy of their home countries."[49]

Adedibu also iterates that BMCs play crucial roles in helping their members cope with settlement in a new land despite their political impact remaining in infancy. He ultimately argues that BMCs in Britain must rethink their missional strategies and pay attention to the British context to have future relevance. Other tasks they must carry out include leadership development, theological training, and planting of missional churches.[50] Adedibu continues to explore and develop all these dimensions of African Christianity in Britain in his writings.

2.2.2.2 Harvey Kwiyani

Currently serving as the CEO of Global Connections (a UK network for world mission) and teaching at the Church Mission Society, Oxford, Harvey C. Kwiyani, a Malawian mission theologian, has more than twenty years of mission and theological education experience traversing Europe and the United States.[51] Having pastored at St. Paul Vineyard Church in St. Paul, Minnesota, and taught missions, theology, and African Christianity across multiple tertiary institutions, Kwiyani is not only a mission practitioner but a seasoned scholar as well. The missiologist holds a PhD in Missions from Luther Seminary and is the founder of Missio Africanus and chief editor of

---

48. Adedibu, "Faith without Borders."
49. Adedibu, 3.
50. Adedibu, "Urban Explosion of Black."
51. Global Connections, "Staff Team."

Missio Africanus: Journal of African Missiology (MAJAM). He is on the editorial team of *ANVIL: Journal of Theology and Mission,* produced by the Church Mission Society. He convenes the Pan-African Theological Roundtable, a scholarly gathering exploring Christianity through an African lens, among other functions.

Kwiyani's primary passions are evident from his multifaceted engagements. He is enthusiastic about missions in the West, especially as this endeavour plays out in the hands of non-Western entities. Hence, his groundbreaking book titled *Sent Forth: African Missionary Work in the West*. In *Sent Forth*, Kwiyani argues persuasively for the significance of the increasing presence of African migrant mission practitioners in the West. Even though the author writes from the United States, he completed his master's degree in Birmingham, UK. Thus, he writes from a rich perspective. The work occupies a new frontline of contemplating mission today, considering the changing face of world Christianity, one that is looking darker by the day. The richness of Kwiyani's works has always derived from the combination of a research process and a lived experience.

The interests of Kwiyani also makes him enthused about African Christianity, both on the African continent and in the diaspora. Since relocating to Britain, Kwiyani has devoted much of his research to exploring missions and African Christianity in the West from a British context. Among his various journal articles, book chapters, books, and co-authored literature,[52] a book published in 2020, *Multicultural Kingdom: Ethnic Diversity, Mission and the Church*,[53] sends a strong message and reveals much about the author's passion. In *Multicultural Kingdom*, Kwiyani emphasizes how twenty-first century Britain is a multicultural setting. Yet, the church in Britain is not taking advantage of the opportunities presented by this cultural diversity.

In the same book, the author observes that the migration of Africans, Asians and Latin American Christians to Britain is having a great influence

---

52. Some of Kwiyani's works include "Exploring Adaptive Challenges"; *Our Children Need Roots and Wings: Equipping and Empowering Young Diaspora Africans for Life and Mission*; *Mission-Shaped Church in a Multicultural World*; "Mission after George Floyd: On White Supremacy, Colonialism and World Christianity"; "Can the West Really Be Converted?"; "African Congregations Adapting to COVID-19: Conversations with African Christian Nurses in Britain," 32–39.

53. Kwiyani, *Multicultural Kingdom*.

on the religious and cultural outlook of the region. Indeed, the form of Christianity these non-Western groups bring introduces diversity to British Christianity. This flow of non-Western Christians to the West, Kwiyani has often reflected, is nothing but the fulfilment of the *blessed reflex* – again, connoting a time when non-Western Christians will refresh Western Christianity.[54] In all, Kwiyani shows that the kingdom of God is multicultural, citing several scriptural examples. Consequently, the British church must embrace and maximize its cultural diversity by overcoming racism and tribalism and developing a multicultural ecclesiology, among other issues. Multiculturalism is the state of twenty-first-century Britain and what the church in the region must grapple with today.

2.2.2.3 Israel Olofinjana

Israel Oluwole Olofinjana is a Nigerian scholar and one of the founding directors of the Centre for Missionaries from the Majority World. The centre is a mission initiative that provides cross-cultural training to those engaged in mission work in the West. Although from a Pentecostal background, he is an ordained Baptist minister who has led two multi-ethnic churches and an independent charismatic congregation. Olofinjana is an honorary research fellow at The Queen's Foundation for Ecumenical Theological Education, Birmingham, and belongs to the advisory body of the Society for the Study of Theology (SST) on matters of race and theology. He is also on the Christian Aid working group for Black Majority Church (BMC) leaders, examining the convergence of climate and racial justice.[55] He has a Bachelor of Arts in Religious Studies from the University of Ibadan, Nigeria, and an Master of Theology in Christian Apologetics from Carolina University of Theology, Virginia, US.[56] His doctoral degree is from the University of Roehampton.

Olofinjana's research interests cut through intercultural mission, focusing on the African congregations' missional engagements in Europe, church history (especially of African Pentecostals and BMCs), contextual theology, biblical hermeneutics, and Christian apologetics.[57] He is very concerned with

---

54. Kwiyani, *Multicultural Kingdom*, 20.
55. Evangelical Alliance, "Rev Dr Israel Oluwole."
56. Langham Publishing, "Israel Oluwole Olofinjana."
57. The Queen's Foundation, "Rev Dr Israel Oluwole Olofinjana."

how ADCs in the UK can do missions better. Therefore, he has written such books as *Turning the Tables on Mission*,[58] a compendium of missionary voices from the global South sharing their missional experiences in Britain and providing helpful tips for improved productivity. Olofinjana's research of nearly a decade on Nigerian Pentecostal church history in 2011 gave birth to the book *20 Pentecostal Pioneers in Nigeria: Their Lives, Their Legacies*.[59] Olofinjana has authored or edited several other books, papers, and journal articles, including *Partnership in Mission: A Black Majority Perspective on Mission and Church Unity*,[60] *African Voices: Towards African British Theologies*,[61] and "Reverse Missiology: Mission Approaches and Practices of African Christians within the Baptist Union of Great Britain."[62]

2.2.2.4 Anderson Moyo

Anderson Moyo is the Senior Pastor of Sheffield Community Church, UK. He holds a Doctor of Ministry degree from Asbury Theological Seminary, Kentucky (USA).[63] His thesis, entitled "The Audacity of Diaspora Missions: The Antioch Multiethnic Church-Planting Model for African Reverse Missionaries in Post Christendom Britain,"[64] which has now evolved into a book,[65] examines the theological explanation for the missional approaches of African diaspora communities in Britain, including their impacts, considering some anthropological realities. In the dissertation, Moyo ultimately formulates a biblical model for growing multi-ethnic churches in the diaspora. Moyo finds the chronicle of the Antioch church in Acts 11 very instructive for planting multi-ethnic congregations in multicultural societies like Britain. He believes strongly in the biblical imperative for churches to be multi-ethnic. Hence, he argues that the expanding ADCs in Britain must adopt this way of doing missions and setting up churches for successful missionary endeavour in their new home.

---

58. Olofinjana, *Turning the Tables*.
59. Olofinjana, *20 Pentecostal Pioneers*.
60. Olofinjana, *Partnership in Mission*.
61. Olofinjana, *African Voices*.
62. Olofinjana, "Reverse Missiology."
63. Langham Publishing, "Anderson Moyo."
64. Moyo, "Audacity of Diaspora Missions."
65. Moyo, *The Audacity of Diaspora Missions*.

2.2.2.5 Johnson Afrane-Twum

The missiology scholar Johnson Afrane-Twum earned his PhD from North-West University, South Africa, in 2018. His thesis reflects much of his passion for and interest in African diaspora communities. Afrane-Twum's thesis, titled "The Mission of the African Immigrant Churches in the Multicultural Context of the UK,"[66] appeals for better collaboration of ADCs and White majority churches in realising missions in the UK. The missiologist believes that ADCs must harness "the historic resources that have informed and governed their existence to date."[67] He adds that if this happens, ADCs' theologies, missiology, and ecclesiology will find enhancement, meeting the host community's needs, as well as those of their own congregations, thus ultimately fostering partnership.

2.2.2.6 Sheila Akomiah-Conteh

Based in Glasgow, Scotland, the Ghanaian scholar Akomiah-Conteh announced herself on the scene of African diaspora Christianity conversations with her doctoral degree from the University of Aberdeen in 2019. Akomiah-Conteh's dissertation, entitled "The Changing Landscape of the Church in Post-Christendom Britain: New Churches in Glasgow, 2000–2016," encapsulates much of her thought on ADCs in Britain, especially in Scotland. In this work, which she has continued to build upon, Akomiah-Conteh contends that though a narrative of decline has characterized the British church, a shift is happening due to the emergence of new churches and Christian communities, mostly African congregations. These new Christian faith groups, found chiefly in urban areas, are altering the composition of the church and introducing fresh patterns of growth, theologies, liturgies, and ecclesiology to the British space, as the researcher evidenced with her studies.[68] Indeed, African congregations have continued to revitalize the religious life of Britain, whether intentionally or unintentionally.

---

66. Afrane-Twum, "Mission of the African Immigrant."
67. Afrane-Twum, 2.
68. Akomiah-Conteh, "Changing Landscape."

2.2.3 Present State of the Discourse

African diaspora Christianity may be generating more attention in academia, yet the discourse on the African missionary movement to the West still appears to be budding even two decades after ter Haar raised the concern in her book entitled *Strangers and Sojourners*. I agree with Kwiyani that "African Christianity is by far the least documented story of all Christianities present in the West."[69] Indeed, the difficulty of tracing the number and history of Liverpool ADCs in connection with this inquiry corroborates Kwiyani's statement. Nonetheless, some positive developments are emerging. For instance, more academic institutions and mainstream mission organizations are creating greater spaces and avenues for engaging with African Christianity, both on the continent and in the diaspora. These include the Andrew Walls Centre for the Study of African and Asian Christianity at Liverpool Hope University and the newly fledged Master's in Theology, Mission, and Ministry (African Diaspora Christianity) programme sponsored by the Church Missionary Society (CMS) in partnership with Durham University.

Consultations, collaborations, and network formations are also multiplying, producing essays and books enhancing the conversations about African Christianity in the diaspora. Some of these important gatherings, which are fast establishing themselves as crucial theological conversations, are: the Pan-African Theological Roundtable, convened by Harvey Kwiyani; the African Diaspora Mission Network, directed by Rev Ebenezer Aryee; and the Centre for Missionaries from the Majority World, steered by Israel Olofinjana. Mission practitioners and ADC leaders are also organising into groups and creating platforms for interaction, however superficial they may sometimes be.

Earlier, African Christian leaders in Britain were very critical of Western Christianity. To them, British Christianity was dead and the continent dark – a description that applied to Africa in the colonial era. In fact, much of these leaders' popular literature, such as Wale Babatunde's *Great Britain Has Fallen: How to Restore Britain's Greatness as a Nation*, published about two decades ago, insisted that Western Christianity was dead and required revival.[70] In the present time, however, more grace and sagacity are reflected in the way

---

69. Kwiyani, *Sent Forth*, 100.
70. Babatunde, *Great Britain Has Fallen*.

ADC leaders are approaching, talking about, and interacting with British Christians and Christianity generally. As Kwiyani words it, there is now "a sombre realization that if they [African Christian leaders] are to be effective missionaries in Britain, African Christians need to work with the British Christians the way they are now."[71] Consequently, these leaders' body language and tone are now less arrogant, and they are more deliberate in missions and partnerships. Their writings[72] are also increasingly highlighting the need to construct cross-cultural bridges with Western Christianity and growing multi-ethnic churches instead of homogenous congregations.[73]

2.3 On Church Growth: Pervasive Ideas

The concept of church growth has hitherto been overladen with American ideas, especially since the founder of the CGM, Donald McGavran, and its foundational proponents are primarily Americans. Moreover, the extant notions of church growth have been applied and adapted to the American context, perhaps in excess, and then propagated as universal. As such, these thoughts have become popular ideas shaping church growth thought.[74]

The overapplication of church growth principles in America is partly seen, for example, in the excessive encouragement and emphasis on numerical church growth (the cardinal belief and teaching of McGavran) by many church leaders. Duncan Forrester, late Scottish theologian and founder of the Centre for Theology and Public Issues at the University of Edinburgh, attests to this reality as he records his observation about many American churches. He writes: huge congregations "crowd in to hear that the Lord will give them success in all their endeavours, healing of body and even miraculous dental fillings" multiple times every week.[75] Yet, a large number of the

---

71. Kwiyani, *Sent Forth*, 101.

72. See, for instance, Omideyi, *Transformed to Transform*; Olofinjana, *Partnership in Mission*; Afrane-Twum, "Mission of the African Immigrant."

73. I have expanded on multi-ethnic churches in a later conversation.

74. I remember how the church growth principles taught in my MDiv days at the seminary (located in South-Western Nigeria) were predominantly, if not all, about the CGM models.

75. The Redwood Chapel of Castro Valley, California; First Nazarene Church of Denver; First Baptist Church of Hammond, Indiana; Thomas Road Baptist Church of Lynchburg, Virginia; and First Baptist Church of Dallas, Texas are all illustrations of the seeming success

adherents may not necessarily belong to the church, as defined by Robert Warren, an former national officer for Evangelism of the Church of England, and Team Rector, St. Thomas Crookes churches.[76] One cannot but wonder if the American influence on church growth principles is the reason for their seemingly limited effectiveness in Britain.

Indeed, Britons exhibit some characteristics which distinguished them from (fellow Western) Americans. For instance, Fox writes about the Britons' distinctive love for moderation. She explains that the English have:[77]

> strict rules about the appearance of modesty, including prohibitions on boasting and any form of self-importance, and rules actively prescribing self-deprecation and self-mockery. We place a high value on modesty, we aspire to modesty . . . Modesty also requires that we try to play down or deny class/wealth/status differences . . . English displays of modesty (whether competitive, hypocritical, or genuine) are distinctive . . .

Fox expands further, in a later edition of the same book, that one could observe the moderation and conservation of the English from a helicopter without even setting foot in the country. Yes, the narrower roads (compared with America) and the smaller residential areas, which appear as small rows of boxes and tiny patches of green, are conspicuous.[78] Contrariwise, the often wider roads and larger residential structures of Americans, among other qualities, make it easy to conceive of the people as more glamorous, liberal, and outward-looking.[79] With the British love for moderation, such church

---

and evidence of the emphasis of numerical church growth in America. See more in Forrester, "Review of *Understanding Church Growth*," 422.

76. Warren defines the church as "a community of people drawn together by faith in and encounter with Jesus Christ as Lord, which leads them to take action in the whole of life, living by a different set of values from what would otherwise have been the case." See Warren, *Healthy Churches' Handbook*, 83.

77. Fox, *Watching the English*, 153–154.

78. Fox, 185; The relative moderation and conservatism of the British is also noticeable in their conversational codes and behavioural codes as Fox classifies them. For more on the British culture, see the works of David P. Christopher, including *British Culture: An Introduction*; Mikes, *How to Be a Brit*.

79. Easton, "English Question." British identity is a relatively recent construct which became superimposed on the national identities of English, Welsh, Scottish, and Irish. For more on British identity and how it differs from America's, see Heath and Roberts, *British Identity*.

growth models as the megachurch[80] will most likely not work well with them, not even in an era when massive church structures are disappearing or being adapted for other purposes. Of course, the same implication arises for other church growth models,[81] which may not align with the British worldview and national characteristics.

2.3.1 Core Teachings of McGavran and the Church Growth Movement

McGavran's teachings and CGM ideas have become almost universal practices and mission concepts. Hence, they require an examination, which this section of the dissertation presents. The following are the fundamental thoughts that McGavran and the CGM propagate.

2.3.1.1 Numerical Church Growth

McGavran and the CGM teach that numerical church growth is God's desire, an expression of the effectiveness of evangelism. Thus, the church and Christians must prioritize it, identify the factors propelling it and allocate more resources to them.[82] This notion resulted from McGavran's observation of how liberal theology was distorting the prominence of evangelism and the little productivity experienced by mission societies despite the massive input of resources in his days.

Certainly, numbers are significant, and statistics could be a helpful guide in identifying the strengths and weaknesses of the church. Nevertheless, McGavran and the CGM's strong emphasis on numerical growth seems to imply, in the words of Forrester, that churches not growing numerically are "failures, and probably faithless as well, while rapidly growing churches are healthy and committed."[83] This evaluation of church growth could not be

---

80. Megachurches emerged in the 1970s. The model describes large congregations with massive structures. The pastors of the churches are usually the founders and have long pastorates, which are characterized by strong leadership. They maintain large organizations and operate like businesses. Some of these churches in America include the Willow Creek Community and Saddleback churches. For more details, see Hong, "Models of Church Growth," 103. See also Niemandt and Yongsoo, "Korean Perspective on Megachurches."

81. See Hayward, "Dynamical Model of Church Growth"; Stark, *Rise of Christianity*, 7; Iannaccone, Olsen, and Stark, "Religious Resources"; Stark and Bainbridge, *Future of Religion*; Morgan, "Ultimate Church Growth Model."

82. McGavran, *Understanding Church Growth*, 31–40.

83. Forrester, "Understanding Church Growth," 422.

more discouraging for minority groups like the ADCs in the UK. Indeed, by being immigrants in a strange land, these congregations battle layered adaptive challenges besides secularization and other church growth difficulties. Moreover, church growth in numbers does not necessarily mean qualitative increase – maturity in grace and faith.[84]

2.3.1.2 Receptivity Principle and Harvest Theology

Having observed the varying degree of gospel reception across different people, McGavran formulated a receptivity principle and harvest theology.[85] He believed mission agents should direct the gospel towards groups that appear more inclined to it than individuals or communities that are less open, mainly because people operate more as a collective body than isolated persons.[86] The missiologist argued for "a vast and purposeful finding"[87] in recruiting people to the Christian faith rather than engaging in a search theology that promotes going everywhere and preaching the Word.[88]

Were the CGM's postulation to be precise, British society, plagued by secularism like most of the West, is already condemned as unresponsive to the gospel and unfit for "purposeful finding." In the words of Ralph Elliot, senior pastor of North Shore Baptist Church, Chicago, Britain is, therefore, "hopeless."[89] By implication, the missionary attempts of individuals or groups, such as African diaspora Christians, have already failed before starting. Besides secularism, the British identity and lifestyle of individualism would also imply fruitlessness in any missionary endeavour in the UK, since missions ought to be more directed at groups or communities, according to the CGM. By the receptivity principle and purposeful finding, McGavran and the CGM forgot to consider the uniqueness of every society, including Britain. Charles Van Engen, professor emeritus of Biblical Theology of Mission, is

---

84. Forrester, 422.
85. McGavran, *Understanding Church Growth*, 27.
86. McGavran, 49–63, 216–232.
87. McGavran, 38.
88. McGavran, 27.
89. Elliott warned against how church growth theology could doom cities to hopelessness with cities' common features of economic mobility, racial mixture, and changing neighbourhoods. See more in Elliott, "Dangers of the Church Growth," 4.

right to assert that the church ought not to overlook unresponsive groups and individuals while contemplating the principle of receptivity to the gospel.[90]

2.3.1.3 Homogenous Unit Principle

The third and perhaps most controversial conviction of CGM is the elastic application of the homogenous unit concept to church growth. Charles Peter Wagner, a devoted follower of McGavran from his student days at Fuller Theological Seminary,[91] defined the homogenous unit principle (HUP) as "a section of society in which all the members have some characteristics in common."[92] The commonalities may be language, tribe, class, culture, nationality, or other forms of shared attributes. By implication, with respect to missions, McGavran and the CGM advocate that people like to become Christians without crossing cultural or racial barriers.[93] Citing biblical and historical instances, such as the Christianization of the Berean Jews (Acts 17:10–14) and that of the Anglo-Saxons in AD 600, McGavran and the CGM crystalized their conviction about group conversion.[94] As Kwiyani observes, McGavran interpreted *panta ta ethne* (translated as "all the nations"), a phrase in the Great Commission of Matthew 28:19, as implying "peoples" of humanity – that is, families, clans, tribes, and ethnicities. Hence, McGavran concludes that group conversion is essential and usually more beneficial than individual conversion.[95]

HUP implicitly suggests that it is alright to have mono-ethnic congregations formed according to tribe, language, class, or other forms of caste. By this, the principle appears to forget a vital theme of the Christian gospel, the message of reconciliation, illustrated in the removal of the wall of partition between Jew and Greek, slave and free, male and female (Gal 3:28). The implications of the wall removal are extensive but include the collapse of

---

90. Van Engen, *Growth of the True*, 454–514.

91. McGavran became the founding Dean of Fuller Theological Seminary's new School of World Mission and Institute of Church Growth in 1965. Wagner was one of his students in 1967–1968. He later joined McGavran as a faculty member in 1971 after serving as adjunct professor between 1968 and 1970. See more in McIntosh, "Life of Donald McGavran," 39.

92. Wagner, *Strategies for Church Growth*, 181.

93. McGavran, *Understanding Church Growth*, 85–87.

94. Kwiyani, *Multicultural Kingdom*, 129.

95. Kwiyani, 129.

gaps between ethnicities, statuses, genders, and other kinds of divisions.[96] The reconciliation message is crucial for ADCs in the UK, which generally exist as closed, homogenous units. The congregations usually do church in favour of the dominant ethnicity in the church (often the pastor's), leading to alienation of *the others* or outsiders.[97]

The HUP has very significant, negative implications for the church. As American pastor John Perkins observes, "it sugarcoats racial segregation with a veneer of spirituality and in practice continues the legacy of segregation that divides whites and blacks into separate churches, relationships and agendas."[98] Modupe Omideyi, a scholar and leader of an ADC in the UK, corroborated this view with an account of a shocking experience of a white couple who had visited an African congregation in Liverpool for the first time. The following is their reflection.

> For a start, Steve and I were the only two white faces in the room . . . There was a lot of noise going on – beautiful singing, but strange to me because although the hymns were sung in English, a lot of the choruses were sung in Yoruba [a South-Western language of Nigeria] . . . Altogether the service must have been three hours long – no one seemed in a hurry to finish. I found it very African and not what I expected of a religious service![99]

I agree with Omideyi that many homogenous churches, like ADCs in the UK, "do not realise the extent to which their own expression of worship is influenced by culture or how alien that culture can seem to others."[100] Plus, this cultural influence is often directly proportional to the number of years since establishment of the congregations.[101] The implication for ADCs in the UK is that they are becoming increasingly irrelevant and strange, finding missions

---

96. Kwiyani explains the implications of being Jew or Greek and the other forms of social and economic segregations mentioned in Galatians 3:28. For details, see Kwiyani, *Multicultural Kingdom*, 86–88.

97. Sturge, *Look What the Lord Has Done*, 41. I have reflected more on the homogenous outlook of ADCs while discussing the research findings.

98. Perkins, *Beyond Charity*, 49.

99. Omideyi, *Transformed to Transform*, 30–31.

100. Omideyi, 33.

101. Kugbeadjor and Kwiyani, "Exploring Adaptive Challenges," 11.

more challenging. Nonetheless, McGavran's HUP is not altogether unhelpful in mission. It could be an easy springboard for starting a congregation. However, homogenous churches are not beneficial to the mission of God in the long run. As indicated in the Scriptures, they are never the ultimate goal for the church (Rev 7:9).[102]

2.4 Conclusion

It is helpful that African Christian leaders in the UK are now more cordial in their perspective, approach, and engagements with their Western counterparts. They are realising the need to collaborate for missional impact in the land. With the increase in consultations, conferences, and other platforms for promoting cross-cultural missions, ADCs in the UK, and of course, Liverpool, have a bright future. A holistic perspective on church growth, shifting focus from a one-sided development of the church, will minimize ADCs' frustrations as they assess their missional activities in modest and secular Britain. By implication, ADCs will find it less stressful to do church in Liverpool and the UK at large. However, generally homogenous African congregations must evolve into multi-ethnic churches. Homogeneity may be handy at the inception of a congregation, but it eventually limits cross-cultural missions. So, while it may be understandable for ADCs to begin as homogenous congregations (as minority communities struggling to adapt in the diaspora) remaining so falls far short of the multi-ethnic agenda of God.

---

102. For more on HUP and its downsides, see Kumbi, *Culturally Intelligent Leader*, 114–116; Stott, *Message of Romans*, 398.

CHAPTER 3

Methodology

3.1 Introduction

This chapter explicates the philosophy and set of ideas that shape the research design. The methodology presentation spreads out, first, into conversation on the rationale for the practical procedure of ethnographically-informed qualitative fieldwork – the approach through which this investigation proceeds. Second is the discourse on the primary data collection method, semi-structured interviews (SSI), which occurred both in person and over the telephone. The experiences of other scholars and researchers like Samson Ayokunle and Philip Oyewale, who have studied different aspects of the African diaspora Christians in Liverpool, were helpful in evaluating the research method.[1] I then explain the data analysis procedure before presenting a reflexive account of my role, as a researcher, in the study. I also reflect on some ethical considerations for the study. The chapter ends with a brief conclusion.

3.2 Theoretical Framework

In conducting a study, researchers usually start with certain assumptions about how and what they will learn during their inquiry, whether in

---

1. Philip Oyewale and Samson Ayokunle's dissertations were of tremendous importance to this study because they provided a similar context and methodology. Ouseph Puthussery's thesis was also insightful. For details of these scholarly records see Oyewale, "A Critical Analysis of Marital Instability"; Ayokunle, "Elements Sustaining Public Worship"; Puthussery, "Marriage and Migration: A Social-Theological Analysis."

paradigms, philosophical beliefs, epistemologies, ontologies, or broadly conceived research methodologies.[2] I processed ideas and reality through a social constructivist approach in this investigation. Social constructivism is the theory of knowledge that emphasizes the creation of knowledge or learning by interpreting the meanings others have about their world.[3] It focuses on the role of culture and context in contemplating happenings within society and builds up knowledge against that backdrop.[4]

Social constructivism theory is grounded in three orientations. First, reality creation is a joint effort of human activity; it (reality) does not exist before that. Second, knowledge is similarly a social and cultural construction resulting from human interactions with one another and their environment. Third, learning is also a social process. It happens as individuals participate in social activities.[5] Therefore, to a social constructionist, meanings are jointly developed with others rather than separately constructed in each person.[6] It is opposed to a post-positivist's approach to knowledge which "begins with a theory, collects data that either supports or refutes the stance, then, makes necessary revisions before conducting additional tests."[7] By implication, in this study, a response to identified church growth challenges only emerges from the field data – interpretations of participants' views on what they believe are elements conditioning church growth in their settings. The response is not a product of an assessment of a prior assumption or theory.

Having clarified how the construction of knowledge happened in this investigation, it is appropriate to consider the research approach. The nature of inquiry and type of information required shapes whatever strategy a researcher employs for any research.[8] With the two general orientations to

---

2. Creswell, *Research Design*, 6–9. Other knowledge claim schools of thought include: post-positivism, constructivism, advocacy/participatory, and pragmatism. For fuller discourse on knowledge claims see Magnus, "General Knowledge Claims," 1–14; Tamar and Koenig, "What I Don't Know," 826–835.

3. Thomas et al., "Applications of Social Constructivist," 2.

4. Kim, "Social Constructivism."

5. Kim, "Social Constructivism."

6. For more on social constructivism see Andrews, "What Is Social Constructivism?"

7. Creswell, *Research Design*, 7.

8. Bell, *Doing Your Research Project*, 8.

social research conduct being quantitative and qualitative strategies,[9] I have chosen the qualitative research approach in this investigation.

3.2.1 Qualitative Research Strategy

In describing qualitative research, Emeritus Professor of Education Keith Punch provides a simple and clear summary as he compares the research design with the quantitative study. He notes that "Quantitative research is empirical research where the data are in the form of numbers [while] qualitative research is empirical research where the data are not in the form of numbers."[10] In other words, qualitative study stresses words and their meanings, significances, and processes,[11] just like the non-numerical phenomenon of church growth this inquiry explores. Of course, numerical data, like participants' frequency of ideas, was not totally insignificant to this investigation. They were helpful in generating themes and categories for data analysis. Indeed, a good qualitative study "reports the range and frequency of actions and meaning, perspectives that are observed, as well as their occurrence, narratively."[12]

Moreover, because qualitative inquiry does not rest on a unified theory or methodological approach but lends itself to a spectrum of theoretical stances and techniques like interviews, observations, document analysis, and questionnaires, a researcher is free to determine the most suitable method for any study, and no one research instrument is privileged over others.[13] Consequently, there is the argument that the individual bias of a researcher – whether in selecting methods or interpreting data – may result in less generalisable, reliable or authentic findings in a qualitative study.[14] To improve the reliability and validity of this investigation, I elicited in-depth responses from participants within an environment that enabled ease of conversation and free flow of discussion – a non-threatening and

---

9. Bryman, *Social Research Methods*, 3.
10. Punch, *Introduction to Social Research*, 3.
11. For further elucidation, see Creswell, *Research Design*, 153–207.
12. Erickson, "Qualitative Research Methods," 1451.
13. Flick, *Introduction to Qualitative Research*, 16.
14. Berg, *Qualitative Research Methods*, 21.

non-intrusive environment[15] – whether during telephone interviews[16] or face-to-face meetings.

3.2.2 Rationale for a Qualitative Research Approach

In addition to the non-numeric nature of the research data, a major reason for undertaking a qualitative research approach for this study is its flexibility.[17] Indeed, I did not have to constrain myself to predetermined analytical categories in processing the field data, unlike questionnaires, for instance. Rather, themes emerged from the collected data, enhancing the study's credibility. In other words, taking a qualitative research approach for this investigation afforded me the liberty of developing a theory from the field data with concepts beginning to emanate from the initial coding phase, converging into broad themes, and culminating in a grounded theory of church growth (for example, the *omolúàbí*-shaped ecclesiology) for the research population.

Even more, the qualitative research's nature of viewing social phenomena holistically makes it suitable for this research.[18] Indeed, the research strategy aided the opportunity to account for various dimensions of church growth phenomena among the ADCs in Liverpool, even when interactions could no longer proceed face-to-face for limitations I discuss later in this chapter. In other words, qualitative research design turned out to be an excellent choice for this inquiry as it allowed the production of a rich, interactive, and encompassing narrative of the study.

The third rationale for adopting a qualitative research strategy for this investigation is its provision for the researcher to systematically reflect on his or her person and how it impacts the study.[19] Indeed, qualitative orientation does not deny the reality of the researcher's role in the final outcome of the study.[20] This feature of a qualitative study made it possible for me to account for my biases, values, and interests in this investigation. For these reasons, qualitative research became the theoretical framework for this study.

---

15. Alshenqeeti, "Interviewing as a Data Collection," 41.
16. I ascertained participants only proceeded with discussions if they were in a preferred environment.
17. Patton, *Qualitative Research*, 14.
18. Seligmann and Estes, "Innovations in Ethnographic Methods," 177.
19. Galdas, "Revisiting Bias," 1.
20. Attia and Edge, "Be(com)ing a Reflexive Researcher," 34.

3.2.3 The Relevance of Ethnography to the Study

While there are many theoretical perspectives available for conducting qualitative research, ranging from a narrative approach to phenomenology, historical research, grounded theory, ethnography, action research, content analysis, and case study,[21] this study employs ethnography[22] to conduct its investigations. However, the fieldwork itself is not a full-fledged ethnography; the inquiry only borrows from ethnographic methods. Therefore, it is ethnographically informed fieldwork. The rationale for conducting this ethnographically informed fieldwork emanates from the following considerations.

First, as a qualitative research approach, ethnography permits the probing of a particular social phenomenon rather than setting out to test an already constructed hypothesis, as in post-positivism.[23] This inquiry did not seek to affirm or disprove any already existing theory of church growth in relation to the research population. Rather, it aimed to probe and unearth any growth concept that may be appropriate to the context through the fieldwork. Thus, ethnography could not be better suited for this investigation.

Second, ethnography tends to focus on investigating, in as much detail as possible, small samples or examples that are considered illuminating and rich for research data.[24] In other words, it concentrates on "a single setting or group and is small-scale."[25] This investigation purposively selected[26] three population samples that were subject to a relatively comprehensive methodical probe and which represented small, interesting portions of the ADCs in Liverpool. For this reason, an ethnographic approach is appropriate for the study.

---

21. Haradhan, "Qualitative Research Methodology," 7.

22. Ethnography is both a research product and a research process in which the researcher engages in prolonged observation and participation to describe and interpret a cultural group's shared and learned patterns of values, behaviours, beliefs, and language. See more in Haradhan, "Qualitative Research Methodology," 13.

23. Creswell, *Research Design*, 7.

24. Vasileiou et al., "Characterising and Justifying Sample," 2; See also Blaxter, Hughes, and Tight, *How to Research*, 64.

25. Whitehead, "What Is Ethnography?," 19.

26. Purposive sampling is a method whereby the researcher uses his or her professionalism to select the research samples so that the data gathered might be able to measure what the researcher sets out to measure. For more on purposive sampling see Rea and Parker, *Designing and Conducting Survey*; Suri, "Purposeful Sampling."

Third, ethnography allows participants to provide a more detailed account of events or stories, unlike a quantitative framework.[27] This aspect of ethnography was especially advantageous to this study as it gave participants the opportunity to buttress arguments, clarify issues, and supply relevant information that could otherwise have been untapped.

The fourth rationale for preferring an ethnographically-informed research approach is that "ethnography is a cyclic iterative process, wherein the ethnographer moves back and forth between observations, interviewing, and interpretation."[28] This iterative attribute of ethnography was particularly beneficial to this investigation because I, as the researcher, had the opportunity to return to the field (mostly by telephone) at different stages of the research for clarifications, supporting or supplementary data, or omissions in previously gathered data.

3.3 Data Collection Methods

Data collection procedures in qualitative research broadly distil into four categories, namely observation, interviews, documents, and visual images.[29] While interviews and questionnaires are most common among researchers, the interview is probably the most widely employed method for researching the social world.[30] The choice and appropriateness of interview over questionnaire is perhaps due to interaction with people being one of the most effective ways of exploring the usually, indirectly observable, in-depth description of individuals and events in their natural settings.[31] Hence, I have engaged semi-structured interviews both in-person and by telephone as my cardinal data-gathering tools. Of course, I was conscious of other data-enriching opportunities through participant observation and document analysis.

---

27. Fusch, Fusch, and Ness, "How to Conduct," 924–925.
28. Whitehead, "Basic Classical Ethnographic Research."
29. Creswell, *Research Design*, 149; Hennink, Hutter, and Bailey, *Qualitative Research Methods*, 10.
30. Davies, *Reflexive Ethnography*, 94; See more in Dörnyei, *Research Methods*.
31. Kvale, *Interviews: An Introduction*, 173.

3.3.1 Interviews

Educationist and social researcher John Schostak provides a clear definition of an interview as "an extendable conversation between partners that aims at having an 'in-depth information' about a certain topic or subject, and through which a phenomenon could be interpreted in terms of the meanings interviewees bring to it."[32] I am aware that choosing the most effective type of interview for specific data is essential, since interview design and question phrasing affect an interviewee's freedom and depth of response.[33] Hence, of the three interview designs, namely, structured (where interview conversations follow a set of questions already drawn out by the researcher in a methodical fashion and with predetermined answers),[34] semi-structured (where discussions take the form of a structured interview but without pre-designed responses),[35] and unstructured (which takes an open-ended approach),[36] I have preferred the semi-structured interview in this study for the following reasons.

3.3.1.1 Why Semi-Structured Interview (SSI)?

The first merit of adopting the SSI in this inquiry is that it allows for depth.[37] By implication, as the researcher, I could probe and expand the interviewees' responses with follow-up questions like *why* or *how*. The interviewees could also build on the ideas they shared and discuss more broadly the queries I raised. These benefits for both the interviewees and myself are easily imaginable considering that the researcher in SSI design usually works with a basic informal checklist of questions and not a formal, rigid one.[38] Indeed, I had a flexible list of questions that covered the issues I sought to investigate with the freedom to probe deeper through sub-questions to elucidate and illuminate matters of concern or new ideas. To the interviewees, the list served as a

---

32. Schostak, *Interviewing and Representation*, 54.
33. Mathers, Fox, and Hunn, *Trent Focus for Research*, 2.
34. Berg, *Qualitative Research Methods*.
35. Rubin and Rubin, *Qualitative Interviewing*, 88.
36. Gubrium and Holstein, *Handbook of Interview Research*. See also Wengraf, *Qualitative Research Interviewing*; Patton, *Qualitative Research*, 339–348.
37. Newcomer, Hatry, and Wholey, *Handbook of Practical Program*, 493.
38. Berg, *Qualitative Research Methods*, 39. The list is informal because the questions do not have to be strictly followed in any particular order for each interviewee. See Denscombe, *Good Research Guide*, 187.

framework to guide their responses to the phenomenon under investigation with minimal constraints. Indeed, this SSI quality helped draw out appropriate information, particularly from less articulate interviewees.

Second, due to the availability of an informal questions list, SSI ensured that the direction or focus of the inquiry was not lost in the interview process. It helped to keep interactions focused while allowing the interviewees' perspectives and experiences to emerge. This is what sociologist Bruce Berg means in his comment that SSI "allows for in-depth probing while permitting the interviewer to keep the interview within the parameters traced out by the aim of the study."[39] The characteristic of SSI's guided interactive sessions was helpful during data collection and analysis as I could gather data more systematically while also addressing all necessary and intended concerns of the study.

Third, adopting the SSI minimized issues that could have emerged from my familiarity with some of the interviewees, and which could have negatively impacted the research. Indeed, some interviewees would not have demonstrated the sort of commitment and seriousness they displayed without the relative sense of formality that comes with SSI, considering the need to make a special arrangement or set up a somewhat formal meeting for interviews.[40] For this investigation, the ambience of a formal meeting, even when conversations were over the phone, added a layer of thoughtfulness to the interviews in general. Familiar participants did not seem to approach the interactions as typical, casual conversations with me. In the end, the chances of garnering relevant data for the study increased, and digressions were greatly reduced.

3.3.1.1.1 Face-To-Face Versus Telephone Interviews

Though inquiries followed the SSI design, interviews did not all proceed in the same format. While the process began as face-to-face interactions, the constraints occasioned by the COVID-19 pandemic later necessitated a change of approach.[41] About two-thirds of the interviews were conducted by telephone. Of course, a telephone interview is not a new research technique,

---

39. Berg, *Qualitative Research Methods*, 39.

40. Denscombe, *Good Research Guide*, 187.

41. Liverpool, the research context, welcomed such restrictions ranging from complete lockdown (including places of worship) to social distancing, the creation of support bubbles, and other forms of control measures introduced by the government.

and this conversation format has its own merits and demerits.[42] As a computer-mediated communication (CMC) tool,[43] telephone interview describes a strategy for eliciting data by permitting interpersonal communication without needing (or providing) face-to-face engagement.[44]

The most significant benefit of the telephone interview to this research was its provision for extended access to participants. In their book, *Internet Communication and Qualitative Research,* scholars Chris Mann and Fiona Stewart highlight five dimensions of this access.[45] The first which concerns this study is access to a broader geographical coverage, unlike the face-to-face technique. With COVID-19 regulations restricting travel and in-person contacts during fieldwork, telephone interviews became handy in reaching various interviewees spread all over Liverpool. Moreover, it was inexpensive compared to face-to-face meetings. Second, it was easier to have a telephone interview with people whose work nature or schedule (for instance, those on night shifts, who needed to sleep in the daytime) further complicated the possibility of face-to-face conversations. Third, telephone interviews permitted the sharing of relatively sensitive stories and better engagement with timid interviewees, who may not have been comfortable, with a face-to-face approach. In all, without requiring a physical presence, the telephone interviews preserved my safety as a researcher by reducing the risks associated with travelling to meeting venues, as the researcher and nurse, Gina Novick, notes.[46]

Despite the above advantages and popularity of telephone interviews, some drawbacks attend this research method. In relation to this study, the foremost possible criticism is in connection with the interviewee's visual and non-verbal cues.[47] Indeed, the telephone interviews might not have provided me with access to interviewees' social signs, thereby eliminating a source of

---

42. In the UK, for instance, telephone interviews became increasingly common in the decades following the 1960s as telephone ownership in Western societies grew to over 90 percent of households. See more in Carr and Worth, "Use of the Telephone," 511.

43. CMC is used by experienced researcher, Raymond Opdenakker, to refer to a process by which messages are electronically relayed from a sender to one or multiple receivers within synchronous (in real time) and asynchronous (time and place notwithstanding) contexts. For further details see Opdenakker, "Advantages and Disadvantages," 1–2, 11.

44. Carr and Worth, " Use of the Telephone," 512.

45. See Mann and Stewart, *Internet Communication*, 12.

46. Novick, "Is There a Bias," 1.

47. See Opdenakker, "Advantages and Disadvantages," 5.

additional information. Yet, the interviewees' voices and intonations were sufficient cues for determining whether a session should end if necessary.[48] Other criticisms of telephone interviews include the likely short duration of the sessions, reduced response rates, and limited telephone coverage in some areas.[49]

3.4 Data Collection Process

In this section, I explicate the procedure for gathering the research data and the way I handled fieldwork challenges that developed during the investigation.

3.4.1 Choice of Congregations and Participants

The exploratory population sample[50] comprised three ADCs with the pseudonyms CH1, CH2, and CH3 for confidentiality.[51] I have only provided a brief description of the three sample congregations, leaving out any history or information that may easily compromise their anonymity and that of the participants because of the kind of data some participants supplied as they shared their stories. Many participants consciously or unconsciously critiqued their own context, spotlighting some unhelpful practices for church growth, as they responded to queries. So, where the pastors wield a lot of power, serving as middlemen between me and some participants, these individuals would end up in a bad light with the church leaders and congregations for seemingly demonstrating disloyalty by criticising some of the church's practices. Moreover, as the research findings would later reveal, there is an unhealthy competition among the research population that makes the subject of confidentiality even more critical. Therefore, I have altogether avoided supplying any information that may expose the identities of the congregations or the participants.

---

48. Mann and Stewart, *Internet Communication*, 13.

49. Novick, "Is There a Bias," 1.

50. Exploratory samples are often used in small-scale qualitative research as representations of a research population with the usual inclusion of interesting, extreme, and unusual examples that can illuminate the phenomenon being studied. For further details, see Denscombe, *Good Research Guide*, 32–33.

51. I have expanded on the matter of confidentiality and other ethical concerns later in this chapter.

CH1 is the first congregation; African male-led with Pentecostal/charismatic orientation and a mix of adult and youth membership. Although the second assembly, CH2, is similarly African male-led and populated by youths and adults, the congregation resembles mission-founded churches[52] in orientation. The third congregation, CH3, presents a variation in both leadership and membership. The church community is African female-led and primarily populated by young people. However, the congregation shares CH1's outlook in orientation (Pentecostal/charismatic).

The selected congregations resulted from purposive sampling against the backdrop of the racial homogeneity of African diaspora congregations.[53] Furthermore, access to the sites also determined their selection, as not all the churches I approached granted permission for investigation. Those who controlled access to the congregations, the "gatekeepers,"[54] consisted of the individual church pastors (almost solely) and other church leaders alongside influential figures within the congregation. With the nature and level of power wielded by these persons, I thought it wise to identify, correctly negotiate, and maintain a solid relationship with them early enough and throughout the investigation. This step, indeed, proved helpful in granting pace to the research and earning participants' trust.

---

52. By this, I imply those denominations founded in Africa through European missionary activities of the nineteenth and twentieth century such as the Anglican denomination, Methodist, Baptist, and others.

53. Scholars often see most African diaspora congregations as types of racially homogenous assemblies; for instance, see Morris, "McGavran on McGavran," 11. The Homogeneous Unit Principle is a term coined by Donald McGavran to refer to a group united by some characteristic. As an elastic term, it can be used to describe a group with educational, economic, ethnic, or social ties. Basically, the Homogeneous Unit Principle holds that "People like to become Christians without crossing racial, linguistic, or class barriers." For an elaborate description and review see McGavran and Wagner, *Understanding Church Growth*, 163; Pickett, "Caste-Sensitive Church Planting"; McGavran, *Bridges of God*.

54. Gatekeepers are key people who can either grant, restrict or deny initial and continued access to the field. For more on gatekeepers, see Denscombe, *Good Research Guide*, 85–86.

Table 1. Key Characteristics of Population Samples

Pseudonym	Orientation	Leader's Gender	Dominant Population
CH1	Pentecostal/charismatic	Male	Mixed (Adults + Youths)
CH2	Mission-founded	Male	Mixed (Adults + Youths)
CH3	Pentecostal/charismatic	Female	Youths

3.4.2 Interview Process

Purposive sampling also applied to the choice of participants, as with the congregations' selection. By this approach, various categories of persons in the sample churches could participate in the research, allowing broader perspectives and reflections. I deliberately excluded minors[55] to avoid the complexity of obtaining ethical clearance for their participation, coupled with their possible inability to fully comprehend the issues the study explores. The interviews proceeded in two different forms, face-to-face interaction and telephone discussions. With CH1, it was almost entirely face-to-face. Conversations with the other two assemblies, CH2 and CH3, happened over the telephone. The interview format was the alternative participant's preference considering government restrictions on in-person gatherings in the wake of the COVID-19 pandemic.

I secured meetings with participants through direct contact or indirectly through telephone or email, whether for face-to-face or telephone discussions. I had spelled out the inquiry's purpose in every instance while the choice of dates, times, and venues for meetings (face-to-face sessions) was mutual. This practice conforms with educationist Dianne Hinds' suggestion that the information the interviewee might reasonably need to know must be considered in planning for an interview. Hence, the researcher must adequately inform the interviewee about the research area with clear guidance on the anticipated length of the interview.[56]

---

55. By a minor, I refer to anyone aged 17 and below.
56. Hinds, *Research Instruments*, 48.

At the start of each investigation, I provided (this was by dictation for telephone conversations) participants with the research information sheet and consent form detailing the research procedure of Liverpool Hope University. I similarly reassured interviewees of anonymity and confidentiality in handling their information. Likewise, I did not rule out the need to arrange more than one interview session to clarify issues raised in previous meetings by participants at any stage of the inquiry, even though it eventually proved unnecessary. I handled postponed interviews by rescheduling them.

In line with SSI's nature, I proceeded into each meeting with some pre-set questions to serve as a guide through the interview process. After each session, participants had the opportunity to raise issues unaddressed during the investigations and that required further development. It was also essential to conduct a pilot[57] before launching the main study. This exercise helped test the interview questions' relevance, scope, and clarity. Moreover, as researchers Hassan et al. hold, the main goal of pilot, feasibility, or vanguard studies is to "identify potential problem areas and deficiencies in the research instruments and protocol prior to implementation during the full study."[58] The interview experiences with each of the three congregations were unique. Hence, I have documented them separately below.

3.4.2.1 Interactions with CH1

At this study's inception, before commencing fieldwork, I had met with the pastor of CH1 at an event and informed him about the research. He was keen on it and immediately shared his contact information so that I could stay in touch. So, when it was time to begin the fieldwork, I reached out to him, and he was still receptive. However, he needed some time to inform the rest of the church's leadership team. After a week, he called me to join the church's Sunday service in order to commence the interviews. It was an added advantage to be a participant-observer, as I had to wait until the end of the service

---

57. Pilot studies are basically trial or preparatory studies carried out to test the feasibility of the full or main study. For more see Moore et al., "Recommendations for Planning Pilot," 332; Cope, "Methods & Meanings," 196; Lancaster, Dodd, and Williamson, "Design and Analysis," 307; Arain et al., "What Is a Pilot," 1.

58. Hassan, Schattner, and Mazza, "Doing a Pilot Study," 70; see also Thabane et. al., "Tutorial on Pilot Studies," 1; Lancaster, "Pilot and Feasibility Studies," 2; Moore et al., "Recommendations for Planning," 333.

before being able to interact with those willing. The pastor was tremendously helpful, making himself available for an interview in the week that culminated in my initial meeting with the congregation. The minister also gave me a soft landing by pleasantly introducing myself and my intention to the church. As such, it was less challenging to find participants comfortable enough to share their experiences. Indeed, I enjoyed the privilege of interviewing four church members during the first meeting alone.

The following Sunday came, and the reception was even better (perhaps word had spread about how I joined the insufficient drummers during my first visit!). I had the pastor's wife on the list of participants, which included some youths (not minors), adults, church workers, and lay members. While the ethnic group of the pastor dominated the church, it was interesting to find a white Westerner in the church who even held a leadership position. Sadly, he could not participate in the research because of his administrative and spiritual duties. Indeed, his view would have enriched the study in many ways, especially as an outsider in terms of race. I also spotted two other African nationalities among the congregation, and they were eager to participate in the study when I approached them. Though the church leader claimed that the congregation was more ethnically diverse, it was not very obvious. Perhaps the sparse attendance (the pastor alluded to this factor) in the two weeks that face-to-face interaction lasted before the unexpected interruption of the COVID-19 pandemic was to blame.

The COVID-19 pandemic came as an unforeseen situation that necessitated a switch in the mode of conducting the interviews. With the introduction of the first lockdown in the UK just two weeks into the fieldwork in March 2020, exploring alternatives to face-to-face interviews was unavoidable. Participants generally preferred telephone conversations. Yet, one participant of the targeted ten could not go through with the interview despite initially setting a meeting time. The individual was no longer responding to further attempts to reach out. In all, rich research data came out of this congregation.

3.4.2.2 Experience with CH2

The uniqueness of my interactions at CH2 is immediately traceable to my shared membership with the congregation. As the fieldwork progressed, the benefits of this connection emerged to outweigh whatever downsides attend such a close relationship between a researcher and the population.[59] For instance, gaining access to the site was more straightforward than the other samples. In fact, CH2's pastor suggested that I proceed with the rest of the interviews before having his own session. Even though he was understandably busy, this sort of access is not likely to have opened up where prior connection or familiarity with the research site was absent.

The church pastor had little or no influence on the selection of participants. The interviews had occurred during the first lockdown in the UK, engendered by the COVID-19 pandemic. So, I only had the privilege of reaching out to potential participants via the telephone. The willingness of these people to be part of the investigation was terrific. In fact, some of them pointed to those who would become additional participants. It was also interesting that the pastor never had to inform anyone before I reached out to them, yet all were cooperative and enthused to assist with the study. I enjoyed the unfettered access that comes from having some form of connection to the research population.

Since the lockdown was just establishing itself at this time, most of the interviewees had not accustomed themselves to the various video conferencing or communication platforms such as the popular Zoom application.[60] Some also felt it was stressful, and others did not want their faces captured. Hence, all interviews happened over the telephone, an alternative provided by participants. With the depth of engagement from the interviewees, video communication or in-person interaction might have denied some people the confidence and courage that accompanied their speech. In one month, all interviews were complete, including that of the pastor, who was last on the list. While this site (CH2) produced quality research data, as with the first (CH1), a few participants may have held back on issues that could portray them as critical of the church or its leadership.

---

59. I have expanded more in a later discourse within this chapter on the benefits and drawbacks of my familiarity with this population. See the conversation titled "My Role as a Researcher."

60. Founded in 2011 with headquarters in San Jose, California, Zoom is a video communications platform that came into the limelight in the wake of the COVID-19 pandemic. See more in Zoom, "About Zoom."

3.4.2.3 Encounter with CH3

Unlike the previous congregations, the majority of the sessions at CH3 happened either on weekends or in the evening. CH3 consisted mainly of students and professionals (a noticeable variation from the other congregations). The church pastor, an acquaintance before the research, was instrumental in securing interviews with her congregants. She publicized the study during one of their church workers' meetings, which was well-attended by those available after the disruptions occasioned by the COVID-19 pandemic. The pastor first granted her own interview, and then her husband's, before suggesting others who might be interested. By contacting these individuals to introduce me and explain the research before I connected with them, the church leader aided the seamlessness of the interview process.

Though the participants were all workers in the church, their ages, gender, professions, and perspectives still varied. Hence, while one may argue that the pastor could have selected these individuals on purpose to a particular end, the non-uniform responses from the participants suggest otherwise. In fact, some hinted at certain weaknesses of the church. In all, seven interviews were successful out of the proposed ten. The telephone interviews (which participants chose over Zoom video communication) took more than a month to complete because of interviewees' limited availability. The field data from CH3 was particularly beneficial in reflecting on issues raised by the other two congregations, which were male-led and dominated mainly by first-generation African migrants (1GM).

3.5 Data Analysis and Synthesis

In qualitative research, data analysis – and, in fact, the entire research strategy – is not usually reducible to distinct stages, nor is there a rigid approach to it. It simply varies based on the context and nature of the investigation.[61] Data analysis generally involves "preparing the data for analysis, conducting different analyses, moving deeper and deeper into understanding the data, representing the data, and making an interpretation of the larger meaning

---

61. Bryman and Burgess, *Analyzing Qualitative Research*, 2–3.

of the data."[62] For this study, again, I have applied the grounded theory (GT) approach to analyse the field data for reasons I shall highlight shortly.

GT is a concept of theory-discovery from methodically garnered data in social research. It is a way of arriving at the theory most appropriate and fitting to its supposed applications because the principle emanates from the associated research data.[63] GT is suitable where knowledge is scanty about a phenomenon or happening, and its goal is to generate a theory that explains a process implicit in the field of study.[64] Since Glaser and Strauss prominently proposed this research and analytic method in their 1967 classic, *The Discovery of Grounded Theory: Strategies for Qualitative Research*,[65] viewing the duo as the first generation proponents of GT has been an increasing trend in the literature.[66] Of course, there have been more recent publications on the data analysis concept.[67]

3.5.1 Rationale for Grounded Theory Approach for Data Analysis

Generally, in sociology, data is crystalized into a theory.[68] Theory breaks down research into a statement about "social life that holds transferable applications to other settings, context, populations, and possibly time periods." It provides modes of conceptualization for describing and explaining data.[69] I have employed grounded theory (GT) as a way of handling data in this study for the following reasons.

First, GT is well-suited for qualitative research, exploratory research, studies of human interaction, and small-scale research.[70] Therefore, it is not appropriate for verifying or disproving pre-existing theories. Since this investigation developed knowledge by social constructivism instead of

---

62. Creswell, *Research Design*, 190.
63. Glaser and Strauss, *Discovery of Grounded Theory*, 1–2.
64. Tie, Birks, and Francis, "Grounded Theory Research," 1–2.
65. Glaser and Strauss, *Discovery of Grounded Theory*.
66. Birks and Mills, *Grounded Theory*, 3.
67. See, for instance, Guetterman et al., "Contemporary Approaches"; Morse et al., *Developing Grounded Theory*; Clarke, *Situational Analysis: Grounded Theory*; Charmaz, *Constructing Grounded Theory*; Bryant, *Grounded Theory*.
68. Collins and Stockton, "Central Role of Theory," 1.
69. Collins and Stockton, 4.
70. Denscombe, *Good Research Guide*, 108–112; Birks and Mills, *Grounded Theory*, 6.

post-positivism, GT became a choice technique for data processing in this study. It provided a framework that guided me into the field with an open mind while anticipating new findings to avoid sliding into pre-theoretically constructed paradigm testing.[71]

Second, a theory generated from GT data is hard to refute or nullify with more data or other means – neither is it usually completely replaceable by another theory, though there is room for modifications.[72] The irreplaceability is due to the close link between the theory (for instance, the dominant church growth factors of ADCs) and the meticulously studied data where it originates (Liverpool). Hence the word *grounded* in the concept. Of course, the hypothesis, codes, themes, and concepts arising from this study were not interpreted in isolation but engaged in dialogue with the existing body of knowledge and ideas.[73]

Third, grounded theory – as with the chief church growth factors of the research population – guides against the devious use of a theory by opportunists who dubiously fit it into inapplicable situations (for instance, beyond the UK) to verify claims that the theory does not originally support.[74] In the end, misapplication of such theories only results in wrongly-defined concepts of the social phenomenon (church growth, in this case) to which they are applied. Indeed, ill-defined concepts "are damaging to both definitive theorising and probative research . . . [and] . . . lies at the heart of the scientific difficulties."[75]

The fourth rationale for preferring grounded theory is that the technique forestalls the danger of a mismatch between theory and the empirical world.[76] Rightly so, the emerging hypotheses and concepts in this research were systematically worked out in relation to the field data during the research process rather than developing theories before the study.

---

71. Timonen, Foley, and Conlon, "Challenges When Using," 6.
72. Glaser and Strauss, *Discovery of Grounded Theory*, 3–4.
73. Timonen, Foley, and Conlon, "Challenges When Using," 6.
74. Glaser and Strauss, *Discovery of Grounded Theory*, 4–5; For further details see Morse et al., *Developing Grounded Theory*.
75. Blumer, *Symbolic Interactionalism*, 171–172.
76. Glaser and Strauss, *Discovery of Grounded Theory*, 5–6.

3.5.2 Data Analysis Process

Data analysis in qualitative research often commences in the pre-fieldwork phase, during the formulation and clarification of research problems, and progresses to writing reports, articles, and books.[77] Plus, with qualitative interviews, the amount of data generated could be so large that analysis becomes overwhelming for some researchers.[78] Therefore, the initial data analysis for this inquiry commenced once a sufficient amount of data emerged.

The analysis was underway with the transcription of recorded interviews and the categorization of the *raw* data. This step is called open coding. It describes the concurrent process of developing a set of analytic categories that capture relevant aspects of *raw* data and assigning certain items of data to these themes.[79] The key criteria that informed the analytic categories were the frequency of ideas, concepts, statements, symbols, events, and specific acts within the data. The next step was the axial coding phase. Axial coding involves the development of concepts to explain the body of thought and the identification of links and relationships between codes or ideas. Scholars Linda Bloomberg and Marie Volpe emphasize the importance of the axial coding phase in their assertion that "efforts should be made to sift through and piece together threads and patterns within categories, compare connecting threads across categories, and compare with issues raised by the broader literature in the field."[80]

---

77. Hammersley and Atkinson, *Ethnography: Principles in Practice*, 158.
78. Neuman, *Social Research Methods*.
79. Hammersley and Atkinson, *Ethnography: Principles in Practice*, 161.
80. Bloomberg and Volpe, *Completing Your Qualitative Dissertation*, 84.

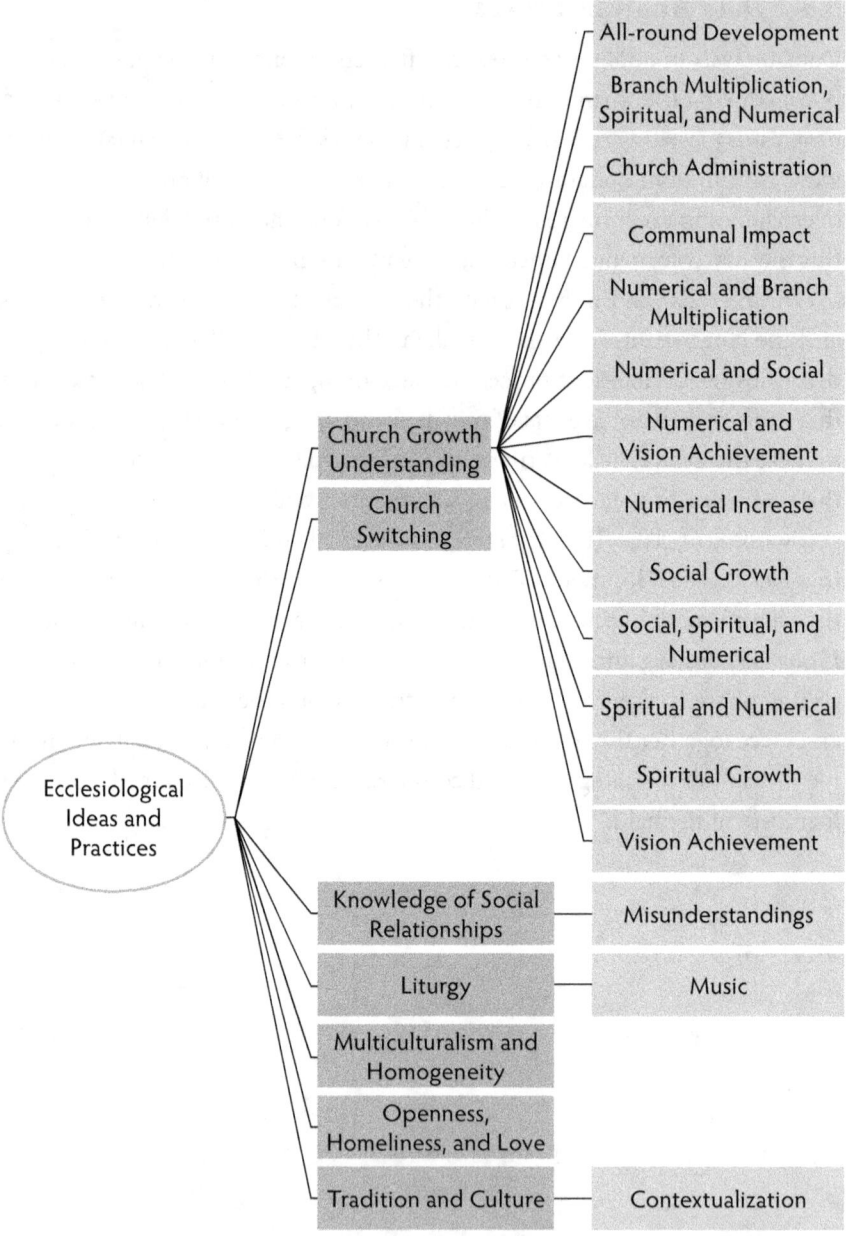

Figure 1. Illustrating Open and Axial Coding Phases in Generating a Theme (Right to Left)

In the final coding phase, selective coding, the linked vital concepts arising from open and axial coding phases crystallize into a story, or grounded theory as in this study. The story or theory is the intended outcome of the iterative data analysis process.[81] In the manner elucidated above, I have analysed the field data for this research.[82] Of immense importance to the entire exercise is the NVivo software. NVivo is a tool designed for computerized data analysis. Its engagement made implementing the data analysis process described above possible and tidy. It is also crucial to note that the nature of the resultant grounded theory from the data analysis process is substantive and not formal. By implication, the theory is not conceptual, with a general coverage beyond its research context.[83] Instead, it has a close link with the empirical situation of church growth of ADCs in the UK and specifically in Liverpool.

3.6 The Reflexive Researcher

In qualitative research, there is no objectivity or neutrality since researchers put themselves in the place of participants in an attempt to understand the world from their perspective.[84] In other words, individual biases are unavoidable in qualitative research because, in the process of interview and interpretation, the data collected are filtered through the perception and subjective opinions of the researcher.[85] In fact, with the researcher and participants engaged in co-constructing a world in the ethnographic research process,[86] worries arise about how a study is influenced by the researcher – in data collection methods and ways of reporting findings. Consequently, reflexivity is

---

81. Denscombe, *Good Research Guide*, 112–113. For more on qualitative research coding see Gläser and Laudel, "Life with and without Coding"; Stuckey, " Second Step in Data Analysis," *Journal of Social*, 7–10.

82. I have provided a full code list in appendix I.

83. Denscombe, *The Good Research Guide*, 116.

84. Hammarberg, Kirkman, and De Lacey, "Qualitative Research Methods," 498.

85. Pezalla, Pettigrew, and Miller-Day, "Researching the Researcher-As-Instrument," *Qualitative Research*, 166.

86. Davies, *Reflexive Ethnography*, 6–10.

a crucial conversation within a qualitative research framework.[87] The reflexive ability of a researcher, as rightly observed by Professor of Education Management David Hellawell, is one of the hallmarks of a good thesis.[88] It is for this reason that I present my reflexive account in this part of the thesis along with considerations of power and gender.

3.6.1 My Role as a Researcher

As I contemplate my possible influence, bias, beliefs, and role in the investigation, I find myself oscillating between the two statuses of insider and outsider.[89] Of course, these two researcher positions often generate arguments among scholars. There is usually a concern as to whether a researcher can distinctly occupy either stance or alternate between the two positions of insider and outsider at different points in the research.[90] I, indeed, assumed the two postures in this inquiry. Of course, neither researcher inclination is more advantageous than the other. The strengths and weaknesses of either standpoint are usually not overwhelming enough to nullify the credibility of a research. In fact, the benefits and appropriateness of a position are suggested and pronounced by the circumstances and purpose of the study.[91] Though I assumed both statuses at various junctures in this investigation, I have only deliberately accounted for my insider stance here and its merits for the research. I have taken this step because of the frequent criticisms insider status commonly attracts in literature.[92]

My reflexive thoughts immediately illuminate the reality of the racial identity I share with the research population. I am an African, investigating

---

87. Reflexivity is the process of demonstrating awareness or paying critical analytic attention to the researcher's role in qualitative research. See more in Palaganas et al., "Reflexivity in Qualitative Research," 427. See more in Berger, "Now I see It," 219–234.

88. Hellawell, "Inside-Out Analysis," 483.

89. The insider is "someone whose biography (gender, race, class, sexual orientation and so on) gives her [sic] a lived familiarity with the group being researched" while the outsider is "a researcher who does not have any intimate knowledge of the group being researched, prior to entry into the group." See Griffith, "Insider/Outsider: Epistemological Privilege."

90. For instance, see Milligan, "Insider-Outsider-Inbetweener," 235–250; Hayfield and Huxley, "Insider and Outsider Perspectives," 91–106; Carling, Erdal, and Ezzati, "Beyond the Insider–Outsider Divide," 36–54.

91. Hammersley, "On the Teacher," 219.

92. For some of the criticisms against insider-researcher see for instance Greene, "On the Inside," 4–5; Saidin, "Insider Researchers"; Unluer, "Being an Insider Researcher," 1–2, 58.

African diaspora congregations – a common characteristic that necessitates an insider label.[93] Even so, this researcher position did not undermine objectivity in the inquiry. Plus, a completely "objective observation is illogical."[94] Moreover, unlike an insider, an outsider has "a structurally imposed incapacity to comprehend alien groups, statuses, cultures and societies . . . [because he or she] . . . has neither been socialised in the group nor has engaged in the run of experience that makes up its life."[95] As such, rather than reducing the credibility of the study, being an African researcher investigating ADCs is enriching for this inquiry.

Another dimension of my influence on the study derives from the tie I have with one of the population samples, CH2, since I am a member of the congregation. This connection to the field of inquiry inevitably impacts the study, as sociologist and anthropologist Davies Charlotte explains regarding insider ethnographic researchers.[96] In this case, one critical implication of the researcher-field link is that accessing the research population was easier and quicker than the other congregations. However, before meditating on other implications of my insider status arising from my relationship with CH2, I find it noteworthy to note an attractive attribute about the congregation that makes it vital to this study. CH2 is one of the largest – if not the most populous – African diaspora congregations in Liverpool. Favourably situated in an area with a relatively dense African population, the congregation boasts a membership size of over four hundred and at least five branches within and outside the UK. In fact, teenagers and children hold their services separately in dedicated properties of the church due to their large numbers. I believe that a site suggesting rich research data such as this should not be side-lined in this study because of insider concerns or other reasons. So, to not undermine the study's quality, I have included CH2 as a sample.

---

93. Ethnicity, and, in fact, race, is only one of the innate and unchanging features of a researcher's identity that may, by default, imply some insiderness. Other dimensions of insiderness of a researcher are identified and discussed in Mercer, " Challenges of Insider Research," 3–4.

94. Gilbert, *Researching Social Life*, 276.

95. Merton, "Insiders and Outsiders," 15. For more arguments associated with and in favour of insider research see also Greene, "On the Inside," 1–13; Kerstetter, "Insider, Outsider," 99–117.

96. Davies, *Reflexive Ethnography*, 7.

My link with CH2 through membership (which, again, makes me an insider) was occasioned, first, by family ties with the congregation. My father was among the founding leadership team of the assembly while in Liverpool. I, therefore, could not easily escape being a part of the congregation since my arrival in the city. In fact, I am one of the serving ministers in the church. This responsibility suggests that I am a close ally of the church leader, with the implication of potentially impacting the free flow of discussion or breadth of reflection with some participants.[97] However, I am still relatively new in the congregation and not fully accustomed to its politics and history.

Second, in addition to a direct family connection, my relationship with CH2 also comes from my shared denominational beliefs, practices, and doctrines with the congregation. The pastor received his theological education from the same institution, The Nigerian Baptist Theological Seminary, Ogbomoso (NBTS),[98] which is responsible for my theological training. Plus, he has maintained a close relationship with the institution and denomination. Despite increasing my insider stance, and contrary to possibly undermining this inquiry's credibility, my acquaintance with the doctrines and practices of CH2 helped reflect on the research data from the congregation. This sort of advantage is in tandem with leadership and management expert Justine Mercer's observation that

> insiders will undoubtedly have a better initial understanding of the social setting because they know the context; they understand the subtle and diffuse links between situations and events; and they can assess the implications of following particular avenues of enquiry.[99]

Nevertheless, I was careful not to allow my foreknowledge of the congregation's possible structure and theological ideas to hinder the investigation, whether in processing research data from that population or other unfamiliar congregations. By implication, I made sure to approach the inquiry, as much as possible, with a curious and open mind, allowing knowledge to be

---

97. I have touched more on the dynamics of power in this research in the previous section.

98. NBTS is the apex theological institution of The Nigerian Baptist Convention. As a tertiary institution, it directly trains and moderates another nine theological colleges of the convention.

99. Mercer, "Challenges of Insider Research," 6.

co-constructed with participants and not from the basis of a fixed mindset or assumptions about ideas shared by the population.

Further reflection on my possible involvement, as a researcher, in this investigation recalls the struggle and tendency to strongly present, emphasize or tailor the research findings to favour my personal or cultural beliefs (as evident in the choice and use of words). Indeed, "being an insider might raise issues of undue influence of the researcher's perspective but being an outsider does not create immunity to the influence of personal perspective"[100] either. All the same, I navigated this likelihood and challenge by providing scholarly reasons in intellectual terms for moral actions where emphasized. I also took care to clarify and state beforehand where and when I have used a personal voice in place of scholarly expression.

3.6.2 Dynamics of Power and Gender

As a deviation from the widespread assumption that the ultimate source of authority in an inquiry lies with the researcher, qualitative research seeks to promote the participants' equal role in the research process.[101] Consequently, the researcher needs to be aware of and account for power distribution in a qualitative study. Power relation or distribution in a qualitative interview refers to "the interrelated power within the interview."[102] Although not necessarily deliberate, this power may emerge from the interviewer's side towards the interviewees.[103] Health scientist Målfrid Råheim and colleagues provide of helpful advice to guarantee the richness of qualitative research, especially interviews. They suggest that the inquiry's atmosphere must be that of equality between interviewer and participants so that the interviewees do not feel inferior or superior to the interviewer. The entire process, they add, should be one of mutual discovery and exploration because power imbalance within the interview could alter the result of the inquiry.[104]

Reflection on power relations brings to mind my identity during the investigation as the son of the Nigerian Baptist Convention (NBC) president and

---

100. Dwyer and Buckle, "Space Between," 59.
101. Karnieli-Miller, Strier, and Pessach, "Power Relations," 279.
102. Alshenqeeti, "Interviewing as a Data Collection," 41.
103. Alshenqeeti, 41.
104. Råheim et al., "Researcher-Researched Relationship," 1–12.

the national president of CAN. I do not overlook the power implications of this status on the research. Indeed, among my own congregation, CH2, which was aware of my identity, recruiting interviewees was quicker and less stressful. In fact, none of the participants invited for the investigation denied access, either before or during the inquiry. There was a one hundred percent success rate. Notwithstanding, I understand that my identity may have hindered the research in some ways, especially where issues concerning the church leadership were involved.

Also, being a minister at CH2 could not have been without some power implications. Indeed, whether at CH1 or CH3, but more importantly at CH2, the probability of participants not freely and deeply engaging certain concerns is undeniable. This possibility is due to the often psychological or perceivable minister-congregation divide, especially with African congregations, where reverence for church leaders is almost palpable. A potential one-directional power flow from myself to the participants thus arose. To mitigate this power imbalance effect, I made sure to appear less formal, not in the classical image of pastors – dressed in a suit with collar or tie. Instead, I was more freely attired, especially for the face-to-face interviews. Puthussery notes that "some [researchers have] suggested that going dressed in clerical clothing can make the [interview] visit very official and they [have] recommended an informal dress code to look like the respondents for a better response."[105]

My youthfulness relative to a number of the participants similarly constituted some power issues. Indeed, some of the internal struggles of the elderly interviewees who had to be interrogated by a younger man were perceivable. Consequently, I was more culturally conscious in handling the sessions with these older participants. For instance, fillers and words that suggested much regard came up often in the conversations. Much more, in conducting all interviews, I bore in mind sociologists Andrea Fontana and James Frey's advice that discussions should proceed with a courteous, friendly, and unbiased attitude and approach.[106]

---

105. Puthussery, "Marriage and Migration," 30.
106. Fontana and Frey, "Interview: From Neutral Stance," 710.

3.7 Ethical Considerations

Just as the qualitative research framework is concerned with the intellectual and ethical dimensions of a study, ethical issues are also vital considerations in social research.[107] The researcher's personal and professional conduct must ensure the safety of participants from harm[108] and "unnecessary stress" throughout the inquiry.[109] Denscombe provides two critical rationale for reflecting on the ethical dimension of qualitative research. First, he observes that in the past, unscrupulous practices have exposed participants' confidentiality without their consent. Second, some researchers have also demonstrated overwhelming bias in interpreting field data. Others have employed deception and exploitation of participants in gathering data.[110]

Unethical research practices and behaviour may not only leave the researcher and participants "feeling vulnerable and exposed in a negative way"; they may also compromise the entire study's reliability and validity.[111] Overlooking ethical concerns in this study would have been too risky considering the sensitive, personal, and organizational information that occasionally emerged from the interactive sessions with participants. Therefore, I was sure to obtain approval from the Ethics Committee of the university before embarking on the investigation. Below, I have highlighted some major ethical issues relevant to this inquiry.

3.7.1 Informed Consent

It is an ethical practice for researchers to never coerce or compel participants into helping with the investigation. Participants' engagement must be of their own free will, and they must have adequate information about the inquiry to make a logical judgement on whether to participate or not.[112] Informed consent is "an ethical and legal requirement for research involving human

---

107. Erickson, "Qualitative Research Methods," 1454.
108. This harm can be physical, emotional, resource loss (including time), or reputational. For more see Fleming and Zegwaard, "Methodologies, Methods," 211.
109. Cacciattolo, "Ethical Considerations in Research," 55.
110. Denscombe, *Good Research Guide*, 306.
111. Cacciattolo, "Ethical Considerations in Research," 56.
112. Denscombe, *Good Research Guide*, 311.

participants."[113] Hence, the Social Research Association (SRA)[114] and British Sociological Association (BSA)[115] reiterate that every participant has a right to be informed of the purpose and potential implications of the research.

Informed consent is a composite term of two elements or words, "informed" and "consent." Being *informed* means that before commencing any investigation, researchers must acquaint participants with what the inquiry is about, how the data they intend to supply will be processed, and the implication or consequence (if any) of their participation. The *consent* aspect implies that researchers obtain a signed agreement or go-ahead from participants, who must be aware of their right to the data they have supplied and withdraw from the investigation at any point.[116] Informed consent ultimately aims at providing adequate information to potential participants in ways and language that they can understand to enhance their decision to participate in the study.[117] In essence, informed consent "reduces the risk of social harm because it affirms the dignity and respects the agency of those who will be involved in the study."[118]

I sought informed consent in this study by providing each participant with a brief, meticulously worded research information sheet using a clear writing style that was easily understood by participants and devoid of complex academic jargon. The information sheet, as required, clearly outlined what the study was about and the potential implications of participants' involvement. Of course, I was aware that the nature of the research is that of discovery; therefore, its implications will never be wholly determinable from the outset.[119] I accompanied the information sheet with a consent form that participants read and signed before proceeding with the investigation. Moreover, for telephone interviews, these steps were conducted orally at the beginning of every conversation.

---

113. Nijhawan et al., "Informed Consent," 134.
114. Social Research Association, "Ethics Guidelines."
115. British Sociological Association, "Statement of Ethical Practice 2017."
116. Fleming and Zegwaard, "Methodologies, Methods," 210.
117. Nijhawan et al., "Informed Consent," 134.
118. Erickson, "Qualitative Research Methods," 1457.
119. Caiata-Zufferey, "Abductive Art of Discovery," 1–9.

3.7.2 Confidentiality and Anonymity

Security of data is a crucial ethical issue in conducting research. Participants' privacy must be recognized and respected. Hence, sociologist Matthew David and University of Plymouth Partnership Manager Carole Sutton opine that a researcher who is obliged to obtain the consent of participants before invading their privacy must "protect that privacy in the storage and the use of any data collected." This protection could be provided either by anonymity or confidentiality.[120] While it is common to find the two terms applied synonymously, they are, in fact, different. The anonymity of participants implies that the personal details (for instance, name, address, date of birth, and others) of those involved in the research are unknown to the researcher or unrecorded.[121] Confidentiality, on the other hand, means that the "participant's identity is known to the researcher, but the data was de-identified and the identity is kept confidential."[122] In other words, the researcher is aware of the participant's personal details but does not reveal them.

This study is concerned with confidentiality since participants' details are known but not revealed.[123] Therefore, before beginning any interview, I assured participants of the confidentiality of whatever data they supplied. Furthermore, I employed coded designations (alphanumeric names) in referring to participants and the three population samples investigated in the study. I also sought participants' feedback on the data collected to avail them of the opportunity to modify any perceived personal details however desired. Moreover, I was cautious with using direct quotations or self-identifying statements that could give away participants' identities while not denying the inclusion of rich research data in the process.

Finally, I made every effort to comply with the General Data Protection Regulation (GDPR) guidelines. I ascertained the careful safeguarding of the field data by storing them electronically in a password-protected folder on a personal computer, which is also PIN and firewall-secured. There was no sharing of participants' data with anyone under any guise. I deleted the research data a year after ending my course of study.

---

120. David and Sutton, *Social Research: The Basics*, 19.
121. David and Sutton, 19.
122. Fleming and Zegwaard, "Methodologies, Methods," 211.
123. It is also not impossible that some participants were able to connect me with the congregation I belong to though I did not expressly seek to reveal this fact.

3.7.3 Non-Invasive Interaction with Participants

I did not underrate the essence of introducing the research topic and purpose to the participants at the commencement of each interview. Participants were not manipulated or forced into deciding to be part of the study or not. Moreover, all discussions were private to avoid invasiveness or intrusion, though some took place within the participants' church building. I also informed the participants that they could at any point retract any information supplied or completely turn down a response to an inquiry if they found it necessary. In fact, the voice recorder, which was combined with a notepad for recording and collecting data, was close to the participants. This setup was to help interviewees have quicker access to the device in case there were portions of the interview they wanted off the record. Similarly, I was cautious in navigating sensitive topics.[124] My goal was not to unsettle participants, nor was it to completely pull the plug on potentially relevant research data.

3.8 Conclusion

In this chapter, I discussed the research design that informed the choice of data generation and analysis approaches that I employed to address the research question. In other words, I have presented a theoretical framework for the investigation to convey my deepest values as a researcher while also giving a clearly articulated signpost or lens for how the study constructed new knowledge. I justified the study's nature, that of ethnographically informed fieldwork. Thoughts on semi-structured interviews as the primary tools for data collection also received focus. I presented the grounded theory procedure as the inquiry's approach for data analysis and synthesis. Finally, to improve the credibility of the research, I mulled over my role as a researcher in the investigation and some critical ethical issues associated with the study.

---

124. Sensitive topics are those issues that are difficult for respondents or participants to discuss such as medical related themes, sexual behaviours, deaths, taboos, and other associated subjects. See more in Powell et al., "Sensitive Topics," 647–660; Becker and Bryman, *Understanding Research*, 69–73; Liamputtong, James, and Dickson-Swift, *Undertaking Sensitive Research*.

CHAPTER 4

Theories of Church Growth

4.1 Introduction

In this part of the dissertation, I present a few of the wealth of theoretical ideas informing the understanding and endeavour of church growth. In other words, the chapter looks through some of the modes of conceptualising, describing, and explaining the agenda of church growth over the years. I must note that the theories discussed are not necessarily the most popular, nor do they line up in any particular order of effectiveness. They only represent and provide some illumination into the broad conception, laws, and strategies underlining the task of church growth today. This discourse is, of course, significant to this research, whose primary task is to investigate the factors impacting church growth phenomenon in a particular context.

4.2 The Strictness Thesis

In 1972 American theologian and legal scholar Dean Kelley published his book *Why Conservative Churches are Growing*.[1] Kelley sought to make sense of the rationale behind the different growth trajectories observable between conservative and evangelical churches and mainline liberal congregations in America during the second half of the twentieth century. From the evidence he gathered, the author noticed that, while long-standing liberal churches were either plateauing or declining in growth, conservative congregations

---

1. Kelley, *Why Conservative Churches*.

were flourishing. Kelley figured that much of the growth occurring in conservative congregations was due to their religious strictness. He added that, unlike the widespread assumptions of sociological theories of secularization and modernization, congregants do not find the practice of permissiveness, leniency, and inclusivism of liberal denominations attractive, and would rather tilt towards the ascetic lifestyle and high level of commitment demanded and enforced in conservative groups. This is because the high expectations reflect "the seriousness of meaning"[2] longed for by people. Gibbs and Coffey corroborate Kelley's position in observing that "increasing numbers of people are already on a personal spiritual search for meaning and a sense of fulfilment."[3] Ultimately, a robust sense of meaning of life engenders religious strictness, which births congregational strength, leading to church growth.[4]

More clearly, the strictness theory holds that non-liberal churches are thriving because, as they place a huge demand on their parishioners, they enjoy more from them and thus, are supplied with resources that facilitate the delivery of a more winsome religious "product."[5] Moreover, as congregants of strict churches subject themselves to a high level of commitment to retain their membership, outsiders would imagine that these congregations must offer meaningful and profitable messages and thus are attracted to them.[6] For Kelley, strict churches express three characteristics: absolutism, conformity, and fanaticism. Absolutism dismisses all accounts of the meaning of life except the explanation provided by the strict church or denomination. Conformity refers to the intolerance of the church to any kind of dissent or non-compliance of its adherents, while fanaticism describes the tendency of these followers to spread their faith or gospel without readiness to listen to other voices.[7]

---

2. Kelley, 174.
3. Gibbs and Coffey, *Church Next*, 169.
4. Thomas and Olson, "Testing the Strictness Thesis," 620.
5. Stark, *What Americans Really Believe*, 29.
6. Tamney et al., "Strictness and Congregational Growth," 363.
7. Flynn, "Are Strict Churches," 1.

Despite the warm embrace the strictness theory received among various CGM popularizers – including Donald McGavran,[8] George Hunter,[9] Charles Peter Wagner,[10] and Lyle Schaller[11] – it did not sit well with sociologists in the academy who, among other issues raised, questioned the thesis' attribution of congregational growth to institutional influence like strictness rather than demographic factors, such as over-the-top birth rate or population shift.[12] Critiques also discountenanced the strictness theory on the grounds of its ambiguity and scantily presented theoretical procedure against its elaborate empirical relationship. David Roozen and Kirk Hadaway's *Church and Denominational Growth* particularly emphasizes this latter criticism and further proposes that the growth of conservative and evangelical congregations is more correlated with their notable "ideological commitment to evangelistic action" rather than strictness.[13]

However, today, the strictness theory may still be one that cannot be totally dismissed. If one observes the flourishing evangelical congregations in many parts of the global South (for instance, Living Faith Church worldwide, Deeper Life Bible Church, and Foursquare Gospel Church) against the high demands they place on their members – in terms of attendance expectation at (usually frequent) church meetings, rendering of service within the church, high financial commitments, and others – one may be inclined to believe that the strictness theory still holds sway today, at least in the global South. Moreover, while I resided in Nigeria, it was not unusual to hear people use the idea of an "opportunity to serve God" as a reason for relocating to another congregation. What this often meant was that the new congregation provided them with a platform to demonstrate some form of commitment to God, especially since the church would usually expect more from their members.

---

8. McGavran, *Understanding Church Growth*.
9. Hunter, *Contagious Congregation*.
10. Wagner, *Your Church Can Grow*.
11. Schaller, *Effective Church Planting*.
12. See for instance Hout, Greeley, and Wilde, " Demographic Imperative."
13. Roozen and Hadaway, *Church and Denominational Growth*, 42.

4.3 Modernization Theory

Modernization theory, often associated with secularization within the sociology of religion,[14] tends to frown upon the strictness theory of church growth.[15] Indeed, beyond the argument about the fading of religious impact in society, modernization theory opines that for religion to blossom in a society, it must adjust itself to the society's phase in the modernization process.[16] In his 2002 book *The Resilience of Conservative Religion*,[17] educator and sociologist Joseph Tamney researched the growth of three middle-class, conservative Protestant congregations, and discovered that their expansion was partly due to adaptation to contemporary ethics – such as individualism – and embracing a new disposition towards affluence.[18] Tamney concluded that with post-modern societies driven by such factors as consumerism, affinity for elegance, and other issues, modernization theory expects the ascetic lifestyle of strict churches to be less popular while permissive liberal churches gain in relevance.[19] In other words, modernization theory suggests an increase in growth for liberal churches while predicting a decline for strict churches that set and enforce rules and a frugal way of life for their members.

While I have observed that a good number of congregations in non-Western regions may be able to account for their growth partly due to their strict approach, Africa, as with the rest of the global South, is still largely influenced by developments in the West. As such, "Africans generally have a strong urge to emulate the European model of modernization."[20] Of course, the venture of colonialism has not helped in this regard.[21] One may therefore argue that as liberal churches in Europe are adapting to contemporary values in response to modernization, some congregations in the global South may already be doing the same, or at least, are tending towards that direction. So, just as strictness theory may be propelling the growth of some churches, it may not

---

14. For discourses on this subject, see the various contributions in the classic work of Bruce, *Religion and Modernization*.
15. Tamney et al., "Strictness and Congregational Growth," 365.
16. Tamney et al., 365.
17. Tamney, *Resilience of Conservative Religion*.
18. Tamney et al., "Strictness and Congregational Growth," 365.
19. Tamney et al., 365.
20. Yirenkyi, "Church and the Quest," 41.
21. Yirenkyi, 41.

be far-fetched to see modernization theory similarly fuelling the expansion of other congregations, especially as Western civilization continues to find acceptance among the younger generation.

4.4 Types of Church Growth

In 2015, when he was president of Portland Bible College, Frank Damazio captured some typologies of church growth in his book *Strategic Church: Changing Church in an Ever-Changing Culture*.[22] I have discussed these widespread church growth forms below, including a somewhat unique perspective from Damazio.

4.4.1 Numerical Growth

In agreement with one of the aspects of growth encapsulated by the definition of church growth in this dissertation, Damazio reiterates the popular opinion of numerical increase that may happen in a congregation. He submits that a congregation experiences this type of growth when there is numerical or geometric expansion of people "by all means of people growth: biological, transfer and conversion."[23] For instance, when a congregation of 200 people welcomes more members and rises to 300, a numerical increase has occurred. Their size in number has expanded the moment one person, at least, joins the congregation.

4.4.1.1 Biological Growth

This dimension of numerical growth is experienced by a congregation when current members persuade their relatives to join the faith community.[24] It also describes the addition that comes from children being born to existing members of a congregation, since the presence of the young ones automatically fortifies the numerical strength of the local assembly.[25] However, one may wonder if by just being born to Christian parents, children may indeed qualify as Christians, and by implication, authentically add to the numerical

---

22. Damazio, *Strategic Church*.
23. Damazio, 65.
24. Damazio, 65.
25. Towns, "Relationship of Church Growth," 65.

strength of the congregation. For this reason, Russell and Veda Locke maintain that biological growth results primarily from the "addition of children of church members who reach the age of decision."[26] In other words, the children must be old enough to make a choice to become a believer in Christ before counting as biological additions to the growth of the church.

4.4.1.2 Transfer Growth

When growth experience is by transfer, people, for one reason or the other, move from a congregation to become members of another, and the new congregation does not have to share religious traditions with the former.[27] The implication of transfer growth, where "some believers come to the church from another church,"[28] is an increase in the numerical strength of one congregation to the detriment of another. Therefore, one cannot but wonder if this is a helpful growth type for the universal church, especially since it does not necessarily account for any new addition to a congregation but a *rotation* of existing believers among different churches. Transfer growth may be unavoidable in today's world, with people having to constantly migrate for various reasons.

4.4.1.3 Conversion Growth

Conversion growth describes outreach to the unsaved and establishing them in the church. This category of growth is determined by the number of enlistments or converts that join the church.[29] Of course, the emphasis on "conversion as entrance" into the church is biblical. Acts 2:41–47 particularly attests to this. In this record, as believers in Christ fellowshipped together, shared their possessions, and evangelized, "day by day the Lord added to their number [the church] *those who were being saved.*"[30] This explains conversion growth – the expansion of a congregation resulting from the addition of new members through salvation or conversion. This form of church growth, I

---

26. Locke and Locke, *Evangelism and Church Growth*, 68.
27. Olaleye, *Strategies for Church Growth*, 135.
28. Damazio, *Strategic Church*, 65.
29. Paas, "Case Study of Church Growth," 42.
30. Emphasis mine. See Mankin, *Four Dimensions of Church Growth*.

believe, is key among other dimensions of growth since it sees unchurched people become part of the people of God.

4.4.2 Organic Growth

Reflected in the gradual metamorphosis of people into "maturity, transformation, and discipleship,"[31] organic growth (same as internal growth), concerns the evangelism of existing unsaved members of the church – the renewal of local congregants. In other words, organic growth covers the nurturing task of a congregation that results in the spiritual development and maturity of its members.[32] Samuel Olaleye, theologian and former rector of Baptist College of Theology Igede-Ekiti, Nigeria, is convinced that without this type of growth, a church misses the "taproot for enduring growth," for it determines "the level and extent of growth of other segments of the church."[33] There is no gainsaying that organic growth models the spiritual aspect of church growth advocated in this study – growth in grace and faith. Even though he referred to it as the "maturity dimension" of growth, scholar and preacher Jim Mankin explains that organic or internal growth describes the spiritual formation and development of a congregation.[34]

4.4.3 Influence Growth

In what translates roughly as the social dimension of growth that this research puts forward, Damazio describes influence growth of a congregation as the "expansion of the church as seen by its effects on its environment, cities, nations and the world."[35] He adds that this sort of growth resulting from numerical and organic expansion is achieved through outreach and church planting activities, and the equipping of more converts such that the congregation then spreads to other communities and nations as one church, but triggering new congregations in the process.[36] I believe engaging in presence evangelism as identified by Wagner in *Strategies for Church Growth*[37] may

---

31. Damazio, *Strategic Church*, 66.
32. Towns, "Church Growth and Systematic Theology," 65.
33. Olaleye, *Strategies for Church Growth*, 122.
34. Mankin, *Four Dimensions of Church Growth*.
35. Damazio, *Strategic Church*, 66.
36. Damazio, 66.
37. Wagner, *Strategies for Church Growth*.

also facilitate influence growth. Indeed, presence evangelism, the pedestal for the other two levels of evangelism Wagner stresses (proclamation and persuasion), covers all the engagements, activities, and interaction of the congregation, as well as individual Christians, with the world.[38] Therefore, arrangements like night shelters, charity breakfasts, foodbanks, and other similar campaigns, whether at a personal or congregational level, which provide aid to the community and enhance interaction with the world, would fall within the bounds of presence evangelism. Engaging in these kinds of endeavours certainly extends the impact of the church, and ultimately draws more people to it.

4.4.4 Google Growth

From his study of the rise, expansion, and impact of Google, Damazio proposes a church growth type after this order of development. He believes Google's growth reflects numerical, organic, and influence growth altogether. His rationale for this assertion is richly expressed in his own words:

> Although Google employs thousands of people, it is as concerned about the health of each individual as it is about the company's stock portfolio, and it understands that individual development is vitally important to the success and growth of the whole company. Each employee must spend 20 percent of his or her time doing innovative thinking . . . sometimes finding ways of doing things better or faster.[39]

With Google growth bringing together numerical, organic, and influence growth, it would have been logical to imagine church growth from this perspective in this study. However, Google growth seems to fall short by not deliberately accounting for maturity in leadership – a dimension of growth that can condition the experience of other forms of developments within the church. Moreover, Google growth can be more likely witnessed by a congregation that employs the *omolúàbí*-shaped ecclesiology (OSE), introduced later in chapter 7 of this dissertation. Rightly so, OSE informs not

---

38. Wagner, 117.
39. Damazio, *Strategic Church*, 67.

just the numerical, organic, or influence types of church growth, but also the leadership dimension, as I will later show.

4.4.5 Other Typologies

There are other equally pervasive classifications of church growth in the literature. For instance, there is *expansion growth,* which happens when evangelism focuses on people in the immediate community or society.[40] It often calls for the church as an institution, as well as individuals, to establish deliberate contact with people in the world, making them disciples of Christ and "bringing them into church membership in their own local congregation."[41] Expansion growth equally covers the enrolment of "unchurched Christians" to become committed participants in church life.[42] There is also *extension growth,* which is the establishment of a new assembly in a similar culture. It is also referred to as church planting since new churches result from those who have been won to Christ, constituting fresh congregations separate from the existing local church.[43] *Bridging growth* describes setting up a new congregation in a culture or community totally variant to the base church.[44] A report from a working group of the Church of England's Mission and Public Affairs Council published in 2004 adds that extension growth is often achieved not just among those with identical culture to the planting churches, but simultaneously targets those who do not go to church.[45]

4.5 The Holy Spirit and Church Growth

Like many – if not all – church growth exponents, Gibbs insists that "the presence and activity of the Holy Spirit is integral to church growth at every phase."[46] The role of the Holy Spirit in realising church growth is so critical

---

40. Locke and Locke, *Evangelism and Church Growth*, 68.
41. Wagner, *Your Church Can Grow*, 106.
42. Locke and Locke, *Evangelism and Church Growth*, 68.
43. Wagner, *Your Church Can Grow*, 106.
44. Towns, Vaughan, and Seifert, *Complete Book of Church Growth*, 103. Wagner adds that because of the cross-cultural aspect of bridging growth, it is more complicated than extension growth. See Wagner, *Your Church Can Grow*, 106.
45. Archbishop's Council, *Mission-Shaped Church*, 107.
46. Gibbs, "Power Behind the Principles," 125.

that educator, Anglican priest, and church growth consultant Bob Jackson observes that while principles and organizational and human changes are meaningful and qualitative, church growth is only possible on the foundation of "a healthy and deepening spirituality."[47] Gary McIntosh, Professor of Christian Ministry and Leadership, is also strongly convinced that "it is the life-giving work of the Holy Spirit that empowers church programs, plans, and strategies."[48] Gibbs echoes the same submission in maintaining that "Authentic church growth requires power as well as principles [because] the principles do not of themselves cause church growth; they simply explain it."[49] Of course, by power, Gibbs implies the Holy Spirit, whom he affirms as the "power behind the principles" of church growth, whether the theories are developed from a biblical viewpoint or practical orientation.[50]

In accounting for the importance of the activities of the Holy Spirit in achieving church growth, McIntosh explains that, in the first place, "It is the convicting work of the Holy Spirit that leads people to Christ."[51] More so, it is the same Spirit that empowers individual members of the church to witness, and by so doing, recruit many more to the body of Christ.[52] Indeed, Acts 1:8 records: "But you will receive power when the Holy Spirit has come upon you; and you will be my witnesses in Jerusalem, in all Judea and Samaria, and to the ends of the earth." McGavran is, therefore, apt to conclude that church growth is "something that takes place in the world through the agency of the Holy Spirit working through countless dedicated servants of God and a diversity of institutions and organizations."[53] In another place, he adds that churches that grow are those that fervently pursue the power of God – the Holy Spirit.[54]

I also believe that when methodologies, principles, analyses, and strategies are void of the Spirit of God, the life-giving Spirit and source of power, the experience of church growth, if any, will only become superficial and temporal. Engaging this supernatural dimension in realising church growth

---

47. Jackson, *Going for Growth*, 29.
48. McIntosh, *Biblical Church Growth*, 85.
49. Gibbs, " Power Behind the Principles," 125.
50. Gibbs, 125.
51. John 16: 8–11. McIntosh, *Biblical Church Growth*, 83.
52. McIntosh, 83.
53. McGavran, "Ten Years of Church Growth," 1.
54. McGavran, *How Churches Grow*, 57.

may come more easily to Africans, who are generally spirit-oriented.[55] As such, African congregations, including those in diaspora, must be aware of their potential bias so that they do not end up trivialising or overlooking the non-metaphysical strategies of church growth in their missional quest.

4.6 Prayer and Church Growth

Jackson is clear and persuaded that "there is no substitute for prayer when it comes to accessing the behind-the-scenes power of God for growing the church."[56] By this he means that it takes prayer to engage the supernatural dimension, the power of God – the Holy Spirit – that drives the effectiveness of any church growth technique. As such, "There is no point in prayer-less church growth strategies,"[57] for the experience of the supernatural, vigour, freshness, and effectiveness are from the crucible of prayer.[58] Recollecting the words of theologian and Wesleyan Methodist minister Samuel Chadwick, Akin-John adds, "The one concern of the devil is to keep the saints from praying. He fears nothing from prayerless studies, work and Christian activities. He laughs at our toil, mocks our wisdom, but trembles when we pray."[59] If any church must grow, prayer must be an essential element in its strategy. McIntosh suggests some tips for effective prayer for church growth. First, he writes that it must be in agreement with God's word (Dan 9:2). Second, it must proceed in humility (Dan 9:3). Third, such prayer must be consistent with God's character and nature (Dan 9:7,15).[60]

As he reflects on how prayer drive can easily fade, Jackson advances some helpful ideas for sustaining the zest.[61] He notes, first, that prayer must essentially be in line with the tradition and condition of the church. Second, it is encouraging to record specific answers to prayers as it helps to reinforce the faith to continue praying. Third, prayer must be present in corporate gatherings as well as in the individual lives of the congregation. Finally, the pastor

---

55. Mbiti, *African Religions and Philosophy*, 97.
56. Jackson, *What Makes Churches Grow*, 266.
57. Jackson, *Going for Growth*, 30.
58. Akin-John, *22 Dynamic Laws*, 69.
59. Akin-John, 69.
60. McIntosh, *Biblical Church Growth*, 90–91.
61. Jackson, *What Makes Churches Grow*, 268.

himself must model an effective prayer life personally and in conducting church affairs.[62] In all, while the potency of prayer is not in contention, it is clear that a church that intends to grow must combine all strategies, natural or supernatural, to flourish and continue to blossom.

4.7 Common Church Growth Models

Several models (images and figures) have also gained popularity in approaching and achieving the task of church growth within different contexts. While not an exhaustive work, in his article, "Models of Church Growth Movement,"[63] Young-Gi Hong, president of the Institute of Church Growth in Korea, surveyed various missionary models of church growth. I explore these briefly with the hope of providing some insight into the myriads of church growth models that mission practitioners and institutions engage today.

4.7.1 Megachurch Model

I recall how my church growth professor in the seminary passionately expatiated this model of church growth, which he felt was very important in contemporary times. Hong equally insists that megachurches which began to mushroom in the 1970s typically constitute a modern church growth model because they are affected by modernity.[64] Megachurches are notable for charismatic leaders who serve in the pastorate of the church for a long time while exercising strong leadership.[65] Churches of this nature generally demonstrate three major qualities: mega-size, location in urban areas, and non-denominational functionality.[66] Additionally, they are known for demonstrating an appeal for evangelism as they maintain large organizations and operate generally as businesses. With the great influence the megachurch model retains over smaller-sized churches that are embracing it uncritically, this approach to church growth has fallen under huge criticisms, particularly for its over-the-top stress on numerical growth.[67]

---

62. Jackson, 268.
63. Hong, "Models of Church Growth," 101–113.
64. Hong, 103.
65. See the work of Hong, *Dynamism and Dilemma*.
66. Thumma, "Exploring the Megachurch Phenomena."
67. Hong, "Models of Church Growth," 104.

4.7.2 Multiplication Model

The second model of church growth Hong describes is the multiplication model. This model is the idea implicit in church planting, which is "the main way in which the Christian Church has grown across the world for 2,000 years."[68] Moreover, contrary to the expansion of centralized churches in the concept of megachurches, the multiplication model of church growth describes the extension of churches across nations and overseas.[69] Those who favour this model of church growth[70] over the megachurch model perceive the centralized megachurches as limiting growth potential and the evangelistic goal of the church to reach the whole world. They also argue that megachurches have mainly thrived in urban and secularized societies that allow religious freedom. They are ineffective in planting indigenous churches, which are more characteristic of rural areas. However, with the multiplication model of church growth, the church can have a global impact, reaching every nook and cranny.[71]

4.7.3 Cell Church Model

There is also the cell church model. Yong-Gi Cho, South Korean Christian minister who cofounded Yoido Full Gospel Church (the world's largest congregation), made this model of church growth popular as a ministry, practising it with home-cell groups.[72] Consequently, he is acclaimed as the originator of cell movements.[73] Hong believes the cell church model has attracted the interest of many church leaders as a new wave of church growth and renewal since the 1990s.[74] The cell church model originated from two contexts – the megachurch phenomenon and the experience of Christianity's suppression. The baseline for the cell church and megachurch models is that they both take small groups seriously. However, in the cell church, each cell functions

---

68. Jackson, *What Makes Churches Grow*, 159.
69. Hong, "Models of Church Growth," 104.
70. Examples are Lim, "Cho Yonggi's Charismatic Leadership"; Simson, *Houses That Change*.
71. Hong, "Models of Church Growth," 104.
72. Cho, *Successful Home Cell Groups*.
73. Comiskey, *Home Cell Group Explosion*.
74. Hong, "Models of Church Growth," 105.

as a church and is expected to multiply within months. The model of the cell church is patterned after the house community in the early church.[75]

4.7.4 Natural Church Development Model

The fifth model of church growth is the NCD, which stands for Natural Church Development model. Christian Schwarz, a German lecturer, researcher, and author, developed the model. He emphasized that as organic church growth, NCD congregations grow by principles of spiritual life just as living organisms develop. From a survey of one thousand churches across thirty-two countries and six continents, Schwarz released a publication in 1996 titled *Natural Church Development: A Practical Guide to a New Approach*.[76] In the book, Schwarz observes that a healthy organism grows "all by itself," and as such, certain developments in the church tend to happen "all by themselves" or "automatically" – growth automatism.[77] Schwarz then proposes eight universal characteristics of healthy, growing churches. The interplay of all these indicators, he insists, is present in all healthy and growing churches.[78] The scholar also maintains that quality (health) impacts the quantity (numbers or size) of the church, but quantity can happen with or without quality. Consequently, Hong believes that NCD tends to overly stress attention to the quality of growth happening in congregations to the point that it downplays the role of megachurches and overlooks the mission and social responsibilities of the church.[79] He adds that by claiming the undesirability of large congregations, the NCD model neglects cultural contexts of churches, especially those places where large churches are popular and well received.[80]

4.7.5 ICGK Model

The sixth and final church growth model surveyed by Hong is the paradigm developed by the Institute for Church Growth in Korea. The ICGK model, named after the organization which developed it, is also referred to as the multi-variance model. It is so described because it suggests various kinds of

---

75. Hong, 105.
76. Schwarz, *Natural Church Development*.
77. Schwarz, 12.
78. Schwarz, 79.
79. Hong, "Models of Church Growth," 106.
80. Hong, 106–107; For fuller discussion, see Schwarz, *Natural Church Development*.

church growth based on church size.[81] Through a careful observation of 175 churches of different sizes, theological emphases, and denominational attachments between 1993 and 2000, the institute proposed some ten indicators of growing churches as follows: excellent pastoral leadership, mobilising laymen, effective organizational system, systematic evangelism, vitalized nurturing system, specialized ministry, meaningful experience of God, social services for the local community, mission-oriented church, and multiplying through church planting. The institute's important discovery from the study is that church size notwithstanding, pastoral leadership and sermons are the most important aspects in church growth.[82] The ICGK also adopts the 4PMC model as a consulting tool for church growth. 4PMC stands for people, prayer, place, programme, mission, and community.[83]

4.8 Brief Critique of the Popular Church Growth Models

While each of the popular church growth models discussed above presents interesting approaches to church development, all seem to have stressed, quite lopsidedly, one dimension of church growth over others. Moreover, it is wise to examine how these mostly Western models fit specifically within African contexts, whether among diaspora congregations or those on the continent. I hope this evaluation would be beneficial for African Christians in deploying relatable and effective missional strategies in their various settings. Hence, I have highlighted how the common church growth models can find enhancement and greater productivity among African congregations, particularly through effective dialogue with OSE.

To begin with, both megachurch and multiplication models tend to place so much emphasis on numerical growth that they appear silent on other dimensions of church development. These strategies push so heavily for numbers that they encourage large church buildings and locations in urban areas (with the likely implication of a thin connection with the often more culturally aware rural dwellers), and replication over wide geographical areas, even

---

81. Hong, 107.
82. For further details see Institute for Church Growth, *Church Planting*.
83. Hong, "Models of Church Growth," 107–108.

beyond national borders. While the spread and multiplication may appear to facilitate cross-cultural missions, especially with overseas expansion, the large numbers often permit weak social connection within the congregation. Yet, Africans, for instance, operate communally, and therefore, cherish the close social interactions that may be missing in churches of large sizes. Thus, adopting OSE may be the needed resource for megachurches in achieving social growth as well as consolidating on other dimensions of development.

Despite the cell church model featuring opportunity for fellowship and, thus, social growth in the church, it focuses a lot of attention on rapid multiplication of the cells (small home gatherings considered as churches) to the detriment of other essential dimensions of church growth. The model's alliance with the megachurch approach makes it even more difficult to dismiss its tendency for overwhelming concern for numerical increase without necessarily paying attention to other aspects of church growth. Nevertheless, when deployed alongside OSE, the excessive preoccupation with size or numbers can balance the remaining aims of church growth advocated in this work.

NCD is perhaps more concerned about the spiritual growth of the church than any of the other popular church growth models presented. Of course, spiritual growth is foundational. Notwithstanding, the seeming unilateral perspective that spiritual growth alone is what is needed to generate numerical increase appears to invalidate other growth dimensions of the church. The social and administrative growth of the church, for example, receive no feasible consideration as if they matter less in the sustenance and development of the church. Consequently, NCD does not adequately model church growth as understood in this work. OSE provides a more robust framework that covers this deficiency.

The ICGK model does well to propose some ten indicators of a growing church, and accommodates the four aspects of church growth suggested in this study. However, it may have come up short with its narrow conclusion. The model tends to claim that pastoral leadership is the most crucial factor in church growth. Certainly, leadership plays an undeniable and central role in church growth, as this study itself reveals, but it may have been overstressed as though all energy must be expended towards this dimension of growth alone. This is where OSE is, again, advantageous in balancing such a seemingly skewed perspective on church growth.

4.9 Multi-Ethic Church

In spite of the homogenous unit principle's (HUP) many decades of success in missions, in relatively recent times, the concept has come under severe scrutiny from scholars, including Ken Davis, Director of Church Planting at Baptist Bible Seminary, Pennsylvania, and Chuck Van Engen, Professor of Biblical Theology of Mission at Fuller Theological Seminary.[84] The principle is mainly criticized for discouraging cultural or ethnic diversity in the church, and by implication, limiting the extensive *mission of God* in reaching all nations and people-groups.[85] Consequently, an alternative to homogenous congregations – multi-ethnic churches – is now found in several literatures.[86] Of course the social institution and concept described by "multi-ethnic church"[87] is also represented by two sister terms: "Multicultural"[88] and "multiracial" churches.[89] In a broad sense, the substitute concept of multi-ethnic church connotes a gathering where members come from various backgrounds without one culture asserting itself over others, unlike the outlook of homogenous congregations.

4.9.1 In Search of a Name and Description

To arrive at a specific and acceptable description for the alternative to a homogenous congregation, it is vital to highlight the challenge inherent in the extant suggestions of *multi-ethnic/racial/cultural* church. For instance, anthropologist Roger Ballard speaks of some conceptual confusion that exists as to the precise meaning of the terms ethnicity, race, and culture.[90] While missiologists are often comfortable applying the terms synonymously,

---

84. Davis, "Multicultural Church Planting Models"; Van Engen, "Is the Church for Everyone."

85. Lane, "Multiethnic Worship Representative," 12.

86. See, for instance, Dunlow, "Disciples of All Nations"; Prill, "Migration, Mission"; DeYmaz, *Building a Healthy Multi-ethnic*.

87. See the works of DeYmaz and Li, *Leading a Healthy Multi-Ethnic*; Gushiken, "Cultivating Healthy Discipleship Settings," 17–26; Marti, "Conceptual Pathways," 1048–1066; Garces-Forley, *Crossing the Ethnic Divide*.

88. Refer to Brouwer, *How to Become*; Kwiyani, *Mission-Shaped Church*; Hibbert and Hibbert, *Leading Multicultural Teams*; Tahaafe-Williams, "Multicultural Church? Multicultural Ministry."

89. Pitt, "Fear of a Black Pulpit," 218–223; Yancey, *One Body. One Spirit*; Marti, *Worship across the Racial Divide*; Perry, "Racial Diversity, Religion," 355–376.

90. Roger Ballard, "Race, Ethnicity and Culture."

sociologists, on the other hand, appear to create some distinctions as to the dimensions of the social order they describe.[91] The latter tend to consider race as some distinguishing, fixed, and somewhat arbitrary physical characteristic between people – such as skin or hair colour. They relate ethnicity more to common ancestry, history, and practices that are often self-asserted rather than assigned by others.[92] Culture, on its own part, reflects in both categories since language, tradition, worldview, and other cultural expressions are embedded within the categories of race and ethnicity.[93]

Indeed, the border lines of race, culture, and ethnicity are often blurred, and the "tug and pull of state power, group interests, and other social forces"[94] continue to redesign the edges. As such, it appears that the tendency of overlap between these three classifications will persist. Of course, history has revealed how groups once considered ethnicities are now seen as race or vice versa (for instance, the Irish, Italians, and Jews who are now loosely seen as White but were previously excluded from the race).[95] In sum, it appears the distinctions often made between the trio of race, ethnicity, and culture by sociologists are more ideological than practical.[96] Therefore, I find it fair to view the three categories as broadly synonymous in relation to mixed or non-homogenous congregations.

Nonetheless, in this dissertation, I have adopted the term "multi-ethnic church" out of the three popular connotations of a mixed congregation. First, beyond any semantic and conceptual distinction argument, examining mixed churches from the standpoint of race alone (suggested in multi-racial church) risks overlooking the diversity of ethnicities present within the congregations. Second, focusing on ethnicity appears even more meaningful and interesting when it is beyond racial boundaries. As such, "ethnicity is often a bigger determiner of a people's identity and worldview than race or nationality."[97] Of course, culture comes to the scene regardless of perspective since categorising

---

91. Garces-Forley, "New Opportunities and New Values," 211.

92. I have discussed more on the perceived differences at the borderlines of race and ethnicity in another chapter.

93. Cornell and Hartmann, *Ethnicity and Race*.

94. Clair and Denis, "Sociology of Racism," 2.

95. Clair and Denis, 2.

96. Ballard, "Race, Ethnicity and Culture," 1.

97. McIntosh, "Defining a Multi-Ethnic Church."

expressions of culture, such as language, traditions, family systems, worldviews, and others, either as racial or ethnic attribute, is often complex.[98]

For a working definition of multi-ethnic church, I find the description of the late, renowned American missiologist Paul Hiebert quite comprehensive and in alignment with the church growth concept pursued in this study. Hiebert considered a multi-ethnic congregation to be:

> a church in which there is 1) an attitude and practice of accepting people of all ethnic, class and national origins as equal and fully participating members and ministers in the fellowship of the church; and 2) the manifestation of this attitude and practice by the involvement of people from different ethnic, social and national communities as members in the church.[99]

The above definition is relevant to this work because rather than focusing on statistics, it reflects the right "attitude and practice" characterising a truly multi-ethnic assembly. Kwiyani maintains that in this sort of gathering, "all cultures – both host and guest – intentionally displace themselves from the centre to allow for the emergence of a new culture that comes out of all cultures present working together."[100] It is not just the presence of many ethnic faces in the church. Rather, it is a collaborative congregation of various ethnicities, resulting in the formation of a totally new approach to and operation of the church: one undominated by any ethnic group – majority or minority. The emerging culture of the church, then, looks more like the all-welcoming kingdom of God, where the contributions of every ethnic group and individual is appreciated and allowed.[101]

4.9.2 Why Multi-Ethnic Congregations?

I believe the concept of multi-ethnic churches is vital to missions and church growth praxis today, as opposed to the popular idea of homogenous congregations. While I have already mentioned some of the limitations associated with homogenous gatherings,[102] in this part of the dissertation, I outline a few

---

98. Garces-Forley, "New Opportunities and New Values," 210–212.
99. Ortiz, *One New People*, 149.
100. Kwiyani, *Multicultural Kingdom*, 117.
101. Kwiyani, 117.
102. Refer to the conversation on Homogenous Unit Principle in chapter 2.

advantages of multi-ethnic congregations. Indeed, there are many reasons for advocating multi-ethnic congregations, and a single piece of writing such as this may be incapable of enumerating them all. To avoid divergence from the focus of this study, I have highlighted only three rationale for multi-ethnic churches.

First, multi-ethnic congregations reflect the multi-ethnic dimension of God's message – his promise – as resounded throughout the Scriptures.[103] As one reads through the book of the beginnings in Genesis 12:3, one discovers the promise of God to Abraham and his descendants through whom he (God) purposed to bless the whole world. Apostle Paul refers to this promise as "the gospel" in Galatians 3:8. He proceeds to assert in Galatian 3:16–18 that the life, suffering, death, and resurrection of Jesus Christ are the fulfilment of the promise. In the final book of the canonized Bible, there is a description of the culmination of the promise where a vast multitude of people from every nation, tribe, tongue, and language stands before the throne of God in the vision of John (Rev 7:9).[104] This suggests that God's desire and expectation for the church is inclusion – and multi-ethnicity by implication – where the church is made up, again, of "every tribe and language and people and nation" (Rev 5:9; 7:9; 13:7; 14:6). This idea of inclusion is also inherent in the concept of Catholicity – one of the four basic marks of the church.[105] Catholicity refers to "the universal scope of the church as a society instituted by God in which all sorts and conditions of humanity, all races, nations and cultures, can find a welcome and home."[106] Multi-ethnic congregations emphasize the catholicity of the church.

Second, multi-ethnic churches "challenge their members to engage with the ethnically 'other' and develop civic skills for living in a diverse society."[107] Omideyi makes this point clear in her recounting of how she worked alongside her husband to see the church they co-lead in the UK become multi-ethnic.

---

103. Williams, "Celebrating Multiethnic Churches."

104. Williams, "Celebrating Multiethnic Churches." Rev 7:9 also dovetails Jesus's final message to his disciples commonly referred to as "the Great Commission" and recorded in Matt 28:19–20. It speaks of spreading the good news of Jesus's life, suffering, death, and resurrection to all nations. Some other biblical passages that reflect diversity and inclusion are Gal 3:28, Acts 17: 26–27, Col 3:11, Ezek 47:22, and Rev 5:9.

105. Cray, *Mission-Shaped Church*, 96–97.

106. Alvis, *Anglican Understanding*, 65.

107. Garces-Forley, "New Opportunities," 209.

She retells how they would both engage with their host communities during their frequent evangelism outings while developing skills for establishing a multi-cultural church and living in a multicultural society like Britain. The result was the emergence of a congregation composed of people from multiple ethnic backgrounds across racial and cultural boundaries[108] – a church that has become more cross-culturally competent since the members are furnished with good intercultural skills.[109]

Third, multi-ethnic congregations gain from a broad range of ideas and insights.[110] John Piper, chancellor of Bethlehem College and Seminary, and former pastor of Bethlehem Baptist Church, Minneapolis, sought to draw from this advantage of multi-ethnicity when he decided to present to his congregation the desire to include a non-White pastor on the staff team of the church. Piper strongly believed that even if bringing a minority on board would reduce the productivity of the organization, it was a loss that was worth it considering God's multi-ethnic message and vision of equality.[111] Of course, a person of different ethnicity and more likely, a variant worldview to the majority culture in the church, may be able to spot a potential problem and develop a more robust solution rather than one who shares ethnicity with the dominant group. In fact, the presence of multiple interacting cultures in the church enriches the congregation's interpretation of the Scriptures as the people encounter God through diverse cultural lenses.[112]

4.10 Contextualization

In realising the intended goal of multi-ethnic congregations, an important conversation that often arises is the concept of contextualization.[113] As one of the central themes in missiology, contextualization is intrinsic to Christianity, and has become a recurring challenge since the inception of the church: arising whenever the gospel migrated and crossed languages and cultures.[114] In

---

108. Omideyi, *Transformed to Transform*, 29–36.
109. Hardison, "Theological Critique of Multi-ethnic," 8.
110. Hardison, 9.
111. Piper, *Bloodlines: Race, Cross*, 257–258.
112. Whiteman, "Contextualization: The Theory," 4.
113. I explain what contextualization is in the next discourse.
114. Magesa, *Anatomy of Inculturation*, 87.

fact, the entire Bible is contextualized consciously or unconsciously with its message originally coming in language and concepts meaningful to sources and receptors in the Hebrew and Greco-Roman cultures in biblical times.[115] There are also several records of the activities of contextualization in various church-related happenings recorded in the Scripture.

For instance, there is the development arising from the gathering of apostles in Jerusalem as recorded in Acts 15. The meeting was to address some confusion following the conversion of Gentiles and their expectations regarding the Law of Moses. The decision of the apostles here was clear: "Gentile believers in Jesus could be received as fellow Israelites without becoming Jews."[116] They could retain their culture as "they did not have to become Jews culturally in order to enter into the new covenant."[117] This was an act of contextualizing the gospel message for the Gentiles with the apostles seeking to answer the question: what does it mean to follow Jesus in the Gentile culture?[118] Yet the term contextualization, in missions vocabulary, did not emerge until the early 1970s[119] and ever since, there has been an increase in writings and conversations about it.

4.10.1 What is It?

The task of contextualization involves the relationship between the gospel, church, and localities.[120] In short, it is the intersection between faith and culture. Literature is replete with vocabularies like "adaptation," "accommodation," "indigenization," and "translation" that refer to this relationship between faith and culture.[121] Contextualization came to the forefront in 1971, together

---

115. Hesselgrave, "Contextualization That Is Authentic," 115.
116. Walls, *Crossing Cultural Frontiers*, 5.
117. Herbert, "Rooted or Uprooted," 131.
118. Bendor-Samuel, "Challenge and Realignment," 277.
119. The first mention of the term "contextualization" was in the publication Theological Education Fund, *Ministry in Context*. The Theological Education Fund (TEF) was launched by the International Missionary Council (IMC) at its Ghana meeting in 1957–1958. The agency's purpose was to evaluate requests for funding according to how contextualized they were in four areas: Missiology, theological application, educational methods, and educational structure. For further details, see Hesselgrave and Rommen, *Contextualization: Meanings, Methods*, 28–35.
120. Whiteman, "Contextualization," 2.
121. Dean Flemming, *Contextualization in the New Testament*, 18; Hesselgrave and Rommen, *Contextualization*, ix.

with a sister term, "inculturation,"[122] in 1974, perhaps because contextualization comes across as a more dynamic, deeper, and more adequate description of the current experience in missions.[123] With the unyielding challenge to seek for ways in which the gospel could be "more deeply lived, celebrated, and shared,"[124] agents of church growth and missions will likely continue to find contextualization relevant in their missionary activities.

In order to make sense of and realize the agenda of contextualization, which seeks the "faithful communication of, reflection upon, and living out the Christian faith in ways appropriate to specific contexts,"[125] missiologists and other scholars have provided various insights about the underlying idea in both classic and more recent literature.[126] In this dissertation, I have adopted the timeless and comprehensive definition of late David Hesselgrave, Professor of Missions (and arguably the founding dean of modern evangelical missiology) for its holistic perspective. According to Hesselgrave, contextualization is:

> the attempt to communicate the message of the person, works, Word, and will of God in a way that is faithful to God's revelation, especially as it is put forth in the teachings of Holy Scripture, and that it is meaningful to respondents in their respective cultural and existential contexts.[127]

The above definition suggests a required interaction and balance between theology and culture when it speaks of communicating the Scripture message

---

122. "Inculturation" first surfaced as a term in the Final Statement, no. 12, of the First Plenary Assembly of the Federation of Asian Bishops' Conference, Evangelization in Modern Day Asia (Taipei, 22–27 April 1974). Refer to Federation of Asian Bishops' Conference (FABC), *Evangelization in Modern Day Asia*. In their statement and reccommendations, the Asian bishops asserted, "The local church is a church incarnate in a people, a church indigenous and inculturated." For more see also *His Gospel to Our Peoples*, vol. 2, 332. The term "inculturation" itself broadly describes the Christian faith translated into a culture. For further readings on inculturation see Magesa, *Anatomy of Inculturation*; Ballano, "Inculturation, Anthropology"; Tovey, *Inculturation of Christian Worship*; Arbuckle, *Culture, Inculturation, and Theologians*.

123. Whiteman, "Contextualization," 2.

124. Schineller, *Handbook on Inculturation*, 3.

125. Ott, "Globalization and Contextualization," 43–44.

126. See for instance Taber, "Limits of Indigenization," 372–399; Kuhn, "Adventist Theological-Missiology: Contextualization," 175–208; Boersema, "Contextualization and the Need," 257–263; Fluegge, "Dubious History of 'Contextualization,'" 50–69.

127. Hesselgrave, "Contextualization That Is Authentic," 115.

in ways that are true to God's revelation, and do not ignore or downplay the receiver's culture and entire context. The uncompromized gospel, the "unchanging Word"[128] and the truth it communicates can only be truly incarnated, understood, and received when it comes to people in concepts and manners that they find relatable and not compulsory from the messenger's worldview.[129] Similarly, by implying a right engagement between the gospel and culture, concerns of syncretism,[130] which, of course, often arise when "developments in non-Western churches . . . do not neatly align with Western Christianity,"[131] are resolved. The related issue of over-contextualization is also addressed in the definition, which pushes for the need to be sensitive to the settings where mission is taking place.[132]

Certainly, the concerns of syncretism and over-contextualizing are valid; hence some scholars and mission practitioners have considered the agenda of contextualization as a "risky business" on a steep cliff of "gospel contamination."[133] These worries of syncretism, over-contextualization, and gospel contamination, then, raise the question of authentic, true, good, and relevant contextualization. Paul Hiebert describes true contextualization as activities that seek for balance between the exegesis of the Scripture and of culture, culminating in a critical response from the recipients of the gospel message.[134] In other words, good or authentic contextualization helps to understand:

> the possibility and capability of Christians in a determined context to make the gospel feel at home in the cultures where people live and communicate God's Word; but at the same time, to take into account that the gospel will always be a pilgrim

---

128. Moreau, *Contextualizing the Faith*, 1.

129. Bowen, ed. *Missionary Letters*, 114.

130. Syncretism broadly refers to the replacement or dilution of the essential truths of the gospel through the incorporation of non-Christian elements. See more in Moreau, *Evangelical Dictionary*, 924–925.

131. Richard, "Religious Syncretism," 209.

132. Craig Ott, Stephen Strauss, and Timothy Tennent also highlight the importance of being true and sensitive to mission context. See Ott, Strauss, and Tennent, *Encountering Theology of Mission*, 276.

133. Greeson, "Comprehensive Contextualization," 425.

134. For more on authentic contextualization see Hiebert, "Critical Contextualization," 109–110.

in every culture since it will confront the sinful and opposing elements in it.[135]

The importance of contextualization to missions cannot be overstressed, given that the church continues to seek to engage societies and localities incarnationally.[136] Moreover, as humans, "our faith is *always* enfleshed because, despite our spiritual nature, we are enfleshed beings (we have physical bodies)."[137] This consideration, I am convinced, is at the heart of contextualization.

4.10.2 The Breadth of Contextualization

Bible translators apply dynamic equivalence in translating the Bible from one language to another because dynamic interpretation implies "the closest natural equivalence to the source language."[138] In the same vein, the scope of contextualization cuts broadly across every form of "dynamic equivalence in all the areas of church life."[139] Of course, this would include both verbal and non-verbal forms of activities involved in carrying out the gospel or the mission of God everywhere the church (the people of God as opposed to buildings) exists as Matthew 28:18–20 emphasizes.[140]

In contemplating the extent of contextualization, missiologist Stephen Bevans posits that contextualization extends as far back as the faith experience recorded in the Scriptures and sustained in tradition and stretches forward to accommodate contemporary experiences that make up the present settings of the gospel.[141] As such, the personal life experience of an individual or group, their culture or community, their social location, and the phenomenon of social change, all speak to the agenda of contextualization.[142] These realities form various aspects with which the activity of contextualization must interact. Thus, the breadth of contextualization.

---

135. Paredes, "Short-Term Missions," 257.
136. Beresh, "Contextualize without Compromise," 1.
137. Moreau, *Contextualizing the Faith*, 2.
138. Hesselgrave and Rommen, *Contextualization*, 62.
139. Chai, "Look at Contextualization," 10.
140. Hesselgrave, "Contextualization That Is Authentic," 115.
141. Bevans, *Models of Contextual Theology*, 5.
142. Bevans, 5–6.

To be more deliberate about the task of contextualization, American missiologist Harley Talman identifies seven specific, critical areas where churches can concentrate their efforts: Theology, bible translation, language, worship, evangelism, church planting, music, and leadership training.[143] Though with different terminologies, Professor of Intercultural Studies Scott Moreau provides similar aspects of church life that the agenda of contextualization should cover. These are: Mythical facet, ethical side, artistic and technological dimension, rituals, experiential aspect (especially in relation to the supernatural), doctrine, and social services and actions of the church.[144] Suffice it to say contextualization applies to all areas of church life apart from its essence or message. As such, an African way of being and doing church as the OSE, developed later in this thesis, could be appropriate.

4.10.3 Functions of Contextualization

Whatever form of Christianity that operates in a given community, place (home or diaspora), and time is necessarily facilitated by contextualization.[145] This is so critical that "the seemingly steadfast refusal or resistance by the church to seriously contextualize the gospel is one of its greatest mistakes and will sadly hasten its declining influence on Western society."[146] Unfortunately, and again, the erosion of church impact in the West is now more conspicuous than ever. It is therefore of utmost importance to meditate on the roles of contextualization in order to appreciate its benefits.

Cultural anthropologist Darrell Whiteman made a good case for the functions of contextualization in his now classic article titled "Contextualization: The Theory, the Gap, the Challenge."[147] In this outstanding piece, Whiteman captured the method and challenge of relating the gospel to culture across localities. He identified three essential functions of contextualization which I outline below.

---

143. Talman, "Comprehensive Contextualization," 6.
144. Refer to Moreau, *Contextualizing the Faith*.
145. Magesa, *Anatomy of Inculturation*, 87.
146. Frost and Hirsch, *Shaping of Things*, 57.
147. Whiteman, "Contextualization," 2–4.

4.10.3.1 Addresses Deepest Needs

Whiteman's words express the first role of contextualization aptly and comprehensively. Contextualization seeks to:

> communicate the Gospel in word and deed and to establish the church in ways that make sense to people within their local cultural context, presenting Christianity in such a way that it meets people's deepest needs and penetrates their worldview, thus allowing them to follow Christ and remain within their own culture.[148]

This function emphasizes the verbal and non-verbal aspects of contextualization, which facilitate the gospel presentation in a manner that addresses people's deepest needs and "penetrates their worldviews."[149] This role of contextualization is critical because mission agents are often unaware of how their understanding and practice of the Christian faith has been shaped by their own context so that they end up passing down their culture along with the faith.[150] So, contextualization ensures that Christianity and its symbolic institution – church – is established in ways that make sense to the localities and not according to the culture of the mission agents. As such, people can become Christians without adopting or learning the culture of the missionary. This is what the Jerusalem council addressed in Acts 15 in encouraging the conversion of Gentiles without the need to imbibe Judaism. By implication, converts did not have to renounce their culture, family, or community to become Christians.

4.10.3.2 Offends for the Right Reasons

The second function of contextualization is that it offends. Good contextualization offends for the right reasons and bad contextualization, or its absence, offends for the wrong reasons. By this, Whiteman implies that when the gospel is not contextualized or is done so poorly, people become culturally offended and are not willing to receive it. McGavran similarly contends that it is not the "offense of the cross" that hinders church growth, but

---

148. Emphasis in original text. Whiteman, 2.
149. Frost and Hirsch, *Shaping of Things*, 83.
150. Whiteman, "Contextualization," 2.

the "nonbiblical offenses" (standards and rules set by men) which does not often permit authentic contextualization.[151] Poor contextualization or its total absence makes people suspicious of the gospel, mission agents, and their new converts as alien.

New converts also get the stigma of being cultural misfits and traitors, having embraced another culture together with the gospel. Consequently, the gospel can no longer offend for the right reasons. That is, exposing sinfulness, the tendency toward evil, oppressive structures and behaviour patterns within culture,[152] such as the Rwandan genocide and South African apartheid.[153] More recent are the prevailing Boko-Haram terrorism and banditry activities in Nigeria, including the gruesome murder of Adamawa state Christian Association of Nigeria (CAN) Chairman Reverend Andimi on 20 January 2020, among other nefarious movements and practices.[154]

4.10.3.3 Enriches the Universal Church

The third character of contextualization in missions is to help develop contextualized expressions of the gospel, thereby expanding the universal church's understanding of the kingdom of God. It reminds all persons, as representatives of different cultures, that no one culture is supreme or has a privileged or ultimate position when it comes to God's revelation and the practice of Christianity.[155] For instance, Africans have something to teach the West about joyful dependence on God in the midst of suffering and poverty, just as Latin Americans also possess insights on celebratory worship and economic justice.[156] In essence, the catholic church can theologize more accurately through contextualization, for "it takes a whole world to understand a whole Christ."[157]

---

151. McGavran, *Understanding Church Growth*, 201.
152. Whiteman, "Contextualization," 3–4.
153. Harrison, "Bridging Theory and Training," 196.
154. See report on Rev. Andimi's execution at CSW, "Boko Haram Executes Chair."
155. Whiteman, "Contextualization," 4.
156. Ott, Strauss, and Tennent, *Encountering Theology of Mission*, 289.
157. Tennent, " Challenge of Churchless Christianity," 176.

4.11 Conclusion

I have mentioned that with the multitude of principles and schools of thought governing the agenda of church growth, it would be a difficult if not impossible task to enumerate all relevant theories in one writing. Therefore, the theories addressed in this chapter are not exhaustive, but an attempt to scan through the general rules, designs, postulations, and strategies that have shaped and continue to influence the activities of church growth in the world. Of course, there were foundational voices, especially from the church growth movement, who popularized the concept of church growth and charted the course of thinking about it long before other contributors arose. As such, a host of the theories presented, and which have formed common missiological concepts today, demonstrate vague or direct connections to the earlier propositions. In fact, in some cases, they seem more like mere reinventions of the same principles.

A deviant, however, is the concept of the multi-ethnic church, which serves as a critique and an alternative to the HUP of the CGM. In discussing this substitute church composition and outlook over HUP, I argued for the preference of the term multi-ethnic congregation over the similar terms of multi-racial and multicultural congregations. I also explored the closely linked practice of contextualization to multiethnicity. It is notable that the OSE this dissertation advances is a contextualized way of being the church.

CHAPTER 5

Church Growth and Development of African Diaspora Congregations in Liverpool

5.1 Introduction

In this section, I explore the emergence and growth of ADCs in Liverpool. I consider it helpful in achieving this task to situate the discourse within the larger British and, ultimately, Western context. I hope that having a sense of the topography of Christianity in the West will provide some hints about the depth of the challenge that attends pioneering an ADC in such an environment. Against this backdrop, I open the discussion by examining the critical role of migration in the spread of God's mission – and, of course, Christianity – right from biblical times. With migration eventually shifting the base of Christianity to Europe, I reflect on the Great European migration that reintroduces Christianity to Africa, the faith that would later expand beyond the continent into the diaspora. After accounting for the presence of African Christianity in the British diaspora, I narrow the rest of the conversation down to Liverpool, musing on the growth of ADCs in the city.

5.2 The Element of Migration

It is perhaps an unforgiveable error to trace the spread and growth of the Christian faith in any era and region without considering the place of migration. Indeed, it is the migration of Africans to the West that makes the presence of African Christians and congregations in the region possible in first place.[1] Migration itself, "a massive movement of peoples," is not a strange phenomenon for humanity.[2] As Hanciles observes, "from little-understood ecological changes (including occurrences of famine and natural disasters) to overly aggressive neighbours and the perennial round of military violence," for thousands of years, the uncertain nature of normal life made migration a fundamental part of human existence.[3] Explaining further, he adds, "as long as human beings have inhabited the planet, relocation, displacement, and population transfers have marked the human condition."[4] There is, indeed, no denying that "human history has often been determined by movements of people."[5] Hanciles, for instance, in his recent publication entitled *Migration and the Making of Global Christianity*,[6] surveys how the spread of global Christianity since its inception has been driven much more by human migration than organized missionary activities. In essence, migration is just "an irrepressible human urge."[7]

5.2.1 Convergence of Migration and *Missio Dei*: Biblical Witness

The norm of migration to human conditions is seen all through the Bible. Both the Old Testament (OT) and New Testament (NT) reflect the unmistakable and inseparable connection between migration and *missio Dei* (the mission of God), and by implication, with Christianity.[8] Right from the ejection of Adam and Eve from the garden of Eden (Gen 3), a case of involuntary migration, to the exile of John on the Island of Patmos (Rev 1:9), migration themes run through the biblical record.[9] In fact, Walls believes that with the thread of migration running through various narratives in Genesis – for

---

1. Kwiyani, *Sent Forth*, 41.
2. Walls, *Crossing Cultural Frontiers*, 49.
3. Hanciles, *Beyond Christendom*, 139.
4. Hanciles, 139.
5. Walls, *Crossing Cultural Frontiers*, 49.
6. Hanciles, *Migration and the Making*.
7. Bohning, "International Migration," 18.
8. Kwiyani, *Sent Forth*, 43.
9. Hanciles, *Beyond Christendom*, 140.

instance, the displacement of Adam and Eve, the wanderings of Cain (Gen 4), dispersion of people from Tower of Babel (Gen 11), and the movements of the patriarchs (Abraham, Isaac, and Jacob, along with Joseph), the first book of the Bible might as well be called the book of migrations.[10]

Moving from Genesis into Exodus, migration continues its appearances in major events of the OT, colouring the story of the journey of the nation of Israel from Egypt. On this trek to their own land, divine judgement results in the serial, forced scatterings of the people to Assyria (2 Kgs 17) and Babylon (2 Kgs 25) before episodes of later resettlement in the land (Ezra and Nehemiah). As Walls insists, all these events represent various forms of migration, whether voluntary or involuntary,[11] and they "set the tone for the rest of the Bible."[12]

The NT also presents evidence of the intertwining of migration and the mission of God. The story of incarnation is certainly a foremost example. John 1:14 explains this interplay of God's mission and migration: "And the Word became flesh and lived among us." (NRSV) In this event, Jesus, the son of the missionary God, migrates down to earth, emptying himself and "taking the form of a slave" to completely identify with mankind (Phil 2:7 NRSV). According to Swiss theologian Karl Barth, incarnation is "the way of a [sic] Son of God into the far country."[13] The triune God does not only become an immigrant God who descended to live on earth (far country) with humans, though. The Spirit of God himself retains the identity of a migrant God as he continues to reside with God's people all over the world.[14]

Another prime phenomenon that reflects the inextricability of migration and *missio Dei* in the NT is the spread of Christianity. Jesus's charge to his disciples to be his witnesses in Jerusalem, Judea, Samaria, and to the far ends of the earth, often referred to as the Great Commission (Matthew 28:19), is with an implication of migration.[15] Hence, the *Jesus movement* (Christianity) has always benefited from migration for its expansion.[16] This reality becomes even

---

10. Walls, "Mission and Migration," 3.
11. Walls, 3.
12. Kwiyani, *Sent Forth*, 43.
13. Barth, *Church Dogmatics*, 157.
14. Groody, "Crossing the Divide," 649.
15. Kwiyani, *Sent Forth*, 48–49.
16. Kwiyani, *Mission-Shaped*, 4.

clearer as one reads through the records of Acts, the Epistles, and other NT books. In these narratives, migration takes the early church from its original Jewish base around the Mediterranean world from Antioch to Corinth, Rome, Philippi, and other well-known centres in the NT.[17] Of course, this mobility of the church is helpful, as missiologist David Bosch argues: "I believe that the church discovers her true nature only as she moves from one human world to another, when she crosses frontiers, whether these are geographical, cultural, ethnic, linguistic, or sociological."[18] In fact, multi-ethnic churches owe their existence and expansion to migration. Hence, scholar and church leader Malcolm Patten insists that, "There is a strong correlation between migration, the expansion of cities and growth in number of multicultural churches."[19]

An important composition that maps and summarizes the intersections of migration and the mission of God throughout the length of Scripture is the "Immigrants Creed," written by José Luis Casal. Casal himself was a Cuban immigrant and the General Missioner of Tres Rios Presbytery of the Presbyterian Church, U.S.A. at the time of authoring these insightful statements of belief:[20]

> I believe in Almighty God, who guided the people in exile and in exodus, the God of Joseph in Egypt and Daniel in Babylon, the God of foreigners and immigrants.
>
> I believe in Jesus Christ, a displaced Galilean, who was born away from his people and his home, who fled his country with his parents when his life was in danger, and returning to his own country suffered the oppression of the tyrant Pontius Pilate, the servant of a foreign power, who then was persecuted, beaten, and finally tortured, accused and condemned to death unjustly. But on the third day, this scorned Jesus rose from the dead, not as a foreigner but to offer us citizenship in heaven.

---

17. Ross, "Non-Western Christians," 6.
18. Bosch, *Spirituality for the Road*, 58.
19. Patten, *Leading a Multi-Cultural Church*, 144.
20. Trinity Presbyterian Church, *Service of Worship*.

I believe in the Holy Spirit, the eternal immigrant from God's kingdom among us, who speaks all languages, lives in all countries, and reunites all races.

I believe that the church is the secure home for the foreigner and for all believers who constitute it, who speak the same language and have the same purpose.

I believe that the Communion of the Saints begins when we accept the diversity of the saints. I believe in the forgiveness, which makes us all equal, and in the reconciliation, which identifies us more than does race, language or nationality.

I believe that in the Resurrection God will unite us as one people in which all are distinct and all are alike at the same time.

Beyond this world, I believe in Life Eternal in which no one will be an immigrant but all will be citizens of God's kingdom, which will never end. Amen.[21]

5.2.2 European Migration and the Renewal of African Christianity

By the fourth century AD, the gains of Christianity in Europe began to explode through migration, leading the continent to become the hotspot of Christianity between 500 and 1500 CE.[22] Therefore, when the Great European migration began at the close of the fifteenth century, Christianity was, again on the move, shifting its base.[23] The European domination of international migration would last for over 450 years and result in 21 percent of Europeans relocating outside Europe and occupying more than a third of the inhabited world.[24] One notable fruit of this era of migration is the reintroduction of Christianity to Africa (in a third phase) in the hundred years between 1850 and 1950 while European missionary enterprise lasted.[25]

---

21. Trinity Presbyterian Church, *Service of Worship*.
22. Hanciles, *Beyond Christendom*, 156.
23. Kwiyani, *Mission-Shaped Church*, 13.
24. Hanciles, *Beyond Christendom*, 157.
25. Kwiyani, *Sent Forth*, 138.

Of course, Christianity existed in North Africa since "late antiquity," when it was instrumental to "the development of Christian tradition." Scholars James Spickard and Afe Adogame add that the "latinized" form of Christianity had faint influence in the south and was eventually overrun by Muslim conquest, leaving only traces behind in Egypt and Ethiopia.[26] The second planting of Christianity in Africa occurred with the efforts of Catholic Portuguese explorers in the fifteenth and sixteenth centuries, resulting in the evangelization of the Congo and parts of sub-Saharan Africa: São Tomé, Mozambique, Angola, Madagascar, and present-day Benin.[27] However, this second phase of Christianity, which was marked by an "innovative cultural embrace of Catholicism,"[28] wound down in the eighteenth century, ultimately seeing the fading of "practically all the missions south of the Sahara."[29]

The third attempt to plant Christianity in Africa, through European Christian mission, ended up being ensnared in colonialism, a practice with an underlining racist ideology that the White race is superior.[30] This unhealthy alignment between Christianity and colonialism was also compounded by Europeans' scramble for and partitioning of Africa at the Berlin Congo conference of 1884–1885.[31] As such, "The whole system of Europe's relations to Africa . . . was to colonise (to extract resources) and Christianise (to make colonialism easier)," and many missionaries were consciously involved in these intertwined activities while others participated unknowingly.[32] To date, Christianity is still trying to disentangle itself from colonialism, perpetually lining up as one of the three Cs (Christianity, Civilization, and Commerce) of the condemnable practice.[33]

The side-effect of white-supremacy-stained European Christianity that found its way to Africa was the limited embrace it had among the African

---

26. Spickard and Adogame, "Introduction: Africa," 3.
27. John Paul II, "Post Synodal Apostolic Exhortation."
28. Kollman, " History of Christianity."
29. John Paul II, "Ecclesia in Africa."
30. Kwiyani, "Mission after George Floyd," 7. I have expanded more on the ideology of race and racism in a later chapter entitled "Church Growth and the Dynamics of Race."
31. Spickard and Adogame, "Africa and Religious Transnationalism," 4.
32. Kwiyani, "Mission after George Floyd," 8.
33. Nzacahayo, "Biblical and Historical Theology," 52.

people, for there was "general aversion to the White man's Christianity."³⁴ Racism was not hidden in the mission churches established by the missionaries, where "even able and experienced ministers remained second-class members of the church, always inferior to the most junior missionary recently arrived from Britain."³⁵ With the resettlement of former slaves (converted) in Liberia and Sierra Leone, African Christians were already championing the evangelization of their homeland. Thus, by the end of the nineteenth century, when European imperialism was gradually attaining its peak, African Initiated Churches (AICs)³⁶ like the South African Ethiopian and Zionist churches, and West African "African Churches," started emerging from within the mission churches.³⁷

Over the course of the twentieth century, AICs multiplied tremendously for many other reasons, which Ayegboyin and Ishola identify, including: nationalist feelings, mass movements occasioned by the emergence of charismatic (prophetic) figures, the desire to indigenize Christianity, passion for a purer form of Christianity, freedom to express gifts of leadership, and circumstantial factors (such as influenza epidemic and subsequent economic depression).³⁸ By the 1950s and 1960s, Pentecostal and charismatic churches were also showing up on the continent in large numbers, either indigenously planted (for instance, Deeper Life Bible Church, The Redeemed Christian Church of God, Church of Pentecost) or established by Pentecostal groups abroad (examples are the Four Square Gospel Church, Campus Crusade for Christ, and Full Gospel Businessmen Fellowship International).³⁹ Benefiting from the global expansion of Pentecostalism since the 1960s⁴⁰ and its flexibility to indigenize itself wherever it is found,⁴¹ most AICs today are "churches of a Pentecostal type that have contextualized and indigenized Christianity in

---

34. Sundkler, *Bantu Prophets*, 37, 300.
35. Hastings, *Church in Africa*, 529.
36. To adhere to the main concern of this work, I have chosen not to engage in the debate surrounding the nomenclature of AIC and instead adopted "African Initiated Churches" as the meaning of the term despite its various nuances.
37. Spickard and Adogame, "Africa and Religious Transnationalism," 4, 5.
38. Ayegboyin and Ishola, *African Indigenous Churches*, 12–16.
39. Spickard and Adogame, "Africa and Religious Transnationalism," 6.
40. Zurlo, Johnson, and Crossing, "World Christianity and Mission," 18.
41. Shenk, "Recasting Theology of Mission," 102.

Africa."[42] The "African expression of the worldwide Pentecostal movement"[43] has also been growing so much since the 1970s[44] that it is fair to say that African Pentecostals now generally represent the face of Christianity in Africa.

5.3 How Christianity Is Looking in Britain and the Wider West

While Western Christianity in general has been nosediving, African Christianity has continued to establish itself and expand since the nineteenth century.[45] In fact, over the last hundred years, Christianity's centre of gravity has not only shifted from the North to the global South; its growth and spread in the new hotspot of the faith has been unprecedented.[46] For instance, in Africa in 1900, there were only nine million Christians while 300 million were present in Europe.[47] By 2021, there were over 600 million Christians in Africa and about 500 million in Europe – a difference of 100 million.[48] This sort of watershed in the history of World Christianity, Ola notes, is only comparable to the Protestant Reformation of 500 years ago.[49]

In Britain, between 2001 and 2011 alone, the population of Christians in England and Wales combined declined by 11 percent, from 37 million to 33 million. Moreover, while the figure of white Christian adherents slid from 35 million to 30 million, those from other ethnic groups rose. One example is the African Christian population increasing by 109.3% from about 300,000 to over 600,000.[50] A few years later in 2017, Kwiyani observed that, "a 14-percent-minority group made predominantly of migrants [accounted] for 60 percent of church attendance in a global city like London." He concludes that Christianity is undoubtedly appearing a lot darker in Britain by the year.[51]

---

42. Anderson, "Evangelism and the Growth."
43. Cox, *Fire from Heaven*, 246.
44. Kwiyani, *Sent Forth*, 111.
45. Ayegboyin and Ishola, *African Indigenous Churches*, 1.
46. Kwiyani, *Sent Forth*, 9.
47. Zurlo, Johnson, and Crossing, "World Christianity and Mission," 23.
48. Zurlo, Johnson, and Crossing, 23.
49. Ola, "Strangers' Meat," 1.
50. Rogers and Gale, *Faith Groups*, 2.
51. Kwiyani, "Can the West," 81.

Church Growth and Development of African Diaspora Congregations 113

The shift in the base of Christianity in favour of the South has, certainly, caused the North, including Liverpool, to become the field of missional activities of African (including Caribbean) Pentecostal churches over the last six decades.[52] Perhaps this growth of African Christianity, which spreads from Africa outwards to other parts of the world, is what Liberian educator Edward Blyden foresaw in the nineteenth century when he commented, as Ola quoted, that:

> Africa may yet prove to be the spiritual conservatory of the world . . . When the civilized nations in consequence of their wonderful material development, shall have had their spiritual perceptions darkened and spiritual susceptibilities blunted through the agency of a captivating and absorbing materialism, it may be that they have to resort to Africa to recover some of the simple elements of faith, for the promise of that land is that she shall stretch forth her hands unto God.[53]

Blyden's insights would be affirmed by Western missionaries at the World Missionary conference of Edinburgh in 1910. It was at this gathering that the missionaries expressed optimism about a future time when Christians from the mission fields of Latin America, Africa, and Asia would energize Western Christianity in what is now known as the *blessed reflex*.[54] The belief was that the zest that facilitated missionary activities in the nineteenth century would engender "a reflex action in the rest of the world that would, in return, benefit Western sending churches."[55] Suffice it to say that the blessed reflex is now here. However, it appears today's reality is just as Hollenweger observed in 1990: "Christians in Britain prayed for many years for revival, and when it came they did not recognise it because it was black."[56]

---

52. Adedibu, "African-Led Pentecostal Churches," 84.
53. Ola, "Reverse Mission," 25.
54. Kwiyani, *Sent Forth*, 71.
55. Kwiyani, 71.
56. Hollenweger, "Foreword," ix.

5.4 Streams of African Christianity in Britain and the Rise of African Diaspora Congregations

Even though African diaspora communities have existed in Britain since the Roman age, not much is known until the sixteenth century, when Africans began to show up in greater numbers, mostly as enslaved Africans, but also as students and merchants of ships.[57] The four-centuries-long slave trade[58] could not but provide a boost to the Black population in Britain.[59] Theologian and educator Paul Nzacahayo suggested that a significant number of these enslaved Africans were Christians. Citing church historian Stephen Tomkins, Nzacahayo notes, for instance, the presence of freed slaves, Olaudah Equiano (Nigerian), and Ottobah Cugoano (Ghanaian) in 1780s London, along with "hundreds of former slaves."[60] There was also an itinerant African preacher, John Jea (born 1773 in Old Calabar), whose evangelistic activities extended across the US to the UK and Ireland. Jea might have planted a church in Portsmouth in 1805 after settling down in the city.[61] David Killingray, emeritus Professor of Modern History similarly speaks of some Black ministers leading white congregations in the nineteenth century at various times.[62]

The Black Christian population in Britain sustained its growth, and by the twentieth century, in 1906, the first known record of a Black Pentecostal church surfaced in London, the *Sumner Road Chapel* at Peckham (now known as Sureway International Ministries).[63] This assembly was founded by the Ghanaian businessman and school master Thomas Kwame Brem-Wilson (1855–1929).[64] A Nigerian, Daniels Ekarte (1890–1964), started the *African Churches Mission* (ACM) some twenty-five years later (1931) at Toxteth, Liverpool.[65]

---

57. Adi, "Pan-Africanism and West African," 70.

58. Bediako, *Christianity in Africa*, 75.

59. For instance, David Killingray and Joel Edwards note that by 1750, there were about 10,000 Africans in London and another 5,000 outside the city. See Killingray and Edwards, *Black Voices*, 21.

60. Nzacahayo, "Biblical and Historical Theology," 54.

61. See more in Jea, *Life, History, and Unparalleled*.

62. Killingray, "Black Atlantic Missionary Movement," 3–31.

63. Adedibu, *Coat of Many Colours*, 26.

64. Adedibu, *Coat of Many Colours*, 26.

65. However, after observing some documents from Nigerian National Archives in Ibadan, Thomas Higgins inferred that Ekarte began his ministry in 1922 near the Liverpool

The era of the two world wars also saw the movement of many more African Christians into Britain, but gained intensity after the Second World War with the *Windrush* migration of the 1940s and 1950s.[66] Haar notes that as workers from the West Indies trooped in to Britain in response to labour market needs, they often encountered an unfriendly reception from their hosts. She further adds that many of these immigrants, being "practising Christians," expected to settle into British mainline churches, since the majority were members of mainstream congregations (Methodists, Anglicans, Baptists, or Catholics) back home. Unfortunately, the same discrimination encountered on the streets greeted them in churches. Hence, it became necessary for them to form their own congregations.[67] The first of these was Calvary Church of God in Christ, which began in London in 1948. Shortly after, in 1953, the New Testament Church of God was started, as well as the Church of God of Prophecy. Five years later (1958), the Wesleyan Holiness Church emerged, just three years before the establishment of the New Testament Assembly in 1961.[68]

The political decolonization of many African nations in the 1960s presented a new trend of migration that brought African students, diplomats, and tourists to England, and Europe in general. The implication was that many more ADCs emerged within the next decade (1960–1970).[69] The ADCs of this period were particularly grounded in "the social and religious traditions of the African communities from which they draw most of their members."[70] Therefore, by 1964, the first AIC was planted in the UK. With the help of Rev. Father Olu Abiola, late Primate Adeleke Adejobi pioneered the Church of the

---

docks. See more in Higgins, "Mission Networks." I must note the obvious here, that Ekarte and his work are of particular interest, having sprouted in Liverpool – the specific setting of this research, so I have explored his story further in a later section.

    66. Nzacahayo, "Biblical and Historical Theology," 54. The Windrush generation gets its name from the *SS Empire Windrush* ship which docked at Tilbury with 492 Caribbean immigrants onboard. See more in Mead, "Empire Windrush."

    67. Haar, *Halfway to Paradise*, 92.

    68. Christian Enquiry Agency, "Contributions of the Black Majority."

    69. Olofinjana, *Partnership in Mission*, 26.

    70. Haar, *Halfway to Paradise*, 94–95.

Lord – Aladura, in South London.[71] Several other ADCs subsequently arose in the 1980s and 1990s. These are classed as African Pentecostal churches.[72]

5.5 African Diaspora Congregations in Liverpool

Hitherto, I have examined the trajectory of African Christianity in the UK in general to properly locate and comprehend the appearance and growth of ADCs in Liverpool. In this section, I focus specifically on Liverpool. To achieve this, I begin by exploring the earliest ADC to show up in the city, as well as the life of its founder in relation to its emergence. Afterwards, I consider other ADCs that have popped up over the years.

5.5.1 Daniels Ekarte and the African Churches Mission (ACM)

Founded in 1207, Liverpool, a city in Merseyside, England with a population of 500,000 in mid-2020,[73] hosted its foremost ADC in 1931 through the pioneering effort of Daniels Ekarte. The Black population in the city had grown from three thousand in 1911, a few years before the First World War, to five thousand after the war, and eight thousand by 1948.[74] These people initially settled mostly around the Liverpool docks in the south before gradually spreading out after World War II due to urban renewal.[75]

Though the population of Liverpool had risen to its highest in the 1930s,[76] not much was attractive about the city in other ways. For instance, unemployment was up by 106 percent between 1930 and 1933 alone, and about one in every ten residents was receiving relief in 1933.[77] In fact, in the nineteenth century, the appalling living conditions in Liverpool were glaring, with unmissable sights of dirty and ragged children begging on the streets, poor

---

71. Olofinjana, *Partnership in Mission*, 26.
72. Nzacahayo, " Biblical and Historical Theology," 55.
73. The population figures are according to the 2020 mid-year census from the Office for National Statistics since the 2021 census is under processing. Liverpool City Council, "Demographics Headline Indicators."
74. Helmond and Palmer, *Staying Power: Black Presence*, 16.
75. Zack-Williams, "African Diaspora Conditioning," 531.
76. Rink et al., "From Long-Term," 167–168.
77. Sherwood, *Pastor Daniels Ekarte*, 7.

sewage disposal systems, congestion, and the absence of home comforts and clothing.[78] Toxteth, which was then one of the slums sheltering 30 percent of the paupers in the city, would become the site for ACM, founded by Ekarte.[79]

Before his migration to Britain, Ekarte, who was born in Calabar, Nigeria (probably in the 1890s)[80] served as an errand-boy for Arthur Wilkie, a Free Church of Scotland missionary in Calabar. This was until his encounter with another Scottish missionary, Mary Slessor (1848–1915), who had such a great influence on him that he quit his service with Wilkie and started working for her. After some time, Ekarte made up his mind to be a missionary. Later, he became consumed with the idea of moving to England, where his mother-figure, Slessor, had come from. Though Slessor cautioned him, citing England's lack of zest for "heavenly things," Ekarte would eventually depart for England after her death in 1915.[81]

On arriving in Liverpool, Ekarte was quickly greeted by the reality of what Slessor had warned about. Immorality was, indeed, conspicuous, and so was another phenomenon Ekarte had not prepared for: racism. He had entered the country at a time when racial tension was very high and Black immigrants in particular were receiving blame for the economic and social woes that were further compounded by the effects of the war.[82] One may wonder whether people merely chose to be oblivious to the attendant, devasting effects of wars or just found it easier to finger the immigrant community as a matter of convenience. Ekarte was so heartbroken by these developments that he initially thought of quitting his missionary quest and returning to Nigeria. However, he soon found his faith again in 1922 and the passion to "minister to the needs of Africans in diaspora" came alive. It was this drive that birthed ACM.[83]

From 1922, when he began a new life, Ekarte started preaching on the streets and holding services in private rooms and public places, attracting

---

78. Sherwood, *African Churches Mission*, 7–8.

79. Law, "White Racism," 50.

80. Sherwood observes that there seems to be some inconsistencies in the interviews Ekarte gave, what he wrote about himself, and repeated stories about his early life. Nonetheless, Sherwood was able to situate Ekarte's year of birth within the 1890s. See Sherwood, *African Churches Mission*, 23–24.

81. Sherwood, 23–24.

82. Higgins, "Mission Networks," 168–169.

83. Higgins, 169.

crowds. However, Sherwood notes that the image of an African man preaching on the streets and amassing a large following was a disturbance to the police.[84] Hence, Ekarte was arrested and jailed twice. Nevertheless, he was be deterred, continuing his preaching even in jail.[85] To avert future clashes with the authorities, Ekarte proceeded with his subsequent meetings indoors, in a hall he hired from two vicars.[86] However, he was pushed out by racist troublemakers. Through the help of the Church of Scotland and an anonymous donation, Ekarte later secured a facility at 122–124 Hill Street, Toxteth, Liverpool. This was the building that became the headquarters of ACM when it opened on 7 July 1931.[87]

Ekarte publicly rebuked British colonialism, and even though this posture pitched him against the government, he sustained his voice for the oppressed and the condemnation of racial discrimination.[88] ACM thus became a place for aiding immigrants and the outcast. The centre also transformed into an orphanage, catering to "children born to African American soldiers and English women after the Second World War [who] were often rejected by society."[89] Ekarte's courage is commendable for the feat he achieved amid the socio-economic challenges of his time (notably racism and economic depression). Within five years of inception the membership of ACM climbed to 558.[90]

Sadly, with the multiple endeavours of the mission, it was still spartan by 1938.[91] The financial challenge of the project lingered alongside the unfavourable disposition of the government towards Ekarte. Before long, Liverpool authorities began to clamour for urban renovation, a move that aided the closure of the orphanage. In "a task callously performed by the Children's Department," the youngsters at the orphanage were retrieved by officials on 3 June 1949. However, other arms of the mission persisted until 1964 when the

---

84. Sherwood, *African Churches Mission*, 25.
85. Sherwood, 25–26.
86. Higgins, "Mission Networks," 169.
87. Sherwood, *African Churches Mission*, 26, 28–29.
88. Olofinjana, "Everyday Heroes."
89. Olofinjana, "Everyday Heroes."
90. Sherwood, *African Churches Mission*, 32.
91. Sherwood, 30.

building was finally shut down by the government. By this time, a dejected Ekarte was old and died few weeks later.[92]

5.5.2 From ACM to Present Time

Africans migrate along with their religions. Moreover, with Pentecostals and Charismatics dominating the scene of church growth in Africa, the "pentecostalization of Christianity in Africa has led to the pentecostalization of African Diaspora Christianity."[93] Therefore, since the emergence of ACM, myriads of African Pentecostal churches have been mushrooming, especially with the 1980s and 1990s influx of ADCs into Britain. The oldest of this wave in Liverpool is the Temple of Praise (TOP), founded in 1980 by Tani and Modupe Omideyi as a small house group.[94]

TOP settled at Anfield in 1991 after relocating multiple times. The congregation had teamed up to refurbish a "disused church building." In 1998, the church purchased an unused cinema and converted it into what is now called the Lighthouse building. TOP moved into this structure in April 2004. The formal registration of the church along with other works it is involved in occurred in 1995 under the umbrella name *Love & Joy Ministries*.[95] The various arms of Love & Joy Ministries range from Temple of Praise church to Liverpool Lighthouse Limited, Harmony Academy, and an AP Free School and Bright Park, a five-acre wooded land currently under development as a valuable community resource. The multi-ethnic promotion, continuous growth, and impact of the church is perhaps affirmed by Omideyi's emergence as the first ethnic minority chair of the Evangelical Alliance board.[96] Moreover, the work of Love & Joy Ministries has now extended to other cities in the UK, Uganda, Gambia, Ireland, South Africa, Pakistan, and Myanmar, where it supports churches and ministries.[97]

---

92. Higgins, "Mission Networks," 170; See also Wilson, "Racism and Private Assistance," 54, 72.
93. Kwiyani, *Sent Forth*, 113.
94. Temple of Praise, "Our Story."
95. Temple of Praise, "Our Story."
96. Evangelical Alliance is the largest and oldest body representing the UK's two million evangelical Christians since 1846. See more in Evangelical Alliance, "About Us." Omideyi has recently stepped down from this position.
97. Webster, "Tani Omideyi Becomes First."

In the last four decades, many other ADCs have surfaced in Liverpool with those of Nigerian nationality dominating the scene. While it may be difficult to trace all these congregations for a host of reasons discussed later in the research findings, some prominent ones are: Redeemed Christian Church of God (with five branches), Pentecost Baptist Church Int'l (PCBC), Christian Gold House Chapel Ministry Int'l, Winners' Chapel International, Glory Worship Church, Deeper Life Christian Ministry, Mountain of Fire and Miracle Ministries Int'l, Alive Believers Church and Community Centre, The Apostolic Church, Love Economy Church, Christ Authority Baptist Church Int'l, Victory Baptist Church (a branch of PCBC), The Gospel Faith Mission Int'l, Christ Apostolic Church, Mountain of Prayer, The Church of Pentecost Liverpool Central Assembly, The New Life International Mission, Ahavah International, Life Changers Empowering Centre, Christian Life Centre, The Faith Ministry, and Apostolic Faith Mission International Ministries.[98]

5.6 Conclusion

The growth of ADCs in Liverpool does not appear to be slowing down. In fact, there is a bright future for their continuous expansion, more so considering the sustained explosion of African Christianity. Plus, migration remains a constant in human endeavours as push and pull factors persist in determining migration trends all over the world. Africans have been actively immigrating to Britain in increased numbers since the *Windrush* wave and bringing their religions with them. Therefore, the face of Christianity in Liverpool can only become darker as the effects of secularism weaken the impact of religion and faith in the West as a whole.

---

98. I have provided a more comprehensive list of these churches, including their nationalities, at appendix III.

CHAPTER 6

Research Findings and Implications

6.1 Introduction

This section presents the outcomes of the research described in chapter 3. The discussion flow ensures that focus remains on critical issues about church growth in the research context despite other interesting matters arising from the findings. Indeed, participants engaged quite richly with the research questions. The chapter is divided into six parts. The first is an introduction to the rest of the chapter. In the second section, I consider the use of NVivo for coding the research data. The third part explores the overarching themes arising from the investigation. Part four presents other ideas that emerged from the research data in addition to the dominant themes. The fifth section is a rumination ob the research findings in connection with the research questions pursued by the study. A brief conclusion ends the chapter in part six.

6.2 NVivo Coding

The study anticipated thirty interviews altogether, ten from each of the three churches recruited for the study. Nine persons out of the desired ten were involved in the first congregation (CH1), while all ten interviews in the second assembly (CH2) were successful. However, the third congregation (CH3) fell short, with only seven completed interviews. As a result, twenty-six transcripts came out of the investigation across the three congregations.[1] Transcripts' importation into NVivo followed, producing nine broad nodes and various sub-nodes after data analysis and coding. While these sub-nodes spread across themes emerging from the data analysis process, significant cross-coding (same text references in more than one node) also occurred. The following is the summary table of broad nodes generated through NVivo.[2]

Table 2. NVivo Codes

Name	Files	References
Contextual Realities of the UK	21	56
Congregation's Demographics	5	6
Ecclesiological Dispositions and Praxis	21	56
Finances	4	4
Leadership	25	109
Spiritual Enablement	5	9
The Church's Poor Image	1	1
Membership Benefits	5	7
2GMs' Allegiance to ADCs	8	13

6.3 Dominant Themes

In this part of the chapter, my goal is to discuss the most conspicuous themes from the analysed data as reflected in NVivo. The three key themes are ecclesiology, contextual realities of the UK, and leadership. These broad categories cascade into various sub-themes. There were also cases of cross-coding, which, made the research data, along with the interview process itself, very enlightening. While other ideas surfaced from the data analysis process, the high number of references to the three broad categories suggest their criticality to ADCs' growth in Liverpool. Consequently, they have attracted greater attention.

---

1. Only one transcript from the twenty-six interview sessions is appended to this thesis. Others can, however, be accessed by reaching out to the researcher through the Department of Theology at Liverpool Hope University.

2. A comprehensive code list is available in appendix I.

Again, CH1, CH2, and CH3 are the pseudonyms for the first, second, and third congregations, respectively. I have concealed the congregations' identities to maintain confidentiality.

6.3.1 Ecclesiological Dispositions and Praxis

There are orientations individuals hold about church growth and how to do church. These views and practices have significant impacts on the development of the church. Indeed, in conversations with participants, the influence of ecclesiological notions and patterns on church growth is evident, garnering fifty-six references from twenty-one persons. I have presented some of the perspectives and praxis below.

6.3.1.1 Homogeneity

A highlight in how ADCs do church, which affects their growth, is the sustained support for homogenous expression in their church structures and membership. Eighteen participants touched on homogeneity, even though it came up unconsciously while discussing other factors of church growth for most. From their twenty-five references and general observation, it is characteristic of an ADC to have the majority of its congregation sharing ethnicity, culture, or race with its leader. Understandably, in two of the three communities interviewed, significant parts of the membership were of the same ethnicities as their pastors. Even for the third congregation, homogeneity still reflected along racial lines. So, where the leader of an ADC is Zimbabwean, for instance, the majority population in the church would be Zimbabweans. This kind of membership formation is unhealthy for cross-cultural missions and multiethnicity; it suggests that ADCs are culturally or racially exclusive to outsiders.

ADCs are more likely to reflect homogeneity considering the minority population of their predominantly African communities in the UK. These African congregants desire safety nets in an unfamiliar land. They want centres where they can find support, including psychological, emotional, financial, accommodation, and otherwise. ADCs fit this picture, for instance, by how they do church, with the louder expressions of African cultures. This way of being church addresses the psychological needs of ADC members (mostly 1GMs), who desire to feel closer to home, as one participant from CH2 affirms:

> Most of the members [of ADCs] are coming from maybe Ghana, Nigeria, Sierra Leone and they want something that feels like or that is closer to what they have back home. So, with the look of that I want to believe that . . . Because let's be honest with ourselves, a lot of people have a way they go to church back in Nigeria. I will use Nigeria as an example. And we are talking of someone about 30, 40 years old. And even though it is good to change and variety is good, if you have an African church or you want to go to an Orthodox or somewhere here, I think a majority of them will choose African churches because it makes them feel at home more, psychologically and emotionally.

The above rationale notwithstanding, homogeneity is unhelpful for ADCs in the long run. It hinders the achievement of God's mission and aspiration to see all nations and peoples gather in the worship of God (Rev 7:9). Again, starting as monocultural groups may be understandable, easy, and fair, but ADCs' refusal or fear to outgrow homogeneous composition, especially racially, culturally, or ethnically, does not facilitate cross-cultural mission.

The overarching demerit of the racially and culturally homogenous ADCs is felt more significantly by 2GMs and a few outsiders (Westerners) who find themselves among the majority 1GM congregations. These two groups of people have grown up in a non-African environment. Therefore, it is understandable that they find the dominant African cultural expressions in ADCs (reflected in language, liturgy, church administration, etc.) challenging to relate to, and thus, often hampering their worship experiences. Hence, 2GMs are quick to move on from ADCs if the opportunity arises.[3]

One 2GM from CH1 passionately voiced the awkwardness of and his disapproval of ADCs' saturation with African cultures. Highlighting that it is mere self-centeredness and insensitivity to others' way of life, the participant protested, "A lot of people are being stuck in this African mentality. If you go to most of these African churches, hardly would you see a white person there; you will only see an African person, a Black person. Why? Because we just want to focus on ourselves." In all, compared with 1GMs, 2GMs appear more aware of the long-term negative impact of the cultural homogeneity of

---

3. I have expanded this discourse in a later conversation on 2GMs' allegiance to ADCs.

ADCs on their growth. It is not too much to reemphasize that ADCs project themselves in a bad light when they hold on to their homogeneity because it suggests that they are not welcoming to outsiders. In the end, church growth stifles as cross-cultural expansion becomes challenging.

Another member of CH3, a 2GM, explained with a business analogy how homogeneity denies the church the benefits of multiethnicity:

> When you're making a business case for diversity [multiethnicity], you see there's the avoidance of group thinking where everybody in one room is thinking alike because they're all from the same place, have the same experiences, have the same background and somehow, unfortunately, have the same ideas. So, when you have a room of people who have come from different backgrounds and have a bag of different experiences with them, you will be able to see the richness of that displayed even in smaller administrative duties, which is very key to growth.

Nonetheless, a congregation does not transform into multiethnicity so easily since change usually encounters resistance, even in the church.[4] Indeed, another participant observed that, "When the church starts to change, the old members who were there before this is being done might feel like, oh no, the church is changing; I don't like it, I'm going to start my own church, I'm going to go to a new church." All the same, if the leader can introduce the right amount of change to the congregation per time, just as with an adaptive leader,[5] the church can enjoy the changes required for its transformation into a multi-ethnic church, and growth will occur more freely.

6.3.1.2 Church Growth Is Spiritual

For at least seventeen participants, church growth is either solely about the spiritual formation[6] of congregants or a combination of spiritual development and other aspects of advancement, such as numerical and leadership.

---

4. I reiterate in a more detailed way how change generates a lot of reactions, including resistance, later in unpacking the Adaptive Leadership style.

5. I detail the practices of an adaptive leader within the Adaptive Leadership Structure later in this dissertation.

6. Spiritual formation concerns giving thought to God, learning about his activities and character, and participating in his life and initiatives. See more in Branson and Martinez, *Churches, Cultures and Leadership*, 62.

The prominence of conceiving church growth as spiritual development of the church is most likely traceable to the spirit-oriented worldview of the participants.[7] Africans believe in the existence of spirits that regularly interfere with the physical world and with whom they must maintain harmonious relationships. In fact, to them, the spirit world strongly influences the material.[8] So, by encountering the Holy Spirit in Christianity, the spirit-centred worldview of Africans is sustained in their Christian experience.[9] As such, church growth, as with any other phenomenon, is first imagined from a spiritual viewpoint.

Moreover, recalling the submission of Gibbs that the Holy Spirit is the power behind the principles of church growth, and hence his centrality to the phenomenon,[10] Africans' conviction that church growth is a spiritual affair finds further validation. The people see themselves as spiritual renewal agents in the West to fulfil the aspirations of blessed reflex. Church growth is, in all ways to them, a spiritual activity. Yet, Gibbs never nullified strategies in church growth endeavour when he argued for the central role of the Holy Spirit in the pursuit. Instead, he posited that both principles and the power behind them (the Holy Spirit) must co-operate for church growth to happen.[11] Consequently, measuring and making church growth a spiritual affair alone is grossly inadequate, and ADCs must come to terms with this fact.

Beyond the spiritual contribution they claim to bring to the West, ADCs must pay closer attention to other aspects of church growth for robust mission work in the UK. One of these areas is the social impact of the church, especially with charity being a fashionable practice in the West. As ADCs seek to better engage in activities that enhance their community engagement and societal contributions, their mission in the UK will become more meaningful and acceptable to their hosts. This sort of exchange, where the West gains spiritually and ADCs become more deliberate in community impact is beneficial to the growth of the UK church as a whole.

---

7. Mugambi, *Christianity and African Culture*, 64.
8. Mbiti, *African Religions and Philosophy*, 97.
9. Mugambi, *Christianity and African Culture*, 64–65.
10. Gibbs, "Power Behind the Principles," 125.
11. Gibbs, 125.

6.3.1.3 Cultural Stereotypes and Traditions

It is not strange to see people occasionally exhibit their cultural stereotypes, traditions and biases as they go through life. This reality is equally observable in ADCs. Eleven participants highlighted church growth challenges arising from stereotypes, fixed cultural mindsets, and behaviours in their contexts. The church leader of CH3 narrated a vivid instance. The pastor, interestingly, is one of the few female leaders of an ADC in Liverpool. Her account illustrates and summarizes the adverse effect of stereotypes and traditions on the growth of ADCs in the city:

> We recently had a scenario like this, where somebody that was heading a very significant department in the church, all of a sudden, came up and said women are not supposed to lead in the church, but she's the woman leader. So, I heard from the daughter who came to meet me after one Sunday morning, "Oh pastor, I just want to ask you. My mom was saying so and so." The mom said a lot of these things and then that just gave me a clue. But it was really damaging because we lost 50 percent of the church members.

Traditions are not bad in themselves. Nonetheless, ADCs must be wary of those ideas and practices that may be eccentric, non-central to their cultural identity, and potentially hindering adaptation to their host environment. One 2GM from CH1 rightly points out the implications of clinging to unhelpful traditions and stereotypes by ADCs and how this practice discourages the 2GMs' participation. His words are worth reading:

> The future would be to leave tradition because tradition is playing a big aspect in why the youth do not want to come [to church] as well. So, if you put tradition aside and focus on worshipping God itself . . . Yes. Because it's an African church so they bring African mentality to a different environment where people have grown up with different expectations and views. So, you have to adhere to that and understand that you have to compromise in some way for the glory of God.

ADCs can employ the AL strategy to identify those practices that are fit for the past and the ones that must persist to facilitate quick adaptation to their new environment. Additionally, ADCs can engage OSE[12] to acknowledge values and behaviours that are core to 1GMs while also listening to and adopting new ways of doing church that 2GMs and the host community find relatable.

6.3.1.4 Relationship Dynamics within the Church

The research also suggests that growth is ultimately affected when the church does not demonstrate a sound awareness of people skills. Even Jesus needed to mature socially – in favour with men – as he grew in other facets of life (Luke 2:52). Therefore, a clear sense of and the practice of social relationship etiquette must be a central ecclesiological concern for any church. Indeed, it dictates the flow of interactions within the church and its social health and growth. So far-reaching is the impact of relationship dynamics that its effect extends across all age groups and ADCs' engagements with outsiders. This factor of church growth was a common thread across most of the experiences of misunderstandings and conflicts relayed by twelve participants.

Often demonstrated in manners of approach, communication, attitude, and other aspects of social interaction, a participant from CH1 affirms the crucial role of the knowledge and honour of relationship principles to church growth. In her reminiscence of the reason for a family's departure from her congregation, she recalled that "it's the way they were treated, maybe by one individual and they felt offended, and they felt like, no, they may not be able to attend [anymore]." Another interviewee from CH2 submits that "we don't know how to approach people. And when you don't know how to approach people, it makes the church disintegrate. When the church doesn't know how to address crisis . . . it disintegrates." Additional illumination comes from another response from a participant at CH3:

> Even if . . . the larger percentage of the population [of a typical ADC] is black, even at that, we still come from different places [not in terms of race but ethnicities, and sometimes cultures], different language, different ways of communicating. So, I think misunderstanding sometimes causes or it's a problem or might be a problem. Because, you want to express yourself or you

---

12. I discuss the *omolúàbí*-shaped ecclesiology in the seventh chapter of this dissertation.

> feel because this person looks at me in a certain way, oh I am offended. Meanwhile, it might not really be, maybe that's just the way the person looks or maybe that's just the way the person says hello to somebody. So, you feel offended. I think I have heard that that's caused some people to leave. Oh, people didn't greet me well, people didn't embrace me well, people didn't do this. So, people misunderstand other people's actions; which is not necessary, because we are from different places.

If ADCs must sustain growth, they must pay closer attention to the flow of interactions within their congregations and towards outsiders. In other words, the ecclesiology of ADCs must address their social engagement strategies internally and externally as they attempt to connect more successfully with their host community and their members. For this step, OSE is helpful. In the end, the church becomes a peaceful community, thereby fostering church growth.

Altogether, the ample citation of tradition and culture within ecclesiological practices suggests that culture will continue to immensely impact church doctrine and functions. Therefore, the subject of contextualization becomes increasingly inevitable in missions and church life. As churches progressively become contextualized, they will be more meaningful to people within their local settings. More so, the effects of globalization and migration continue to alter the church's colour and composition. As such, the importance of multi-ethnic congregations will only grow. The concept will increase in relevance within ecclesiological and missional conversations and multi-ethnicity will become the normative order and outlook of any growth-inclined congregation in the near future.

6.3.2 Contextual Realities of the UK

The happenings, habits, and practices consistent with the UK and most Western nations, where ADCs are evolving, are not without significant contributions to their (ADCs') growth and development. Fifty-six references from twenty-one participants were strong enough to consolidate this observation. With this frequency, contextual realities in British societies come on the heels of leadership as major elements influencing the growth of ADCs in Liverpool and, by extension, the UK. Some of the consistent happenings in the UK that participants identified are as follows:

6.3.2.1 Racism

Racism[13] remains the perennial experience of Black people generally in the West.[14] It is an inescapable reality shaping all of life, including church growth, for Black people. The stench of racism was perceivable in almost all participants' narratives about their congregational growth, even though only four people were bold enough to name the evil. One of the participants from CH2 gave an insight into how racism subtly and blatantly plays out against ADCs in the city. Reflecting on a few of his congregation's confrontations with racially motivated attitudes and actions, the individual reveals:

> I mean, our church, we faced racial attacks in the beginning, at the inception. And I can still say that we are still facing it [racism] until now. But it has become reduced, as it were. But we had to face a lot of . . . I mean, our church was burgled several times, our car was burnt down, our church bus was burnt down . . . And in the past, we had to endure being called n***a, all sorts of ridiculous names in the past. So, we've been there; we've experienced all sorts in terms of racism. That is just the consequence of living in the country and trying to . . . I mean, so many times we've been reported to the police for making noise, all because the people could not stand the fact that Africans are worshipping. So, that is one of the challenges.

Racial injustice cannot but make a considerable impression on ADCs' growth where congregants see themselves as a community or family.[15] Racial offence against one is an attack on the entire family or congregation. One participant rightly looked back at the experiences of his church, saying "I think there was also a racist remark before . . . [and] . . . if you make it to

---

13. In this dissertation, racism is defined as all consciously and unconsciously cultivated attitudes and/or actions undergirded by false beliefs, assumptions, misconceptions, stereotypes, and prejudices about other people or cultures, leading to their subordination, discrimination, vilification, and marginalization. See more in chapter 8.

14. I have explained this assertion and expatiated the issue of racism in chapter 8.

15. There were allusions to communal sense of ADCs across the three congregations recruited for the research.

one person, you're making it to everyone." The church growth disruptions that attend these acts of racism are only best imagined across congregations because people's tenacity and ability to endure derogatory statements and actions differ.

6.3.2.2 Challenges with Place of Worship

Participants equally showed that having a stable location or property for regular worship is pivotal to retaining and attracting members to the church. CH1's leader, for instance, explained how possessing a permanent meeting venue or structure affects church growth numerically: "if you're starting to have let's say a group or a cell meeting and you don't have a permanent place, or you don't have the fund to rent the place where you'll be able to gather, it brings limits, and it scatters the people as well." Another participant from CH1 added that it is a popular perspective among the host community (UK) to relate churches to dedicated conspicuous properties such that "if they see like a small community hall or whatever [temporary meeting venues of many ADCs], they might feel like this is a private organization." Therefore, ADCs are at a loss with the inability to secure permanent meeting venues or buildings. The suspicion that they are homogenously closed groups or a selective organization only intensifies. The implication then is that church growth (and, of course, multiethnicity) becomes more challenging. The reflection of one participant from CH3 consolidates this point even more:

> For every organization, whether church or business, whatever it takes, once you begin to move from one place to another, it definitely cripples you with numerical growth. Even those who lived at the back and you've just moved say two minutes away, would complain that church has moved and they're not able to make it. So that's one of the challenges that we've experienced because we've moved quite a lot. And we're just about to move again. So, that in some way has affected the growth [of our congregation] numerically.

Another response from a participant at CH3 maintained that "people would be more trusting" of a pastor and the church when a stable structure is in place. Sadly, Black people's racially shaped, poor socio-economic conditions in the West will continue to sustain their incapacity to conveniently secure permanent meeting venues. As long as racism persists, manifesting itself in the denial of specific accommodations to Black people and other non-White races and their restriction to odd and minimal remuneration jobs,[16] ADCs may continue to find it hard to acquire buildings for their services. Church growth then becomes a luxury they cannot afford or experience.

6.3.2.3 Secularism

Secularism not only gained fifteen references from eleven participants; it equally underlaid thirteen participants' discussions that captured work-family-life balance's impact on church growth. The displacement of religion from most Western nations' centre is easily observable in the extended work hours that have replaced the time commonly available for family engagements and religious practices in many non-Western countries. By implication, African Christians find their family relationships and church commitments under strain by coming to the UK. Interviewees, indeed, bemoaned the stress of juggling work, family, and church life in the UK, all pointing back to the increasing secularization of Western societies. One of the participants from CH1 painted a vivid picture of how work patterns in the UK affect the growth of her congregation. She said,

> Work is a big factor . . . To me, that's one of the major things that stop the church from growing. It's work time. Because I think in Africa where you just work from Monday to Friday, sometimes Saturdays and Sundays are like normally free. But in England, I think since Christianity is going downhill, it's like now there are jobs where they are saying you have to work on a Sunday, and if you do get a job, you can't say no because you need the money.

Someone else from CH1 who included the element of family commitment in the equation lamented, "People want to serve God, but they are caught between family responsibilities, workload, financial burden, and God. This is the problem." Yet another response from CH2 came out with some sense of guilt: "We are all so busy getting shifts, doing work to pay our bills and doing all the things we need money for. Only God will help us." Someone else from the same congregation (CH2) concluded quite strikingly. In what

---

16. Brown, "Same Difference," 48.

sounded like the voice of the helpless, surrendering to fate, the individual declared, "That is the way they [the British] have structured their economy."

By and large, the subtle appearance of race in the life dynamics of the UK, and indeed, the entire world, suggests that the intersection of faith and race will increasingly dominate conversations within world Christianity in the coming years, to the end that multiethnicity will gain ground as a better representation of the church. Therefore, the church must not downplay or overlook the negative impacts of racial categorization on the life of its victims as it engages in cross-cultural ministries and progressively becomes multi-ethnic. Doing the above will undoubtedly require deliberate moves to constantly express love to the marginalized and ethnic minorities within the church. Sustained deliberations are helpful in this regard to facilitate a better understanding of both sides: the marginalized and the privileged majority. In the end, black and white people will be able to worship more comfortably together without suspicion or condescension.

6.3.3 Leadership

One of the most significant illuminations (109 references) from the research was the unanimous citing of leadership[17] (twenty-five of twenty-six interviewees) as a church growth driver of Liverpool ADCs, in addition to other principal factors. Participants were sure that leadership plays a notable role in shaping the growth of the research population. As they pointed to various leadership-related matters directly and indirectly in their conversations, the conviction became clear. I have explored some of the leadership issues below in no particular order.[18]

6.3.3.1 Vision

The subject of vision, a clear sense of purpose, and the leader's philosophy of ministry attracted twelve references from participants as a church growth catalyst of the research population. Those from CH3 particularly demonstrated a strong persuasion that vision, also expressed as goals and targets,

---

17. In this writing, I define leadership as a process of collective participation through which a person inspires or influences a group towards achieving a shared goal. For more discussion on leadership, refer to chapter 9 of this dissertation.

18. A detailed list of all factors can be found in appendix I.

developed and communicated by the church pastor, is a vital facilitator of growth in their context. There was hardly an interviewee from CH3 that failed to affirm the significant role of vision in fuelling any congregation's growth, citing instances about their own assembly. The church pastor argues this point quite well as she recounts a time when a situation sought to destabilize the church, reducing its membership strength:

> How God does the thing is that if your people come and they're grounded in the vision – that's why when I started, I was mentioning that I did spend a lot of time investing in the people – even when they go, if they're meant to be here, they would not leave to stay anywhere else because they are so engrossed. They bought into the vision; they've seen our hearts; this is who we are. Although we lost about 50 percent of the people, the young people went all out. They didn't want that gap to be felt.

Another interviewee from the same congregation connected vision with the demographics of the church. This participant explains that in their context, where the goal of the church (or pastor) is to reach out to young people who it believes to be critical evangelistic agents in the city, church growth is the degree to which this category of people has joined and become committed members of the church. As such, CH3 is essentially a youth congregation. The exact words of the participant are worth a read:

> I think the pastor was very adamant that she wanted youth because she believed that the revival would start within the city, and we needed young, energetic people to lead the match. And so, our target audience were mainly students, young adults, young married couples and so on . . . And so, for us, church growth would mean, how well have we been able to advertise ourselves to our target audience and how would they have been able to engage with us over time?

The link between a church's vision and its demographics also shows in CH2's leader's comment. He asserts that God's mandate to him is to "prepare a generation" for Jesus in the diaspora. By generation, this minister implied 1GM. Therefore, CH2 has a high percentage of 1GM membership. No one at CH1 established a connection between vision and the kind of population in the church. However, the church pastor agrees and hints at the vital role of vision in shaping the church and its growth. He says:

> My ministry, the area of my specialization, is the prophetic and the deliverance . . . It's a bit of challenge in this area that we live in . . . [but] . . . Those who want it, those who are interested, what I do is that I book a special day for them, counsel the person, teach him or her and if he's willing, then I take the person through deliverance. So that is what I've been doing for 10 to 11 years now with CH1.

Vision is essential to every organization because it clarifies its purpose and direction.[19] It does not just exist as a beautifully crafted arbitrary statement on the walls of establishments but possesses the power to influence people's behaviour.[20] It is, therefore, beneficial for ADC leaders to develop accurate visions for their churches. However, there must be caution in doing this since "*Focus often creates blindness.* [By implication] When you are looking north, you cannot see south."[21] So, while CH1, CH2, and CH3 have crafted visions that propel them to target specific groups of people consciously or unconsciously, the same pursuit could make them blind or closed to other categories of people within and outside the church. The ways these congregations do church may be alienating the ethnically other or any *other* people within and outside the congregations. CH1, CH2, and CH3 then become unintentionally homogenous communities along the lines of age-group, ethnicity, or culture. Yet, as I have previously argued while discussing HUP, homogeneity should never be the church's goal, for it creates exclusivity that frustrates the inclusive message of the *missio Dei*.

6.3.3.2 Synergy

The impact of collaboration on the growth of the research population was also strong. Twenty-two pointers supported this observation from fourteen participants. The general notion from interviewees was that cohesion is broadly weak among ADCs (and their leaders, of course) in Liverpool, and

---

19. Wheatley, *Leadership and the New*, 53.
20. Wheatley, 13.
21. Emphasis in original text. Murdock, ed., *Law of Recognition*, 43.

this has prevented any ground-breaking missional achievements or growth of the churches. The lament of the pastor of CH2 says it all" "we are becoming disjointed, disunited . . . [hence, the inability] . . . to make the kingdom of this world the kingdom of our Lord and Master Jesus Christ." The church leader adds that lack of adequate collaboration has hampered the missional agenda of "winning the locals." So, what many ADCs are recording as numerical growth is only a "recycling" of congregants.[22] This participant's cry for synergy, along with others, suggests that African ministers must engage and be more deliberate about collaboration for their impact to be felt, sustained, and multiplied in their host community.

While several issues may be responsible for the weak collaboration among ADCs in Liverpool, the matter of unnecessary competition among the church leaders was notably inferred by the leader of CH1. In retelling how his congregation emerged, the pastor notes, "when I came in [to the UK], I was just travelling [between] Manchester, Liverpool, Birmingham, London, preaching for other churches and doing deliverance for other churches. So, I found out that I needed just also to do something that in the future would have my footprints on it." This mentality is mainly responsible for the constant sprouting of "mushroom churches" as one participant described the pockets of ADCs showing up everywhere in the city. More so, there is a backdrop of a mission mandate that many 1GMs provide as the impetus for their migration to the West.[23]

In light of this, earlier voices on African diaspora Christianity, such as Kwiyani and Olofinjana (as indicated in the literature review) – could not be more apt in observing the need for collaboration in missions today. The yearning for improved synergy is not limited to engagement among ADCs only, but also across cultural barriers with Western counterparts. Partnership will indeed make missions less stressful and more productive for ADCs in the West. It is as "kindred live together in unity" (Ps 133:1) that the mission of God and church growth find quick results. Encouragement to collaborate

---

22. By this, the interviewee refers to the fluidity of ADCs due to migration across churches for various reasons.

23. For instance, in an interview session with Dupe Adefala, the pastor of Word Fountain Christian Ministries, the Nigerian discussed how her migration to the UK, together with her family, was mostly motivated by God's call (through a prophecy) to do missions in UK rather than economic benefit. See in Adefala, "How Rich the Kingdom," 60.

will also come from Westerners when it is no longer an awkward feeling for them to accept the leadership of a Black person since a host of ADCs are still African-led. Then the saying, "mission seems more convenient when it is directed at people below us and not those eye-to-eye with us"[24] will no longer be valid.

6.3.3.3 *Charisma*

Another important discovery was the significant role of leaders' charisma in advancing their congregations. Participants (twelve with seventeen references) generally thought their pastors' specific abilities, graces, attitudes, and behaviours have been instrumental in drawing many more people to their congregations, translating to a numerical increase. One participant from CH3, for instance, recalled how she had joined and remained in her church because the pastor "is a very friendly person. He will go to any extent for anyone. He has a very large heart. And he sees the good in everybody." CH1 and CH3's leaders seemed better aware of the impact of their charisma on the growth of their congregations. This awareness is clear from the assertion of the pastor of CH1, who sees himself as having a special kind of grace in the prophetic ministry. He submits, "my specialization is the prophetic and the deliverance [gifts]" and that people come to him to experience this grace, leading to the flourishing of his ministry. Hence, he delightfully concludes: "So, that is what I've been doing for 10 to 11 years now with CH1."[25] That ADC leaders are admired and in demand for their charisma is not a strange observation. Anderson argues that African Pentecostal churches are generally marked by "charismatic . . . men and women who are respected [and sought] for their preaching and leadership abilities."[26] More so, Africans usually demonstrate a preference for charismatic, value-based leadership.[27]

6.3.3.4 *Homiletics*

ADC leaders' art of preaching and delivering sermons also came to the fore as an essential driver of church growth, with eight participants alluding to

---

24. Reifsnider, "Lessons from South-Asian Christians."
25. The pastor's assembly name is replaced with CH1 for confidentiality.
26. Anderson, *African Reformation*, 19.
27. Bolden and Kirk, "African Leadership," 72.

this factor ten times. Second-generation African migrants (2GMs), those born to 1GMs, were particularly concerned about the homiletics of ADC leaders, which they complained were too often overwhelmed by the theme of "evil, evil, evil." More so, the delivery of these sermons is usually too loud and passionate for the 2GMs who have matured in the West. The comment of one of the youths in CH1 is quite revealing in this regard:

> African churches make you scared like someone is attacking you. Those things they say, you don't trust a lot of people around. Even sometimes, you start looking at your friends, thinking they might not be your friends. That's why I even feel like in the church, you can be sitting next to someone, and you still don't trust the person even though you both go to the same church and the same pastor preaches to you . . . I feel like if they [ADC pastors] bring more positivity into it [the messages], it makes people feel like yeah, let me go. Not more negativity. You say you're going to go to hell. Everything is to do with someone is attacking you back from home. It has got to the point where all in the church are . . . we don't even help our own families back home because you're scared; they've told you so many negative things that you don't want to send money back.

It was, however, unexpected but a courageous move by the pastor of CH2 to validate the concern of 2GMs regarding the strange sermons of ADC ministers in general. This church leader confessed, "I discovered, not until very recently, that most of the time, we are not preaching the main thing; we are not preaching Christ. Christ is different from culture. We preach more of culture than Jesus Christ himself."[28] Sadly, the generally awkward homiletics of ADC leaders according to 2GMs is not without far-reaching implications. It ultimately results in such a sharp disconnect between the youths and the churches that they are eager to leave at the slightest opportunity. As one 1GM from CH2 reinforced the general concerns of most 1GMs, "when they [2GMs] have flown the nest, they hardly, hardly, hardly, come back to church."

---

28. By not preaching Christ and contrasting Him with culture, the CH2 leader appears to be bemoaning the alienating tendency of cultures to the outsiders, especially where certain manners and customs are more favoured to the detriment of the all-encompassing gospel of Christ.

This situation, unfortunately, is a reality that is common to many ADCs and affects their growth.[29]

6.3.3.5 Mission Strategies

While the focus here is not on leadership style, which gained five indirect references from the interviews, it is important to note as a background to the subject under exploration that the typical approaches to leadership in most African communities rely heavily on centralized power or authority.[30] By implication, nothing happens without going through the leader, whether within smaller family settings or broader political architectures. In the same vein, since most ADC leaders sustain the leadership techniques they have practised from home in the diaspora, it is hard to imagine any activity in the church without their strong influence. As such, the church's approach to missions becomes a leadership subject.

Sixteen participants repeatedly suggested (a total of twenty-eight times) that the current mission strategies of many ADCs, more often, serve as inhibitors to their growth since they are mostly inapplicable within the UK context. A participant explained it well:

> What I noticed is, back in Nigeria, you know when you share flyers, you have a detached section where people can write their names, their phone numbers and all that. But in this place, you can't do that. People will tell you, why do you want my detail, why do you want this? Yeah. And also, when you are inviting them to church, it is difficult for you to stand with them for five minutes, ten minutes. "Oh, I am busy, I am busy, I need to . . ."
> So, all those things, those are also barriers

As with many others, this participant's comment implies that ADCs must reimagine their mission methods if they are to have any ground-breaking work in the UK and move beyond the cyclic exchange of members amidst themselves. To this end, some suggestions for more productive mission

---

29. This subject of unattractiveness of ADCs to 2GMs is expanded a bit more within the conversation of 2GM's allegiance to ADCs later in this chapter.

30. Bolden and Kirk, "African Leadership," 73; See also Blunt and Jones, "Exploring the Limits," 19.

strategies in the UK emerged during interactions. There is, for instance, the following fascinating contribution from one participant at CH3:

> We do evangelism; we go out. We reach out two different ways to the community. We do coffee morning, trying to reach the people in the area. The first time we moved into the venue we are currently using, we went out to the neighbours to ask them what they would want the church to do or create for them. They said there used to be a community centre around here, but it was burnt down. So, we had an idea of what they wanted in that area. So, we created the coffee morning; we created classes like English class for those with difficulties in the language. So, we were doing training for people. So those are what we did at the beginning. It serves as a tool for evangelism . . . Another thing we do from time to time is going out to the city centre to sing. We knew that people love music. So, our calling is also music, to attract the people to God through music. So, we go out from time to time to sing. You'd see that when we are singing, people are attracted. People stand and start recording, "What is this?" they start asking questions. We used those as an opportunity to begin to tell them about Jesus and tell them about the church. So those are the tools we're using to reach out to people, which I believe have led to the growth.

In addition to the preceding conversation, many other leadership-related factors impacting on church growth of the research population arose during the investigation. There were, for instance, mentions of the role of the minister's training, age and gender, church administration, and other issues. By and large, ADC leaders must pay close attention to their current leadership approaches to make a mark in their environments and ultimately experience growth. To this end, in chapter 9, I propose the adaptive leadership strategy (AL), deployable within a contextualized African ecclesiology, as a practical leadership approach that can enhance Liverpool ADCs' growth.

6.4 Other Ideas That Emerged

While the themes discussed above were most prominent in participants' reflections, other ideas arose during the investigation. I have briefly contemplated this subject matter here.

6.4.1 2GMs' Allegiance to ADCs

The matter of the commitment of 2GMs to ADCs mainly appeared in connection with culturally shaped practices, attitudes, traditions, and mindsets permeating church life in most ADCs. Eight persons, thirteen times, cited the disinterest of 2GMs in ADCs as a perpetual growth challenge of ADCs. This growth hurdle was a deep concern to 1GMs. Indeed, the lamentation was easily perceivable in their voices, as with that of the leader of CH2. The minister had disclosed how he often must metaphorically drag his children to church because of their apathy towards the African congregation. The minister, however, believes that this struggle with his children is not unique to him but an experience shared with other African parents.

Another 1GM from CH2 corroborated the above minister's perspective. The individual, who considered the present disposition of her adult son towards her church, the same congregation the child had matured in, regretted that "he doesn't see my church as his church . . . And I know a lot of our children feel that way." The sad implication, as she continues, is that "If our children are not coming to church, it means they are not bringing their mates, their colleagues to church. And that is one of the things that caused the death of the British churches."

On the one hand, 2GMs have defended their apathy towards ADCs because of the unrelatable, African cultural practices and traditions pervading the church life of many ADCs. On the flip side, 1GMs do not often see any shortcomings in their manners of being church. The way forward would be for 1GMs to discontinue cultural practices that are nonessential elements to their Christian faith and impede adaptation to their new setting (For instance, loud preaching style, seeming disregard for time in services, and vernacular dominance in communication). 2GMs must similarly be more open to receiving the blessings of *strange* African cultures. Their attitude towards the cultures must not be as though they are unneeded, defective, and inferior ways of life that they must despise. Otherwise, the tension between the two groups (1GM and 2GM) will remain, while the poor allegiance of 2GMs to ADCs will also linger on. To overcome these challenges more easily, OSE is, again, a helpful tool.

6.4.2 Spiritual Enablement

No less than five persons also felt that beyond any church growth strategy, the presence of God, the influence of the Holy Spirit, and prayers are vital pillars upon which church growth rests in their contexts, or any other, for that matter. In other words, Gibbs' observation finds validation again, that while principles are great, it takes the supernatural, the Holy Spirit, to power them to effectiveness. A participant from CH3 echoed this and concluded that spiritual enablement of church growth must happen before deploying any strategy. The exact reflection of the individual is worth a read:

> I would say it's because – we cannot ignore the call of God and the grace of God. That's the first thing. So, the call and the grace of God, once it's there, every other thing would align though it's also required of us. For other things to align, we're also required to do our own part, because for every miracle, there is the human side and there is the other side. So, first is God, the grace of God.

From CH1, someone else highlighted the necessity and urgency of prayers in realising church growth. He noted that, "We need to pray. We really need to pray. Because, when the Bible said to 'pray to the Lord of the harvest that he may send labourer into the harvest,' He wasn't joking." However, the response of another participant from CH1 appears to summarize the crucial role of supernatural forces in the expansion of the church more precisely:

> If I should summarise it, I'll say what makes the church grow – I will generalize it to every church – is mainly the Holy Spirit for one, the presence of God being there. That's very important because the Bible says many are called, but few are chosen. So, there are a lot of churches who were not chosen but are still there. So, first of all, it will be the presence of God.

By and large, participants demonstrated an awareness of metaphysical enablers in church growth realization. While the majority mentioned God's presence or grace, the workings of the Holy Spirit, and the power of prayer as effective supernatural enablers of church growth, a distinct perspective included the devil's activities as an inhibitor to growth. The response from a participant at CH3 noted that "the devil is fighting hard. He knows that if the church stands; if the church grows, his own kingdom will go down." Therefore, the church must always be alert to the devil's schemes and relentlessly pursue growth. Participants' belief in the metaphysical drivers of church growth reemphasizes, among other implications, the need to welcome ADCs' spiritual contributions to Christianity in the UK.

6.4.3 Membership Benefits

Some churches also grow due to people's benefits and opportunities from belonging to such congregations. As with the acknowledgement of metaphysical influence in achieving church growth, no less than five persons also alluded to the role of some churches' membership privileges in facilitating their expansion. A participant from CH1 explained:

> I've come across people that have said to me that they'll stay in like [the] Catholic Church because if they need help with things, they can get it done. Like if they need paper signing off by the pastor, they can do it for them. If they need a reference, they can do it for them and all this. Our church has been growing, so we've been in this building for like a year. Before then, we were in a different building that didn't belong to us. So, I don't think people trusted that they could get all those extra benefits.

Similar stories pervaded other participants' reflections. For instance, one person who contemplated the facilitator of numerical growth of her local church (CH3) said:

> ... the other thing about the church is that there are a lot of opportunities, which I think is really good. At one point, the kids were being taught how to play the piano or keyboard by one of the instrumentalists . . . They were teaching the kids how to learn the sound works and stuff. So, I feel that was good in terms of community outreach and helping people feel that the

church is definitely benefiting their lives and that they would do better to stay and bring maybe a couple of their friends in. So, that can help church growth a little bit.

The instances above suggest that, indeed, holding membership at some congregations comes with certain privileges that become positives for the growth of such churches. These benefits would have to transcend the spiritual alone and include other emotional, psychological, and social contributions. ADCs must, therefore, pay closer attention to various ways in which they can be a plus to the lives of their members.

6.4.4 Congregation's Demographics

The investigation also suggests that the demographic of a church has a significant influence on its growth. CH3, which consists almost entirely of a youthful demographic, demonstrated the validity of this observation more clearly. Five participants from the congregation reflected on how the youthfulness of the community impacts the sustenance of its numerical strength. In the words of one of the church members:

> We have faced a few challenges. So, for instance, because the majority of the leaders that you find within our church are either recent graduates or university students, and so, therefore, these are the people that you have given responsibilities to. Now, as young people, it's very difficult to manage young people. That's one of the challenges that the pastors have faced in trying to manage and deal with these energetic, young people who have lots of ideas about what they think is the best way to move. So that is a challenge. I think another challenge that we've had is also the fact that they are students. So, they come to university, they do the three to five years and then they graduate, and then, they may go back home. So, retention of the numbers that we have, fluctuates year on year, because some graduate and stay here in Liverpool or some graduate and go home. Then, it becomes a cycle in terms of numbers – rising and falling. And so, we have to implement ways in which we can attract the best talent and also keep them. That is a challenge by itself.

Another congregant further explained how the church's predominantly youthful demographic affects its growth by citing a particular instance:

> A friend of mine came to the church. He's more mature and he was like, yeah, it's a good church, loved the music, loved the message, but it's more for youth because the majority of our members are youth. So, he classifies it as a youthful church, and he doesn't see himself as a youth. So, he's like, yeah, this is not the church for me.

The above reflections reiterate the downsides of homogeneity, in this case, after the order of age group. The disadvantages certainly outweigh the merits, as in the stories shared above. It is not helpful when one age group overwhelms a congregation in numbers. Indeed, when a gathering is proportionately mixed, comprising all ages, social classes, races, and other forms of caste, it can avail itself of the various kinds of contributions that the wide range of people groups can offer. To this end, ADCs must strive towards outgrowing homogeneity to improve their chances for sustainability and expansion in the diaspora.

6.4.5 Finances

Participants were equally convinced about the weighty implications of finance on church growth. Four persons notably identified the limitations resulting from a lack of adequate finance for realising church growth. One of them from CH1, who summarized the position of others, said, "When a church doesn't have the financial capacity, a church can fold up. To run a church is capital intensive. And when you don't have that financial capacity, unconsciously, you will just discover that the church is running down." Indeed, church administration, sustenance, and multiplication become difficult without adequate finance. This submission is what a member of CH3 also stressed as he brooded upon how taxing the growth journey of his congregation has been in the absence of sufficient financial resources. The individual reflected, "starting a church is very expensive. We've experienced the mercy of God. But having said that, we know that it has been difficult. If we have finance – money – maybe it would have been better and stronger than what we have."

The financial scarcity that characterizes many ADCs may be connected to the colour bar racism prevalent in the West, which, in addition to other areas of life, conditions the kinds of jobs available to Black people.[31] While there are exceptions, many Black people still find it hard to penetrate specific lucrative industries and secure employment with substantial financial remunerations. I have witnessed this reality within my few years of residence in the UK. Moreover, where they get the rare opportunity to attract such employment, climbing the career ladder is often a luxury they do not enjoy.[32] ADCs are affected by these harsh realities since most of their members are the victims. Hence, many ADCs struggle with adequate finances to attend to church growth demands.

6.4.6 The Church's Poor Image

How people perceive the church is indispensable to its growth and expansion, for a congregation with a good or positive impression is naturally appealing to people.[33] Hence, the imprint of a poor image on church growth also ranked among the range of issues participants raised regarding church growth in their contexts. One participant from CH2 specifically spoke of the harm that bad publicity from ex-members of the church is causing the image of the church and its growth:

> For my church, the major challenge has been . . . unfortunately, I have to say this, but it's the truth . . . defamation of character. When people have left the church for whatever reason, then they go out, they start to talk bad about the church. So much so that people who don't even know the pastor would start talking . . . But such a person that has heard that bad report would never – well, don't let me use the word never – would hardly come to join the church.

---

31. Colour bar racism is the term used in this work and by British author and journalist Peter Fryer to describe various measures restricting and negatively impacting the Black population's life in the UK, evolving between the world wars. I have expanded on this subject a bit more in chapter 8. See also Fryer, *Staying Power*, 361–362.

32. While elaborating how racism plays out in the UK's major societal sector in chapter 8 of this book, I cite some classic and recent instances and reports attesting to Black people's discrimination in the UK's employment sector with serious negative implications for the marginalized community.

33. Akin-John, *22 Dynamic Laws*, 109.

The image a church communicates is vital to its growth. Bad reports about a church are unhealthy for its expansion. Therefore, ADCs must ensure that when people contact them, they leave with good memories of their congregations. While it is impossible to please everyone, a deliberate arrangement must be in place to evaluate methods and practices within the church. This assessment will foster accountability and help the church listen to feedback and critique itself, identifying areas for improvement in the process. In the end, conflicts fade in the church and chances of membership retention increase with positive recommendations of the church.

6.5 Mulling over the Research Questions

The primary pursuit of this investigation has been uncovering prime elements shaping church growth among ADCs in Liverpool. Achieving this aim, of course, has meant seeking answers to two questions. Through the issues raised by these queries, I reflect upon the research findings in this section.

6.5.1 What Are the Overarching Church Growth Factors?

The research identified some key elements dictating how well or poorly ADCs flourish in Liverpool. A primary shaper of the growth of ADCs in Liverpool is ecclesiology. Matters of ecclesiology shared the same frequency of occurrence with the contextual realities of the UK. Generally, ADCs see church growth more from a spiritual lens. Therefore, they are often so focused on their spiritual contribution to the West that they overlook other church life and growth aspects. One area of growth ADCs seem to disregard is strengthening their social impact on their members' lives and the host community. This dimension of church growth is particularly crucial because the West has an affection for charity. Hence, if ADCs focus more on their social development by engaging in charitable works and other activities that translate to community impact, they may be able to win over their hosts more easily. The implication is that church growth eventually finds enhancement.

The overwhelming display of cultural practices in most ADCs is another critical ecclesiological concern arising from the research. Indeed, it is a significant highlight of ADCs discouraging the allegiance of their 2GMs. The very expressive African cultural practices in the church life of most ADCs similarly raises the suspicion of their Western hosts that they are homogeneously closed groups. As such, sustenance and expansion of ADCs become more difficult since the 2GMs are disinterested in the homogenous congregations, as with the host community. A need for a robust ecclesiology to accommodate the concerns of all parties (1GM, 2GM, and Westerners) then arises. So important is this issue that the future of ADCs hangs on it.

Another critical church growth factor for the research population is the awareness of context-specific phenomena of the UK. Racism is one perpetual undertone of several contextual realities of the UK that participants identified. Indeed, the impact of racial discrimination spreads into all of life for Black immigrants in the UK.[34] As such, church growth must be directly or indirectly affected by racism, which plays out, for instance, in the poor financial capacity of most ADCs and the unavailability of permanent structures to hold meetings. The issue of race then becomes a crucial conversation for any individual or organization hoping to establish a flourishing congregation in the UK.

The pervasiveness of secularism as a contextual reality of the UK and the entire West is also an indispensable consideration for church growth in the UK. Secularism is a deeply rooted, perennial problem ADCs have continued to grapple with as they try to carry out missions in their environment. Participants pointed out the unenthusiastic attitude of their Westerns host toward church or faith matters. This cold reception to religion makes the task of missions even harder, and more so for church growth. Anyone attempting to sustain a flourishing church in the UK must be aware of the menace of secularism that continues to spread like wildfire.

References to leadership recurred the most, suggesting the high impact of leadership on the growth of ADCs in Liverpool. It is, therefore, critical for ADCs to pay keen attention to the leadership models they employ as they lead their congregations to carry out missions and establish enduring churches in the UK. Of course, the leadership approach needed in the diaspora must proceed within OSE and favour adaptation to the new environment. Church leaders will most certainly need to reevaluate their philosophy of ministry and ensure that their ministerial practice now accommodates the additional skills, befitting missional strategies, leadership styles, and behaviours that their diaspora environment demands.

---

34. I have touched more on this subject in chapter 8 which explores church growth and the dynamics of race.

CH2's leader spoke about some of the adaptations he is going through and which he felt were necessary for any intending ADC minister in the UK. He noted that such a minister must "become the father, you become the mother, you become the counsellor" of the church members. A participant from CH2 rightly attested to the pastor's claim that he is "one man that will not have money, that will go and borrow money so that they can be happy. They know one man that will go the extra mile for them. And you see, these are the things we don't do in Africa." Just as this participant concluded, ADC leaders cannot afford to resist or overlook new learnings and approaches to ministry in leading their congregations in the UK. They must pay conscious attention to their leadership practices.

6.5.2 What Solutions Are Emerging?

The first pursuit of this inquiry has been to answer what primary elements enable or discourage church growth among ADCs in Liverpool. In addition to this query, the study has also sought to unearth possible solutions to church growth challenges from the research data identified by participants during the investigation. The research findings have generated the grounded theory that ecclesiology, contextual realities of the UK, and leadership issues are the primary drivers of church growth for ADCs in Liverpool. To this end, *omolúàbí*-shaped ecclesiology emerged, nesting the adaptive leadership strategy, as a data-rooted solution to church growth issues identified by the study.

ADCs must also pay close attention to their context as they do church. Paying attention means that their views about church growth and church functions reflect an awareness of the realities of the UK (racism and secularism being prominent). Therefore, a new approach to being the church becomes imperative to experience the kind of growth advanced in this thesis. The alternative modus operandi, OSE, developed in this thesis, draws from the richness of the African (Yoruba) culture to allow 1GMs to be Christians, yet comfortably African, even in the diaspora. The OSE also addresses the yearnings of 2GMs as it contextualizes the ways ADCs do church in the UK. Plus, the ecclesiology aids productive engagement with the Western hosts. As an extensive concept, the *omolúàbí*-shaped ecclesiology is also beneficial to the global church.

OSE also promotes the practice of AL in response to leadership concerns arising from the study. AL encourages adaptation and helps to deal with unfamiliar challenges, as with the church growth difficulties confronting the research population. AL is similarly helpful to Liverpool ADCs because it encourages collaboration instead of the hierarchical leadership model many of the ADC leaders have brought from their home countries into the UK, a model that is strange to the West, and thus, scarcely effective.

6.6 Conclusion

The inquiry has revealed several factors affecting the growth of ADCs in Liverpool. Of all these issues, three stand out, with significant references from the research participants. They are ecclesiology, contextual realities of the UK, and leadership. Through analysis, the need emerged for an alternative leadership technique to handle the unfamiliar church growth challenges confronting ADCs in the UK. However, this leadership style must align itself with and present within a new approach to church that is meaningful to the UK environment. The suggested contextualized African ecclesiology, OSE, aids ADCs comfortability to do church in ways that are meaningful to them and their Western hosts to experience growth. It equally addresses the issues arising from the creation of race and its effects on the lives of Black people, particularly ADCs' expansion. In the following chapters, I unpack the OSE concept, the dynamics of race in relation to the research population's growth, and the AL structure.

CHAPTER 7

Omolúàbí-shaped Ecclesiology

7.1 Introduction

The research findings have emphasized the need for ADCs to reimagine their way of being church in the UK to experience the kind of growth this dissertation advances. Moreover, such ecclesiology[1] must aid the African's comprehension of the Christian faith. It must be able to speak to the African soul and needs, even in the diaspora, while also fostering contextualization. It is then appropriate and meaningful that such ecclesiological design derives from an African, and specifically Yoruba, context. After all, at least eleven of the twenty-six ADCs this research identified are not only Nigerian but also Yoruba-led.[2] Therefore, this chapter presents a manner of doing church that derives from the Yoruba concept of *omolúàbí* in response to the various church growth concerns arising from the investigation. The rationale for such an African ecclesiology receives more detailed attention and opens conversations in the chapter before exploring the idea of personhood in the African thought system. The identity discourse presents the *omolúàbí* framework, which the study builds upon to construct a contextualized African ecclesiology to respond to the church growth hurdles identified during the fieldwork.

---

1. While I am aware of the more comprehensive meaning it has in theological discourse, I have applied the term "ecclesiology" loosely in this study to refer to the lifestyle of the church; a way of doing or being church. I have taken this approach to avoid any theological argument that may be associated with the concept and to retain the focus of the research.

2. See appendix III.

I adopt the norm-setting dimension of personhood among the Yoruba people of South-Western Nigeria as a general representation of African identity in the entire conversation for at least two reasons.[3] First, I am of Yoruba ethnicity. So, I am quite familiar with key concepts within the culture. Second, *omolúàbí* as a moral aspect of personhood in Yoruba cosmology perfectly dovetails with the common theme of *ubuntu*[4] in discussions of African identity. One may even conceive of the *omolúàbí* framework as a Yoruba rendition of *ubuntu* social ethics and ideology because of their unquestionable similarities. So, in this chapter, I borrow from the *omolúàbí* concept of African (Yoruba) identity to formulate a genuinely African ecclesiology for ADCs in the UK moving towards church growth realization.

7.2 The Need for a Contextualized African Ecclesiology

The research has revealed that ecclesiology is critical to ADCs' expansion in Liverpool. Moreover, to be productive in the UK, ADCs require a way of being church that is meaningful to their 1GMs and 2GMs alike, as well as to their Western hosts. Yet most ADCs continue to do church the same way they knew and practised back home, ignoring the peculiarities of their new environment. The implication is that their inappropriate ecclesiology ends up only benefiting their 1GM population, leaving others dissatisfied and eventually disengaging from the African congregations. Of course, church growth then suffers.

James McKeown (1900–1989), an Irish missionary to the Gold Coast (present-day Ghana), who planted the Church of Pentecost in that country,

---

3. The Yorubas are arguably the largest ethnic group among Black Africans with historical consciousness and widely researched history. Famous for being the most literate group in Africa and having an impressive rate of urbanization, the Yoruba people have a well-established traditional structure and religion. For more about the Yorubas, see Akintoye, *History of the Yoruba*, 12.

4. Ubuntu is from the popular Zulu maxim of the Nguni people, *umuntu ngumuntu ngabantu* which means that a person is a person through other persons. As a concept, ubuntu stresses that no one is self-sufficient, and that interdependence is a reality for all. In essence, ubuntu implies that a person only discovers her own human qualities, behaviours, and traits through bonding and interacting with fellow human beings. For more details, see Nussbaum, "African Culture and Ubuntu," 2; Antwi, "Koinonia in African Culture," 68; Shutte, *Philosophy for Africa*, 46.

observed that "It would be difficult to grow an English oak in Ghana. A local species, at home in its culture, should grow, reproduce and spread; a church with foreign roots was more likely to struggle."[5] McKeown's warning is instructive to ADC leaders, who seem to be growing an African oak in the UK by the way they do church – excessively dominated by African culture, with little or no attempts at contextualization. As the research data and McKeown stress, this practice only leads to struggles and stunted growth. Hence, to experience growth in the UK, ADCs require a ecclesiology contextualized for the environment.

However, to fashion such an ecclesiology, Africans must first acknowledge the "over-Europeanized" Christianity they have received from Western missionaries.[6] Just as there has been Judaization, Hellenization, Romanization, and Europeanization of Christianity, resulting in the Christianization of these cultures, Africanization of Christianity must also happen.[7] Otherwise, as the missiologist Nigel Rooms insists, African Christians will continue to find themselves "in the difficult position of having one foot in their (somewhat neutered) African culture and one foot in European Christianity (which doesn't sit happily with them)."[8]

The Africanization of Christianity should not seem far-fetched since the "African moral system [itself] has a religious foundation."[9] In fact, *omolúàbí* values broadly overlap the attributes constituting the "fruit of the Spirit" in Galatians 5: 22–23.[10] The *omolúàbí* principles also form a cultural portrait of 2 Peter 1:5–7, which lists some necessary additives to the lives of believers in Christ.[11] The indigenization of Christianity will aid Africans' complete grasp of the Christian faith and how it connects with them, addressing their deepest

---

5. Christine, *Giant in Ghana*, 69.
6. Ayegboyin and Ishola, *African Indigenous Churches*, 14.
7. Mugambi, *Christianity and African Culture*, 4–8.
8. Rooms, *Faith of the English*, 2.
9. Mbiti, *African Religions and Philosophy*, 62.
10. The qualities are "love, joy, peace, patience, kindness, generosity, faithfulness, gentleness, and self-control" (Gal 5:22–23).
11. Here Peter notes: "For this very reason, you must make every effort to support your faith with goodness, and goodness with knowledge, and knowledge with self-control, and self-control with endurance, and endurance with godliness, and godliness with mutual affection, and mutual affection with love" (2 Pet 1:5–7).

needs, including psychological and sociological.[12] It is only then that African Christians can properly contextualize a well-understood Christianity and the way they do church, wherever they find themselves. Consequently, in this chapter, I formulate an ecclesiology from the African concept of *omolúàbí*, which ADCs can then nuance in the UK to experience growth.

7.3 Personhood in African (Yoruba) Thoughtform

Literature broadly views personhood from a dualistic viewpoint, as a concept with both a descriptive anthropological aspect and a moral dimension.[13] By implication, a person consists of both physical components and non-bodily elements. In most African traditions, the idea of personhood is even more comprehensive, with three dimensions: "the material, the non-material, and the quasi-material."[14] Nigerian scholar Olatunji Oyeshile rightly observes that the African concept of personhood is generally more holistic; it "goes beyond the mind-body dualism . . . because it provides not only a satisfactory origin of man [but], it also pays sufficient attention to the relationship between the mental and physical aspects of man in relation to his moral and social status."[15]

Many African cultures' moral sense of identity implies that an individual is not considered a person by just being human, but by necessarily acting in morally acceptable manners in tandem with responsibilities within society.[16] As such, among the Yorubas, one could hear such remarks as *ki ise eniyan* (he or she is not a human being) or *eniyan lasan ni* (he or she is an ordinary or caricature person). These statements do not proceed from evaluating the physical features of the addressee, but his or her ethical demonstration. The declarations attest to a moral inadequacy in the individual that makes the affirmation of his or her personhood impossible.[17] This understanding of per-

---

12. Ayegboyin and Ishola, *African Indigenous Churches*, 14.

13. Adekanye, " Critical Analysis," 2. I am aware that there are several viewpoints about what constitutes a person. The irreconcilable difference in the various schools of thought, however, makes it sometimes difficult to sufficiently articulate the concept of personhood.

14. Adekanye, 2. Adekanye explains quasi-material as African concept of "disembodied existence." This is a phenomenon where the soul of the dead continues to exist albeit without the former body.

15. Oyeshile, "Towards an African Conception," 104.

16. Ikuenobe, "Good and Beautiful," 128.

17. Gbadegesin, *African Philosophy*, 27.

sonhood emphasising the norm-setting aspect of an individual over physical features is common across African cultures, unlike the English philosophical construct.[18]

7.3.1 *Omolúàbí* Concept

A highly valued philosophical and cultural construct concerned with the moral aspect of identity among the Yoruba people is the *omolúàbí* concept.[19] For this people group, the culmination of all conversations aimed at teaching moral lessons is the notion of *omolúàbí*. The same truth resounds in the affirmation of educationist and social scientists Grace Akanbi and Alice Jekayinfa, that "the end of Yoruba traditional education is to make every individual 'Omoluabi.'"[20] Philosophically and culturally, *omolúàbí* represents someone who possesses good virtues. The concept provides a yardstick for determining the morality or immorality of any act in society.[21] To refer to someone as *omolúàbí* is to recognize and affirm that such a person is well-cultured, mannered, honourable, and respectful – a well-behaved person.[22] An *omolúàbí* embodies all virtues that facilitate the sound expression of wisdom, knowledge, and skills for his or her betterment and by necessity, the betterment of society.[23]

As with the concept of *ubuntu*, *omolúàbí* is applicable either as a noun, where it refers to a "person," or an adjective, when describing the good virtues a person must possess.[24] For instance, a person may say to another, *omolúàbí ni e*. This assertion is translatable as "you are an *omolúàbí*," meaning that the subject of the conversation embodies good virtues or behaviour; hence, he or she is *omolúàbí* by being (applied as a noun). At other times, when used as an adjective, the same speaker could say *o o soro bi omolúàbí*, translatable as "you have not spoken in an *omolúàbí* way." The implication is that the addressee's use of words is inconsistent with *omolúàbí* tenets.

---

18. Gbadegesin, 27.
19. Olanipekun, "Omoluabi: Re-thinking the Concept," 219.
20. Akanbi and Jekayinfa, "Reviving the African Culture," 15. See also Akinyemi, *Orature and Yoruba Riddles*, 231.
21. Adebowale, "Aristotle's Human Virtue," 6.
22. Osoba, " Nature, Form and Functions," 49.
23. Adebowale, "Aristotle's Human Virtue," 5.
24. Adeniji-Neill and Ammon, "Omoluabi: The Way," 1.

7.3.1.1 Omolúàbí *Etymology*

In addition to usage variation, *omolúàbí* also differs in semantic construction. For instance, Joseph Osoba, a Yoruba scholar, believes that the concept is from the phrase *omo + ti + Noa + bi*, meaning "the child Noah birthed." Noah, here, refers to the biblical character Noah, the righteous man who, along with his seven family members, experienced preservation from the great flood that ravaged the entire world in his days.[25] Consequently, *omolúàbí* is a warning to keep good company, just as the Yoruba proverb *agutan to ba baja rin a jegbe* avers, literally meaning that "a sheep that walks with the dog will eat faeces." Even so, I consider Osoba's interpretation grossly misleading because it seems to suggest that the Yorubas had no concept of moral identity, like the *omolúàbí*, before exposure to the Bible. However, although arguably the "largest cultural aggregation in West Africa with a history of political unity and a common historical tradition," the Yoruba people lived harmoniously in the pre-colonial era by "elaborate code of manners and etiquette," as with the *omolúàbí* tenets.[26] Because of this seeming oversight in Osoba's theory, I have not aligned with it in this dissertation.

Omolúàbí can also take the form of the phrase *omo + ti + olu-ìwà + bi*, which is translatable as "the child that the chief or master of character gives birth to."[27] In this construction, the master or chief of character (*olu-ìwà*) may be a dignified parent with outstanding character. It follows, then, that the offspring of such a progenitor would be quintessentially perfect in character, an *omolúàbí*, since every living creature produces after its kind.[28] Nonetheless, this construct of *omolúàbí* as *omo + ti + olu-ìwà + bi* also presents some ambiguity. For instance, another Yoruba intellectual, Segun Gbadegesin, interprets *olu-ìwà* as "God, the creator of every baby." As such, every child is an *omolúàbí*.[29] Gbadegesin's translation does not only seem controvertible in Yoruba language structure, but it further affirms the vagueness that surrounds the construction of *omolúàbí* as *omo + ti + olu-ìwà + bi*.

---

25. Osoba, "Nature, Form and Functions," 49.
26. Olatunji, "Postmodernist Critique of Omoluwabi," 65; see also Fadipe, *Sociology of the Yoruba*, 301.
27. Fayemi, "Human Personality and the Yoruba," 2.
28. Fayemi, 2–3.
29. Gbadegesin, "In search of *Agbasanko*," 87.

Nigerian (Yoruba) philosopher Sophie Oluwole provides yet another rendition of *omolúàbí* as *omo + ti + o + ni + ìwà + bi*, translatable as "a child who behaves like."[30] For at least two reasons, this interpretation is more semantically illuminating and apt for this dissertation. First, it is possible to argue concerning the previous *omolúàbí* constructions that the offspring of Noah, or chief of character, may not necessarily become as exemplary in character as their parents. While Oluwole's version raises the question of who a child behaves like, she immediately completes the build-up with two additional phrases. The full expression of *omolúàbí* then becomes *omo ti o ni ìwà bi + eni ti a ko + ti o si gba eko*, translated as "a child who behaves like + someone who is well trained/nurtured + and lives by the tenets of the training."[31]

Second, Oluwole's presentation of *omolúàbí* addresses the possible ambivalence and concerns in the previous constructions. It focuses on the impact on a child's character formation of training, rather than the parent's character excellence. The interpretation reflects the concept of *omolúàbí* in the Yoruba culture more perfectly. Indeed, it suggests that a person possesses wisdom, skills, disciplines, and learnings displayed in private and public engagements, and by which affirmation of personhood is possible.[32]

7.3.2 Fundamental Attributes of *Omolúàbí*

Omolúàbí must demonstrate certain basic qualities before their affirmation. In this part of the dissertation, I briefly discuss the essential characteristics of *omolúàbí* since a single volume of work is incapable of a more detailed exploration. In no particular order of importance, *omolúàbí* must embody the fundamental attributes below for their recognition in society.

7.3.2.1 Relationship Dynamics

Omolúàbí showcases a sound understanding of the workings of relationships so that they are beneficial to everyone involved.[33] Maintaining harmony in all relationships, whether at work, school, or home, is essential to an

---

30. Oluwole, "Who are (We) the Yoruba?"
31. Oluwole, 13.
32. Fayemi, "Human Personality," 168.
33. Adeniji-Neill and Ammon, "Omoluabi," 4.

omolúàbí in attaining individuality, identity, or self-actualization.[34] Therefore, an *omolúàbí* operates by the guiding principles of social relationships in the Yoruba cultural system. The first is *àjobí*, meaning blood relations, and the second, *àjogbé*, which translates as co-residence.[35] To an *omolúàbí*, everyone relates together from the viewpoint of "shared humanity."[36] Hence, the Yorubas encourage a communal life through the "sharing of common social life, commitment to the collective good of the community, appreciation of mutual obligations, caring for others, interdependence, and solidarity."[37] For relationships to be enriching to all parties, *omolúàbí* longs for some social values in all relationships. These gains appear to resonate significantly with the African diaspora aspirations. They are *ire àìkú* – the value of healthy life into old age, *ire omo* – the value of parenthood, *ire owó* – the value of financial prosperity, *ire oko-aya* – the value of love and companionship (as in marriage), and *ire aborí-òtá* – the value of confident self-actualization.[38]

To *omolúàbí*, harmony in social relationships extends to the spirit world since African cosmological understanding accommodates the interaction of the spirit world and the physical world.[39] Spirits are real, and part of human life in the African worldview, and the spiritual and the physical universe form a whole that is not easily or necessarily separatable.[40] Mbiti argues that the existence of human life is spiritual such that death is not an end but an upgrade into the assembly of the "living-dead," the ancestral realm.[41] This consciousness of the immortality of human beings drives the Yorubas' belief that dead people continue to be a part of the community even after transitioning to the realm of the spirits. Hence, *omolúàbí* must maintain equilibrium in relationship with the spirit world. Some of the acts that symbolize the recognition and fellowship with the spirit world are pouring libations (usually

---

34. Payne, "Akìwowo, Orature and Divination," 180.
35. Akinwowo, *Ajobi and Ajogbe*, 10.
36. Shared humanity refers to the nature or attributes common to all human beings. Howard Grace emphasizes that these shared behaviour and qualities are not necessarily positive, but also include negative aspects of human nature. See more in Grace, *Vision of a Shared Humanity*.
37. Awoniyi, "African Cultural Values," 8.
38. Akinwowo, *Ajobi and Ajogbe*, 13–14.
39. Nel, "African Background of Pentecostal Theology," 8.
40. Mbiti, *African Religions and Philosophy*, 97.
41. Mbiti, 34.

symbolized by spilling some liquid like milk, beer, or water on the floor) and leaving food portions for the dead.[42]

7.3.2.2 Inú Rere

The second fundamental virtue of *omolúàbí* is *inú rere* (goodwill, having a clean and good mind towards others), which is both a moral and mental quality.[43] *Inú rere* pushes *omolúàbí* to give easily to the community in deeds and action.[44] It readily finds expression in the principle of hospitality, which creates "the desire for, a welcome without reserve and without calculation, an exposure without limit to whoever arrives."[45] The unbiased and unrehearsed benevolence does not happen on a surface level of duty for an *omolúàbí* but emanates from the innermost being.[46] To emphasize the importance of *inú rere* evident in hospitality and benevolence, the affirmation of personhood among the Yorubas does not occur without considering deeds linking individuals with their families, friends, community, and others.[47] In essence, *inú rere* is responsible for the love, care, kindness, and concern that an *omolúàbí* shows towards other people instead of overly focusing on himself or herself. As such, society refers to an *omolúàbí* as "a different individual."[48]

7.3.2.3 Cultural Integration

Another distinctive of *omolúàbí* is cultural awareness and integration.[49] Only a cultured person is fit for recognition as an *omolúàbí*. The uncultured is an *omo lásán* or *omokómo*, suggesting a worthless child. *Omokómo* is socially unincorporated, culturally deviant, or a misfit in the community or set-up.[50] Chief among the implications of being cultured is to have *iteríba* (respect).[51] An *omolúàbí* has self-respect (including recognition and setting boundaries)

---

42. Mbiti, 33.
43. Abimbola, "Iwapele: The Concept," 389, 393.
44. Adeniji-Neill and Ammon, "Omoluabi," 1.
45. Derrida, " Principle of Hospitality," 6.
46. Olanipekun, "Omoluabi: Re-thinking the Concept," 224.
47. Adeniji-Neill and Ammon, "Omoluabi," 2.
48. Adedayo, "Concept of Omoluabi," 2.
49. Adeniji-Neill and Ammon, "Omoluabi," 4.
50. Oyeneye and Shoremi, "Concept of Culture," 253.
51. Abimbola, "Iwapele," 389.

and honour for others, including parents, elders, other authority figures, peers, and even younger ones.[52] In other words, an *omolúàbí* is aware of and quick to acknowledge others' rights regardless of their age or status. Everyone is deserving of his or her respect based on their humanness.[53]

Ìwàpèlé or *ìwàtútù* (gentleness or gentle character) also comes to the fore as a vital element of being cultured. *Ìwàpèlé* expresses itself in "being mindful of the individuality of others, treating others gently and being tolerant and accommodating of the peculiarity of the existence of others."[54] Consequently, *ìwàpèlé* often makes the list of critical ethical behaviours and moral conduct admired and approved within the Yoruba moral system.[55] An *omolúàbí*, who has high regard for culture, demonstrates *ìwàpèlé* in communications, business, musical constructions, religious actions, and other aspects of life.[56]

7.3.2.4 Òrò Síso

The spoken word (*òrò síso*) is so significant among the Yorubas that it forms another key characteristic of *omolúàbí*.[57] *Òrò*, meaning "words," can convey disrespect or hurt to others when used frivolously or unguardedly. *Omolúàbí* has this understanding and therefore uses *òrò* with dexterity. Referring to it as language, Yoruba scholar John Bewaji provides additional insight into the importance of *òrò* among the Yorubas. He notes that:

> The demand for, and expectation of, decent, responsible and insightful use of the language is reflected in all aspects of communication, be it in verbal salutations, musical constructions, poetic performances, religious and spiritual displays and

---

52. Adeniji-Neill and Ammon, "Omoluabi," 1.
53. Fayemi, "Human Personality," 169.
54. Dada, "Aristotle and the Omolúwàbí Ethos."
55. Bewaji, "Ethics and Morality," 339.
56. Bewaji, *Beauty and Culture*, 159.
57. Òrò is a composite of *ogbon* (wisdom), *imo* (knowledge), and *oye* (understanding), the creative companions of Olodumare, the supreme being in Yoruba cosmology. Òrò is the source of speech, meaning and communication, potent enough to "create order out of existence." It finds utterance primarily through owe (proverbs) and by implication, other range of communicative properties of the Yoruba people viz: "sculpture, àrokò, dance, drama, song, chant, poetry, incantations like ofò, ògèdè, àyájóèpè, odù, èsà and many others." See more in Abiodun, "Verbal and Visual Metaphors," 254–256; Opefeyitimi, "Ayajo as Ifa," 25; Abimbola, "Iwapele," 389.

utterances, or in the negotiations of important formal and non-formal pacts, deals, treaties and business, etc.⁵⁸

It is admirable for *omolúàbí* to demonstrate intelligent use of *ọ̀rọ̀* by engaging Yoruba proverbs (*òwe*) in communication. Indeed, without *òwe*, "speech flounders and falls short of its mark, whereas aided by them, communication is fleet and unerring."⁵⁹ Yoruba proverbs are the channels through which *ọ̀rọ̀* finds expression, as evident in the popular notion among the people that, *òwe lesin òrò, bi òrò ba sonu, òwe la fi n wa*. The literal translation of this clause is that, metaphorically, proverbs are the horse of *òrò*; when *òrò* is lost, proverbs are the means for searching it out. Just as horses were reliable means of transportation to distant lands and battlefields in ancient times, proverbs function as suitable and effective verbal communication tools.⁶⁰ In summation, *omolúàbí* is that cultured person who can "optimise the efficaciousness of speech,"⁶¹ leveraging proverbs amidst other communication tools and consequently demonstrating cultural appreciation and awareness.

7.3.2.5 Ìwà

The fifth hallmark of *omolúàbí* is *ìwà* (character). Even in *omolúàbí*'s etymology, *ìwà* is central.⁶² *Ìwà* can either make one more valuable when exhibiting *ìwà rere* (good character/moral goodness) or less desirable when demonstrating *ìwà buburu* or *ìwà ibaja* (bad or terrible character). Good character may not be the sole determinant of personhood, but it certainly attracts a lot of admiration for the Yorubas. In fact, they often link good character and *ewà* (beauty). For them, moral goodness acts as the "normative necessary condition for a person to be truly and strictly considered beautiful, and to be a person in the robust sense."⁶³ Bad character, however, receives condemnation and reduces an individual's personhood or humanness to the level of

---

58. Bewaji, *Beauty and Culture*, 159.
59. Owomoyela, *Yoruba Proverbs*, 12.
60. Osoba, " Nature, Form and Functions," 46. Osoba further notes that Yoruba proverbs are marked by "shortness, sense, and salt." The implication is that Yoruba proverbs are usually brief but deep, and therefore require sharp perception to fully grasp the intended meaning or sense. Plus, the proverbs engage figurative language, which adds poetic flavour to speeches.
61. Owomoyela, *Yoruba Proverbs*, 12.
62. Abimbola, "Iwapele," 389.
63. Ikuenobe, "Good and Beautiful," 129.

"ordinary things" such that one attracts the tag *èniyàn lásán* (worthless fellow) or *eranko* (animal).[64] African philosopher Ademola Fayemi also resounds the vitality of *ìwà*, especially in rites of passage and integrity development. He explains that even though a person may be human, deficiency in *ìwà* results in their reckoning as unfit for trust or responsibilities in society. Consequently, he concludes that *ìwà* is the "fulcrum of human personality."[65]

7.3.2.6 Isé *and* Akínkanjú

Another set of connected elementary qualities of *omolúàbí* is *isé* (hard work) and *akínkanjú* (courage or bravery).[66] *Omolúàbí* puts a lot of care and effort into work because, without a strong work ethic and diligence, a person attracts the tag of *òle* (lazy or indolent person), making other *omolúàbí* qualities meaningless.[67] Indeed, Yorubas hold that *isé l'ogun isé, eni ti ko sisé yio jale*. This popular saying literally translates as "hard work is the panacea for poverty; whoever does not work hard will become a thief or robber."

Isé and *akínkanjú* virtues ensure that an *omolúàbí* courageously navigates tough times and develops *ìfaradà* (fortitude) to endure and rebound when knocked down.[68] Rightly so, life is not a bed of roses and can be unpredictable. As such, without the extra virtue of *akínkanjú* to support *isé*, it may be difficult to remain hardworking or exhibit other core qualities of *omolúàbí*. *Akínkanjú* is opposed to "escapism, self-condemnation, abandonment and indulgence in vices to circumvent life obstacles."[69] The Nigerian educator and poet Joseph Odunjo, in his Yoruba poem, "Ise Loogun Ise," richly summarizes the importance and broad-reaching implications of the qualities of *isé* and *akínkanjú* as shown below.[70]

---

64. Fayemi, "Human Personality," 170.
65. Fayemi, 170.
66. Adeniji-Neill and Ammon, "Omoluabi," 2.
67. Dada, "Aristotle and the Ọmọlúwàbí Ethos."
68. Oyebade and Azenabor, "Discourse on the Fundamental," 48.
69. Oyebade and Azenabor, 48.
70. This poem is an excerpt from Odunjo's Yoruba book series Alawiye first published in the 1940s, as presented by Jadesola Babatola. See Babatola, "Literary Inquiry," 4–5. The translations are my adaptations of Jadesola's English interpretation of the poem.

Ise l'ogun ise	Work is the remedy for poverty
Mura si'se re, ore mi	Put diligence into work, my friend
Ise la'fi ndeni giga	It is by work that we become great
Bi a ko ba r'eni fehin ti	If we have no one to rest on
Bi ole laari	We appear lazy
Bi a ko ba reni gbekele	If we have no one to trust
A te ra mo se ni	We commit more to our work
Iya re le lowo lowo	Your mother may be financially wealthy
Baba re le lesin lekan	Your father may own numerous horses
Ti o ba gbojule won	If you make them your resort
O te tan ni mo so fun o	You are doomed, I say
Ohun ti a ko ba jiya fun	Whatever we do not persevere to obtain
Se kii le to'jo	It does not last
Ohun ti a ba fa'ra sise fun	Whatever we work hard to acquire
Ni npe lowo eni	It lasts longer in one's hands
Apa lara igunpa ni iye kan	Our arms are our friends, elbow, our siblings
B'aiye ba fe o loni	If you are loved by the world today
Ti o ba lowo lowo,	If you remain financially prosperous, they will love
won a tun fe o lola	you tomorrow as well
Abi ko wa nipo atata	Even better when you occupy an esteemed position
Aiye a ye o si terin terin	The world will honour you with laughter
Je ki o deni ti ra ngo	Just become penniless and destitute
Ko ri bi won ti nyin mu si o	Then, see how they will wink their noses in scorn
Eko si tun n s'eni d'oga	Learning or education also makes one a master
Mura ki o koo dara dara	Strive to learn very well
Bi o ba ri opo eniyan	If you see many people
Ti won ni fi eko so erin rin	That ask you to abandon education
Da kun ma fara we won	Please, do not copy them
Iya mbe fomo ti ko gbon	Suffering awaits the foolish child

> *Ekun mbe fomo ti nsare kiri*   And sorrow for the aimless child
> *Mafowuro sere ore mi*   Do not waste your early years, my friend
> *Mura sise ojo nlo*   Work hard now, for time waits for no one

7.3.2.7 Òtító

Òtító (truth), integrity, and honesty are a group of related, basic characters of *omolúàbí*.[71] Integrity conveys a sense of wholeness or completeness in line with the Latin word, *integras*.[72] The implication regarding an *omolúàbí* is that he or she must exhibit coherence and consistency in principles, values, thoughts, speech, and actions. *Omolúàbí* must be honest, straightforward, incorruptible, truthful, and accountable.[73] Thus, he or she becomes "a good and dependable person who stands above board at all times."[74] *Omolúàbí*'s integrity and *òtító* reflect in his or her private and public endeavours that such an individual does not indulge in or support fraudulent activities.[75] Truth and integrity are central to being an *omolúàbí* because, ultimately, they are the "stuff of moral courage and even heroism."[76]

The implications and tenets of *omolúàbí* are extensive, and I have only covered the essential elements in this conversation. Indeed, *omolúàbí* also models principles of self-discipline and control, humility in success, and high self-esteem in sorrow and failure.[77] It further makes personal ambitions align with that of the community, fostering harmony and guiding every member of the community to make significant contributions to the general well-being of the society. The mindset of an *omolúàbí* is "one for all and all for one."[78]

---

71. Abimbola, "Iwapele," 389, 393.
72. Montefiore and Vines, eds. *Integrity in the Public*, 9.
73. Patrick Dobel includes many of these attributes among values accommodated within integrity. For further details, see Dobel, "Integrity in the Public Service."
74. Akanbi and Jekayinfa, "Reviving the African Culture," 15.
75. Oyerinde, "'Omoluabi' - The Concept," 200.
76. Brenkert, ed. *Corporate Integrity and Accountability*, 5.
77. Olanipekun, "Omoluabi: Re-thinking the Concept," 226.
78. Oyebade and Azenabor, "Discourse on the Fundamental," 49.

7.4 What *Omolúàbí*-shaped Ecclesiology Would Look Like

Considering the religious foundation of the African moral system, it is convenient for Christianity and, indeed, ecclesiology to draw from the *omolúàbí* concept. Moreover, since every theology, ecclesiology, and missiology is contextual,[79] an ecclesiology "brewed in an African pot"[80] is more likely to have meaning in African communities than Western ecclesiology. By permitting a dialogue between the *omolúàbí* principles and ecclesiology, enrichment can come to the current contemplations and practices of the church. Both church leaders and congregants would find the product of such interaction instructive and beneficial. Below, I have highlighted five crucial ways in which the *omolúàbí* philosophical and cultural understanding can inform the lifestyle of the church; that is, the features of *omolúàbí*-shaped ecclesiology (OSE).

7.4.1 Recognition of and Harmony with the Spirit

Perhaps OSE's spiritual emphasis is its most crucial element. Just as an *omolúàbí* is conscious of the participation of the spiritual world in the physical, engaging OSE would imply that the church recognizes the influence and necessity of the Holy Spirit in its life. The church cannot be "unidimensional" in its orientation, as with the Western interpretation of life events, but must be multifaceted, acknowledging spiritual reality alongside the physical.[81] African Pentecostals, as with most of the research participants, are confident that church growth is spiritual and passionately demonstrate this belief in the supernatural, in alignment with the African worldview. Hence, it should not be strange that Pentecostalism has taken over the face of Christianity in Africa.[82] The global church can learn from the multi-dimensional worldview of an *omolúàbí*, who acknowledges spiritual reality along with the physical. In practical terms, OSE's supernatural emphasis would imply that the church

---

79. Kwiyani, *Multicultural Kingdom*, 109.

80. This phrase reflects in Agbon E. Orobator's book title to metaphorically describe a theology constructed from African cultural and sociological resources. See Orobator, *Theology Brewed*.

81. Ayokunle, *Communities of Faith*, 69.

82. I have stated this in another part of this dissertation. See the conversation on European Migration and the Renewal of African Christianity in chapter 5.

believes, permits, and demonstrates the Bible's teachings on divine healing, angels, visions, miracles, prophecies, dream interpretation, and other spiritual possibilities through the power of the Holy Spirit. Then, the church can truly begin to "live by the Spirit, [and] . . . be guided by the Spirit," according to Galatians 5:25.

As the *omolúàbí* concept seeks harmony with the spirit world, OSE would also insist that the church maintain peace and fellowship with the Holy Spirit. This "communion of the Holy Spirit" (2 Cor 13:13 NRSV) will more than likely require a vibrant prayer life since prayer is a vital channel to "truly connect with God [or his Spirit]."[83] Maintaining unity with the Holy Spirit will also see a church grow in the fruit of the Spirit and "grieve the Holy Spirit" (Eph 4:30) less every day. Sustaining a working relationship with the Spirit will also see a church increasingly experience productivity as it deploys various growth strategies, for the Holy Spirit remains the enabler of biblical church growth principles. Ultimately, through OSE's emphasis on spiritual consciousness and persistent alliance with the Holy Spirit, the church will continue to experience spiritual maturity.

7.4.2 Building Relationships

Second, OSE expects that the church operates with a rich knowledge of relationship dynamics. Being the church in this way will undoubtedly aid the social growth of the church. Indeed, as one participant from CH2 puts it, "when you don't know how to approach people . . . [or] . . . the church doesn't know how to address crisis . . . it disintegrates." Living by the *omolúàbí* ethos of *ìwàpèlé* and *ìteríba* would translate to congregants respecting themselves regardless of age, social status, race, or other classfications. The implication is that the 2GMs and youths, in general, would find it more convenient to contribute to the church's development without being disdained or silenced. In the end, they would be more likely to give their allegiance to their African congregations. Moreover, adults would also enjoy the benefits of learning from the younger generation, besides the opportunity to pass down their much-needed wisdom in an atmosphere of respect for individuality. As a result, cross-pollination of ideas and learning would increase, culminating in church growth.

---

83. Omartian, "Foreword," 9.

An awareness of relationship dynamics would also mitigate conflicts and misunderstandings in the church. There would be more forbearance in social interactions since people would be better informed that, although constituting a church, "we are from different places," as a participant from CH3 notes. Against this consciousness, the other's attitudes, behaviour, and actions would filter, reducing the tendencies for offences and misunderstandings. As such, leaders and members would engage more effectively without distrust, bitterness, anger, hypocrisy, pride, or prejudice as they respect relationship etiquette and boundaries while operating in love with one another. Congregants, regardless of their divide, would equally be able to serve more lovingly together as they apply the social principles of àjobí and àjogbé within the omolúàbí framework. Highhandedness would find little expression in the church that models àjobí and àjogbé. As with the early church, everyone would live as comrades and a true family. No one would shy away from assisting the less privileged, just as Luke describes the brotherly love of the early church: "There was not a needy person among them, for as many as owned lands or houses sold them and brought the proceeds of what was sold. They laid it at the apostles' feet, and it was distributed to each as any had need" (Acts 4:34–35).

7.4.3 Stress on Social Ministry

Third, OSE would mean that the church gets involved socially in the life of its members and community. It would not only be concerned with or measure its growth almost exclusively from a spiritual perspective, as most participants perceive church growth. Rather, the church would also be aware of and deliberately seek to address the welfare and social needs of its members and of society. This imperative for the church's social engagement derives from *omolúàbí*'s virtues of hospitality and benevolence – both offshoots of *inú rere*. The leaders of a socially involved church will be cautious to prevent the formality of their professional backgrounds from getting in the way of the church's social commitments. Indeed, there is the tendency for ministers with professional experiences to style their congregations as business environments, preferring their highly skilled members on which they focus most of their efforts, including social ministry. These church leaders may also not favour any gathering or fellowship that brings the professionals in close contact with the church's unskilled, marginalized, or less privileged population. Theologian Tim Chester and church planter Steve Timmis tell of a minister like this in their book, entitled *Total Church*, who wants a church that reflects his background as a professional. The pastor reveals, "I don't want to be opening my home to people. I don't want to get involved in people's lives. I don't want needy people in my church."[84]

OSE is opposed to such bias and segregation, which prevents social interaction and opportunities for congregants to meet one another's material and non-material needs. Instead, the *omolúàbí*'s goodwill implicit in OSE will ensure that church leaders put away preferences in administering the church and its resources. By implication, the body of Christ will be open to all and show concern and care, even to the marginalized. Church growth will no longer be almost solely a spiritual pursuit, as many of the participants indicated, but measured also by the extent to which the church is socially involved. As in Luke 4:18, the poor, prisoners, blind, oppressed, and other overlooked groups in society will find aid through the church's services. The widows will not be left behind, as the early church had to choose people who specifically attended to the material needs of its widows (Acts 6:1–6). Moreover, as the church becomes more intentional in its social engagement, especially beyond its congregants to strangers, it will begin to live up to its expectation as "the light of the world" (Matt 5:14) instead of just a shining light to itself. In the end, the acts of love will open up possibilities for the recipients to join the church, increasing its numerical strength.

7.4.4 Excellent Leadership

OSE also speaks to leadership issues, which this investigation has exposed (with 109 references from twenty-five of twenty-six interviewees) as part of the prominent factors influencing church growth among the research population. The African-shaped ecclesiology suggests that pastors stay on top of their game through *ìṣẹ́* (hard work) and *akínkanjú* (courage) to remain relevant in a fast-developing and changing world.[85] Pastors may need to add to their ministerial training, both formally and informally. David not only led the Israelites by integrity or personal charm, but also with skill (Ps 78:72). The

---

84. Chester and Timmis, *Total Church*, 67.

85. Of course, these are necessary qualities emphasising the leadership and administrative growth suggested in the working definition of church growth for this dissertation.

COVID-19 pandemic has exposed the need to acquire some technological expertise, an unusual field for many church leaders. Learning an unfamiliar skill will likely require *iteríba* (humility and respect) from pastors. Indeed, as in the technological world, facilitators of new learning may be younger individuals or "pew members" who are professionals in the relevant areas of knowledge.

ADC leaders will also need to extend training or discipleship to their church congregations in keeping with *omolúàbí*'s emphasis on training (Oluwole's interpretation and that of this work) and the Great Commission's charge to "make disciples of all nations" (Matt 28:19–20). It is only after investing in training their congregants that pastors would be ethically correct to expect improved lifestyles from their members, patterned after Christ. Designing a methodical discipleship process is helpful in this regard. This systematic training would be in addition to ministers consciously living exemplary lives that show the congregation how to live daily like Christ, just like coaches or trainers would model to their trainees.

OSE would also ensure that through excellent leadership, delivered on the platform of *isé*, ADC leaders apply themselves to the thorough and consistent study of the Scriptures and other helpful materials for their ministries. This would align with Paul's advice to Timothy in 2 Timothy 2:15, to "Do your best to present yourself to God as one approved, a worker who does not need to be ashamed and who correctly handles the word of truth." Demonstrating courage (*akínkanjú*) would also mean that pastors speak out bravely when they feel helpless, lonely, depressed, or discouraged. Asking for help would no longer be a sin or an abomination. When ministers have support systems as above, they will continually enjoy refreshments, thus always giving their best and having a better nourished and spiritually mature church.

7.4.5 Holistic Salvation

OSE seeks a comprehensive or holistic experience of salvation. It not only emphasizes salvation as a spiritual phenomenon, but one that must find demonstration and affirmation in complementary moral living, as with the aspirations of Paul in Galatians 5:22–23. In the passage, Paul presents some of the virtues a Christian must exhibit, constituting the "fruit of the Spirit": "love, joy, peace, forbearance, kindness, generosity, faithfulness, gentleness, and self-control."

Just as *omolúàbí* provides a system for validating personhood from a moral viewpoint in Yoruba culture, Christian identity would only be meaningful, recognized, and whole with an exemplary ethical life. Titus 3:8 affirms the same truth that Christians must not be lacking in moral goodness or "good works."[86] While the advocacy here is not for perfectionism, it will be awkward for anyone to belong to the church while being morally deficient. James 2:18 records it this way: "But someone will say, 'You have faith and I have works.' Show me your faith apart from your works, and I show you my faith by my works." Defaming the character of a pastor or church, as one participant highlighted in discussing the hindrances to church growth in her context, is not the good works that edify the body of Christ. The holistic salvation that OSE advocates rejects such harmful behaviour because one's faith profession must be evident in sound ethics and morality.

To church leaders, holistic salvation would translate to a balance in presenting God's ability and desire to provide for his people, as Jehovah Jireh (Gen 22:14). By implication, modelling and teaching this dimension of God would no longer be an issue that attracts such negative tags as "prosperity gospel."[87] Indeed, scholars have identified and condemned the prosperity gospel as promoting greed and materialism.[88] Yet the "prosperity gospel" also challenges us to recognize the power and willingness of God to supply all the needs of his people, including the material, knowing that he is a God who "delights in the welfare of his servant" (Psalm 35:27).

This aspect of God cannot but be particularly emphasized in regions without adequate social amenities or other physical needs. To Africans, a religion (or God) that does not meet their multifaceted needs besides the salvation of

---

86. Titus 3:8 – "I want you to insist on these things, so that those who have have believed in God may be careful to devote themselves to good works. These things are excellent and profitable for people" (ESV).

87. Critics tag this gospel that attests to God's power to provide and his willingness to display the same grace towards its people as *the prosperity gospel*. They consider it a mono-directional exportation of North American Christian-oriented movements. Moreover, to the critics, it is a post-war or Cold War Pentecostal re-invention that originated within the Pentecostal faith particularly of the United States descent with a tendency towards materialistic orientation. See more in Hunt, "'Winning Ways,'" 331. See also Heuser, "Religio-Scapes of the Prosperity Gospel," 21; Gbote and Kgatla, "Prosperity Gospel," 6.

88. See, for example, Niemandt, "Prosperity Gospel," 206–210; Ijaola, "Pentecostalism, the Prosperity Gospel," 137–158; Togarasei, "Pentecostal Gospel of Prosperity," 336–350.

their souls is meaningless.[89] What OSE then suggests by holistic salvation is that church leaders make their people see and engage God's ability and eagerness to address even their material needs without becoming materialistic. Jesus's moderate lifestyle would always be the yardstick, as the pinnacle of *omolúàbí* and "the pioneer and perfecter of our faith" (Hebrews 12:2).

The implication of holistic salvation is also in spoken words. Church leaders would need to demonstrate tact in using words so that people may find their communications and sermon delivery more positive and less offensive. This skill with words would stem from *omolúàbí's* grasp of *ọ̀rọ̀*. Paul also understands the importance of sound speech and lists it among the crucial qualities young men must exhibit in Titus 2:6–8. In all, pastors must never forget that words are delicate and must, therefore, proceed with wisdom and discretion to achieve their intended purposes while also minimising offence.[90]

A helpful tip for African ministers in communicating with tact is to engage proverbs, especially in conveying complex messages. Proverbs remain rich treasures of Africa's oral literature and are vital to contextualization among its people. They are "the drum of God."[91] So, by engaging proverbs in their communications, African church leaders would likely reduce offences in their conversations. Their speeches would more accurately model Paul's admonition to the Colossians: "Let your speech always be gracious, seasoned with salt, so that you may know how you ought to answer everyone" (Col 4:6). Moreover, as Joseph Ola queries, "An African preacher who is neither familiar with nor appreciative of African proverbs, what will be African about his preaching?"[92] Indeed, even Jesus's teachings were replete with parables and wise sayings.

Where holistic salvation marks a congregation, the church would certainly experience the multi-dimensional aspects of church growth this dissertation

---

89. Ayegboyin and Ishola argue that this is one of the rationales for the emergence of AICs, a desire to make Christianity speak to African worldview and concerns. See Ayegboyin and Ishola, *African Indigenous Churches*, 14, 21–22.

90. Tactical use of *ọ̀rọ̀* certainly includes the awareness of key elements of rhetorical theories in communication as identified by Aristotle, the Greek philosopher. There is the Logos, which refers to the logic or rationality of the message. Ethos concerns the credibility of the speaker, while Pathos refers to the state of the listeners – their psychological state, language, mood, and others. See more in "Aristotle's Rhetoric," in *Stanford Encyclopedia of Philosophy*.

91. Heerden, "'Proverb is the Drum,'" 462.

92. Joseph Ola, *Christ as 'Ọ̀rọ̀' ('Word')*.

proposes. The implications of a necessary spiritual experience and complementary moral life for affirming Christian identity will result in more spiritually mature Christians. These congregants would make the church attractive to outsiders through their moral goodness, leading to a numerical increase for the church.

7.5 OSE as a Useful Tool for ADCs' Growth in Liverpool

The applicability of OSE to ADCs in Liverpool and the UK is quite extensive. Understandably, the *omolúàbí* concept itself has broad relevance. In this part of the dissertation, I discuss ways the OSE can address the research population's impediments to growth and facilitate successful missional activities and expansion of the congregations.

7.5.1 Responding to Issues of Race and Homogeneity

OSE could effectively discourage the white superiority complex which prevents cross-cultural pollination of the church and, by implication, multi-ethnicity. Understandably, in OSE's framework, as with the *omolúàbí* construct, the individuality of every person, whether young or old is acknowledged. No one is considered second-class or not good enough regardless of their caste. While it does not deny of racialization in the world, OSE echoes Galatians 3:28,[93] "There is no longer Jew or Greek, there is no longer slave or free, there is no longer male and female; for all . . . are one in Christ Jesus." The implication for Africans doing missions in the UK is that they would find it more favourable to introduce the sparks of newness they claim to have brought to Western Christianity. Western Christians would equally be able to confront and overcome their inherited and learned white-privilege mindset as they unreservedly embrace African Christians in their land. The relationship between the two groups would be different from the 1960s when the

---

93. I am aware that this verse, within the entire book of Galatians, has received a lot of attention from scholars, and therefore a host of interpretative angles exist. I have only attempted to find a contemporary application for the widely translated and used text. The work of Francois Tolmie is a good read on the various interpretations of Gal 3:28. See Tolmie, "Tendencies in the Interpretation."

Church of England, for instance, did poorly in welcoming members of the Commonwealth, as the Archbishop of Canterbury, Justin Welby, recollects:

> The Anglicans in the UK did not trust the newcomers, and when they came to church, they were not welcomed . . . we did not recognise that we belonged to one another . . . And so the Church of England lost the new life that they brought and that God was trying to offer us through them.[94]

Recognising the individuality of everyone would also mean that no culture in the church, including that of the church leader or majority group, considers itself more important than others. Neither would the African congregants nor their Western counterparts (where available) think of themselves as the sole custodians of God's revelations. Similarly, skin colour or cultural bias would cease to shape the face of leadership in the church. Instead, its make-up would genuinely reflect the acknowledgement of God's revelation to every culture and other contributions they can bring to the church to enhance growth. In the end, homogeneity would fizzle out at all levels and aspects of church-life and multi-ethnicity would take root.

7.5.2 Leveraging the Goodwill of *Omolúàbí*

Inú rere, as a fundamental attribute of *omolúàbí*, would constantly remind African diaspora Christians to keep loving relentlessly. The goodwill virtue would help ADCs remain magnanimous in reaching out to their Western hosts against the odds of perpetual racism that attempts to dissuade them. As African Christians in the UK sustain goodwill and loving and friendly attitudes towards their host community, the inequality that racism suggests would gradually give way. Hospitality "brings the host down to the stranger, and at the same time elevates the stranger to the level of the host."[95]

There is power in love, and the wedding of Prince Harry and Meghan Markle (a mixed-race American) in May 2018 is a testament to what love can achieve. In his address, Bishop Michael Curry, quoting Martin Luther King Jr., proclaimed: "We must discover the power of love, the redemptive power of love. And when we do that, we will make of this world a new world, for

---

94. Davies, "'We Failed '60s immigrants.'"
95. Kwiyani, *Multicultural Kingdom*, 139.

love is the only way."[96] The cleric added, "There is power in love. Don't underestimate it. Don't even over-sentimentalise it. There is power, power in love."[97]

ADCs can demonstrate kindness by caring for the homeless, drug addicts, widows, and the less privileged in society. With goodwill likely to thrive better where forgiveness rules, ADCs must persist in forgiving the racial discrimination of the West and continue to grow in the uncomfortable virtue of forgiveness. By so doing, ADCs' interactions with the host community would happen more deliberately and productively, leading to greater effectiveness in cross-cultural missions and church growth.

7.5.3 Paying Attention to Training

OSE does not underplay the role of ADC leaders' charisma and graces in experiencing church growth in the UK. However, it also calls for the importance of theological training (where lacking) and other relevant learning for these leaders. *Omolúàbís* do not merely rely on their charm to get work done but maximize their effectiveness by putting in the required work in their profession, demonstrating the virtues of *isé* and *akínkanjú*. Training is critical for ADC leaders because the West is notably scientifically oriented, unlike the more spiritually-conscious Africa. As such, any communication of the gospel message in the West must be rational enough. The more spiritually minded African leaders, then, have a challenge that will more than likely require conscious and continuous training and retraining to be relevant in the UK. The pastor's charisma or anointing may be a factor in an ADC's development, as the research data have indicated. Yet downplaying the place of skill and training in ministry will undo any ADC leader in Liverpool. Even if they are not keen on cross-cultural missions (which would be a disadvantage to their growth), ADC leaders would still need to find ways of communicating the gospel message understandably to the 2GMs in their congregations.

OSE's training accentuation would also imply that ADC leaders ensure their church members' deliberate, sustained discipleship and training. It would be paramount for ADC leaders to consciously model Christ's life to their church members so that, together, they will all look more like Christ daily. Establishing a learning environment that permits a systematic discipleship

---

96. Peters, "Bishop Michael Curry's."
97. Peters, "Bishop Michael Curry's."

process is also helpful. Such structured training will dissolve gaps in the knowledge and spiritual formation of the congregants. In the end, discrepancies in the faith-life and maturity of church members would collapse. One Christian would not be different in form from another, whether within the same congregation or across churches. Smoother relationships would also more likely result from a congregation that learns and grows together.

7.5.4 Dealing with Secularism

OSE can equally aid ADCs in addressing the widely spreading secularism in the UK and the West. The research findings have suggested that ADCs approach church growth and missions mainly from a spiritual angle. Again, this spiritual contribution to the UK is critical considering the region's extensive secularism. With OSE promoting the spiritual consciousness of the church, ADC can sustain the spiritual reawakening gift they have brought to the UK church and territory. As every congregation becomes more spiritually aware, the Holy Spirit's influence will extend to society, and secular thoughts and impacts will be drastically reduced. However, such spiritual contribution to the UK must proceed from a place of love rather than pride from ADCs considering their spiritual orientation by culture, as against the rationally inclined West. ADCs must be patient, gentle, and understanding in communicating their gift to their Western hosts, as *omolúàbí* is known for *ìwàpèlé* or *ìwàtútù* (gentleness). Love must wrap up their truth, not judgement or condescension, as Paul advises in Ephesians 4:15 about the believers' communication of truth.[98]

7.5.5 Addressing Accountability Concerns

The OSE would be responsive to the yearning for better accountability in ADCs. *Omolúàbí* demands truth, integrity, and humility, and these qualities facilitate accountability. As OSE insists on a working relationship with the Holy Spirit, it would provide ADC leaders with the avenue of drawing from the grace of "the Spirit of Truth" (John 16:13) and to demonstrate integrity in all their dealings. The *omolúàbí*'s humility quality in OSE would also make it easier for ADC leaders to establish structures around their lives and

---

98. "But speaking the truth in love, we must grow up in every way into him who is the head, into Christ." (Eph 4 :15)

ministries to check highhandedness and excesses. They would not continue to favour a centralized leadership style that aids highhandedness and lack of accountability in leadership. Congregants will be more trusting in their leaders, thus increasing their commitment to the church, even financially. In fact, the church's growth would be evident in other areas as well since checks and balances would exist to minimize corruption, distrust, laziness, and other forms of misconduct.

7.5.6 Managing Conflicts

OSE would also be suitable for reducing conflicts within ADCs as all engagements proceed with a rich knowledge of relationship dynamics. The leaders and the people would be mindful of and demonstrate *omolúàbí*'s dexterity in *òrò síso* as they relate. Interactions would proceed from the viewpoint of shared humanity, as intrinsic in the concepts of *àjobí* (blood relations) and *àjogbé* (co-residence). Thus, OSE's way of being the church would encourage commitment to collective good and the joint vision of the church. Rendered services would also receive acknowledgement and appreciation regardless of the culture, age group, or person that offers them. The church would operate as one big, loving family, creating an atmosphere of sincerity and love favouring peaceful co-existence, multi-ethnicity, and church growth.

Living by the Spirit would also see the congregation relate more lovingly, thereby reducing conflicts. As the people seek to maintain a sweet fellowship with the Holy Spirit, they will avoid strife, for it is antithetical to the Holy Spirit. In the end, the church will experience sustained and increased activities of the Spirit in the life of its members, leading them to be forgiving, kind, patient, joyful, peaceful, and self-controlled in their interactions with one another. Instead of quarrels, through the power of the Holy Spirit, all congregants will "Pursue peace with everyone and the holiness without which no one will see the Lord" (Heb 12:14 NRSV). Church leaders will also be able to draw from the grace of leadership that only the Spirit gives (1 Cor 12:28), guiding the people with more accuracy and minimising the chances for misunderstandings and conflicts.

7.6 Conclusion

In this chapter, I have developed an African ecclesiology, the OSE, to respond to the church growth issues identified by this study. The OSE is not only appropriate to the research population, but its comprehensive nature makes it equally beneficial to African congregations everywhere. OSE helps ADCs to Africanize Christianity so that they can properly contextualize it in their Western setting. In other words, it provides African Christians with a resource for doing church in more relatable ways instead of the notably foreign approach they have received from European missionaries. OSE equally advocates attention to other cultures to foster multi-ethnicity and collaboration. The contextualized ecclesiology specifically seeks the recognition of and harmony with the Holy Spirit, the building of relationships, emphasis on social ministry, excellent leadership, and holistic salvation. OSE is, indeed, a highly effective missional tool for ADCs in Liverpool, and a significant theological resource for the global church. By and large, the applications of the *omolúàbí* idea to the practice and doctrine of the church are quite extensive. The exercise done in this chapter is, at best, an introduction to the rich possibilities of the intersection of the *omolúàbí* concept and ecclesiology.

CHAPTER 8

Church Growth and the Dynamics of Race

8.1 Introduction

The research data has shown that the dynamics of race shape all aspects of life for the Black population in the UK. Yet ADCs must carry out cross-cultural missions, establish churches, and grow within this racialized context. The implications of racism, a creation of race, for Black people in the West and around the globe are very severe. Therefore, in this chapter, I explore how the adaptive challenge of racism affects ADCs' expansion in the UK. The remaining discussions are attempts to grasp the depth of racialization of the research context, where ADCs are making efforts to thrive. The conversation proceeds by looking back into history, contemplating the unnecessary creation of race. This discourse spreads out into the examination of race as a social construction. Then, I differentiate race from ethnicity and spotlight the historical events of slavery and racial riots in the UK, focusing on Liverpool.

8.2 How Racism Hampers ADCs' Growth in Liverpool

In discussing the manners of expression and impacts of racism on ADCs' growth in Liverpool, I have approached the conversation from sociologist Eduardo Bonilla-Silva's perspective on racism. Bonilla-Silva identifies three components of racism. He posits that, conceptually, racism could exist at the level of *beliefs* (usually false) about another race. When these wrong beliefs escalate, they form *attitudes*. Prejudicial attitudes feed into the third dimension of racism, *discriminatory actions*.[1]

At least two of the three components of racism are evident in psychologist and educationist Derald Sue's definition of racism. Sue sees racism as "attitude, action, or institutional structure or any social policy that subordinates persons or groups because of their color."[2] A consideration of Bonilla-Silva's view and Sue's definition of racism gives rise to a detailed description of racism in this dissertation. I have considered racism in this writing as consciously and unconsciously cultivated attitudes or actions undergirded by false beliefs, assumptions, misconceptions, stereotypes, and prejudices about other people or cultures, leading to their subordination, discrimination, vilification, and marginalization.

Having defined racism, I now begin exploring how the phenomenon of racism impacts the growth of the research population. Indeed, recalling one participant's observation, racial offence to one congregant is an attack on the entire ADC congregation, and with implications for its growth. In accord with the three levels or components of racism, I have examined, first, the beliefs or mindset of Europeans, in general, about Africans and how this hinders the missional endeavour of ADCs in Liverpool. Second, I consider the other two aspects of racism, attitudes and actions, of white British hosts towards Black immigrants and how these behaviours and habits influence the growth of ADCs in Liverpool.

8.2.1 The Mindset Barrier

From the first contact of Portuguese explorers with Africans in 1444, whom they abducted for enslavement in Europe, to the nineteenth-century era of European missionaries, European Christians have disdained African cultures and religion.[3] After all, Europeans have, since the fifteenth century, held wrong assumptions and biases about Africans.[4] In the centuries that followed (especially the sixteenth and seventeenth), when they suddenly encountered

---

1. Bonilla-Silva, *White Supremacy and Racism*, 22.
2. Sue, *Overcoming Our Racism*, 31.
3. Kwiyani, *Black Light*.
4. White, "History of Blacks."

Black people on their territorial expansion voyages, their reaction was the peddling of myths resulting in defamation, demonization, and contempt for Black people.[5] Europeans formulated ugly ideas about Africans more consistently during those two centuries.[6] For instance, one Professor of History, Winthrop Jordan, who wrote about the unexpected contact of Europeans with Africans in West Africa and Congo, observes:

> One of the fairest-skinned nations suddenly came face to face with one of the darkest people on earth and at a time when the accepted standard of beauty was a fair complexion of rose and white . . . [certainly, Africans] not only failed to fit this ideal but seemed the very picture of perverse negation.[7]

There was also the popular perception about Africans that enjoyed false scientific backings. Europeans held that Africans were in the late stages of the line of evolution and therefore primitive; they lacked intellect and were inferior.[8] The demeaning perception of Europeans about Africans abound in many of their philosophers' quotes.[9] Whether one reads Georg Hegel's (1770–1831) reference to Black Africans as a "race of children who remain immersed in their state of uninterested naïveté" or Emmanuel Kant's (1724–1804) comment that Africans lack talents and possess a "religion of fetishes,"[10] the inferior perspective about Africans is clear.

These dehumanising thoughts about Africans became the foundations upon which nineteenth century European missionaries considered African traditions "pagan, heathen, savage, primitive and barbaric."[11] Kwiyani insists that the Europeans never thought of Africans as having a religion or the idea of God.[12] He illustrates his conviction by retelling the story of a conversation that occurred between the Swiss-German biographer Emil Ludwig (1881–1948) and the South African-born British missionary Edwin Smith

---

5. White, "History of Blacks."
6. Fryer, *Staying Power*, 135.
7. Jordan, *White over Black*, 6, 9.
8. White, " History of Blacks."
9. Kwiyani, *Black Light*.
10. Kwiyani, *Black Light*.
11. Mugambi, *Christianity and African Culture*, 8.
12. Kwiyani, *Black Light*.

(1876–1957). According to Kwiyani, Ludwig was shocked as he listened to Smith discuss his efforts at evangelising Africans and how Africans were already sure of the reality of God. Ludwig's condescension was evident when he wondered aloud how "savages" (referring to Africans) could grasp the "philosophical concept" of God.[13]

It was generally more convenient for Europeans to sustain the belief that Africans were not humans.[14] After all, this ideology was the justification for the transatlantic slave trade that greatly benefitted Europe.[15] Nonetheless, with the advocacy against the slave trade gaining ground and Protestant missions evolving in the nineteenth century, the abduction and slavery of Africans eventually came to an end.[16] Europeans had to reconsider and accept the humanness and religions of Africans. Sadly, Africa's religious heritage would never be good enough for the West as they immediately tagged it primitive and pagan.[17]

A superiority mindset persists in shaping the interactions of Europeans with Black people or other non-white races around the world. Indeed, many European Christians still sustain the mindset that mission should proceed from "people in positions of power or privilege, or from the expansive dynamism of a superior civilization."[18] It is then understandable, besides other factors, why there were close to no white faces among the congregations involved in this research. Many may just not be able to bring themselves to sit under the leadership of a Black person. Sadly, a white supremacy mindset makes the cross-cultural missional activities of Africans in the West more difficult. The way forward for successful missions would be for the West to jettison any form of white supremacy ideas and remember that all men represent God's image (Gen 1:26). Moreover, every culture, race, or tongue is welcome in God's presence (Rev 7:9).

---

13. Kwiyani, *Black Light*.

14. Kwiyani, *Black Light*.

15. I have expanded on the subject of slavery later in this chapter under the conversation titled Racism and Slavery.

16. Kwiyani, *Black Light*.

17. Kwiyani, *Black Light*.

18. Escobar, *Time of Mission*, 17.

8.2.2 Attitudes and Actions Speak Louder

Research findings have revealed that an implicit white supremacy mindset is not the only way racism impedes the growth of ADCs and their missional engagements in Liverpool. Racism equally presents itself in discriminatory attitudes and actions against Black people and these are not without severe implications for ADCs' sustenance and thriving. In this section, under three categories, I discuss the UK's unfriendly attitudes and practices towards its Black population.

8.2.2.1 Harsh Immigration Policies

This study has traced the critical role of migration in spreading Christianity across different world regions (Europe inclusive) and in various eras. African Christianity in the UK could not have been possible in the first place without migrating Africans and their religions. Therefore, African migration to the UK must continue for the sustained existence and expansion of ADCs in the environment. Besides, most ADCs are still struggling to win their Western hosts over, so they remain significantly dependent on immigration flow. Hence, governmental policies that constrain the movement of Black people into the UK will continue to impact the growth of ADCs dramatically.

Meanwhile, racism still holds a firm grip on the West with the evolution of structures abetting racist mindsets. Indeed, those who wield power and design systems are often the perpetrators of individual acts of racism.[19] For example, following the world wars, when there was no longer a need for the services of Black soldiers, hostile government policies have risen and multiplied (with increasing strictness) to check the increasing Black presence in the UK.[20] These laws, which limit the immigration of Africans to the UK, ultimately affect ADCs' growth. Therefore, I have briefly explored their introductions in the following conversation.

8.2.2.1.1 Post-war Legislations

Once the Second World War was over in 1945, the immediate need to rebuild the British economy was a foremost concern, but addressing this pressing

---

19. Emerson, " Persistent Problem," 12–13.
20. White, "History of Blacks."

situation would require the support of immigrant labour in large numbers.[21] Hence, by 1949, the Royal Commission on Population had announced that "immigrants from 'good stock'[22] would be welcomed without 'reserve.'"[23] This call opened the door to Black immigrants who had realized the urgent requirement for labour in Britain, especially in the transport industry and the newly established National Health Service.[24] Unfortunately, Britain was already on a quick journey of adapting to racism from the end of the First World War to the second.[25] By the 1950s, debates had flooded the media and parliament about the necessity to check Black people's immigration, a development that became the excuse for social ills (housing deficit, crime, and unemployment) in the land.[26]

The general assumption by the British government was that fewer Black immigrants in the land would imply easier integration into the English lifestyle and a reduction of racial conflict.[27] Despite a lack of concrete evidence to justify the hypothesis, the validation of racial prejudice still progressed through direct state intervention in the formulation of legislation – strict policies limiting the influx of Black people.[28] These immigration laws that surfaced between 1945 and 1968 meant that Britain had eventually "institutionalised, legitimised, and nationalised" racism.[29]

The British Nationality Act of 1948 not only granted independence to India, but also created a distinction between British subjects. It differentiated UK citizens from its colonies and Commonwealth countries and conferred legal rights of entry, settlement, and work on British subjects in the

---

21. Fryer, *Staying Power*, 373.

22. Whatever "good stock" meant and however it was determined is better left to imaginations even though it appears to suggest a sort of derogatory racial classification.

23. National Archives, "Postwar Immigration."

24. BBC, "Reconstructing Britain."

25. Fryer, *Staying Power*, 361.

26. Blaming all societal problems on Black people's immigration became even more pronounced in the 1960s and 1970s with the fall of traditional industries, when permanent employment was no longer certain. See more in Mustad, Huseby, and Lambine-Christensen, "Post-War Immigration." See also Solomos, *Race and Racism*, 53–54.

27. Solomos, 81.

28. Solomos, 53.

29. Fryer, *Staying Power*, 387.

two latter categories.[30] However, this discrimination was just beginning and would become even more pronounced with the introduction of subsequent legislation. By 1962, the first Commonwealth Immigration Bill emerged to transform Britain's immigration narrative forever. This Commonwealth Immigrants Act conferred the inferior status of *immigrants* on the Black population in Britain and limited the entry of Commonwealth citizens to individuals with employment permits.[31]

Britain's immigration restrictions only grew tighter by the year, with additional measures passed in 1968 and 1971.[32] The 1968 Commonwealth Immigration Act implied that Britain disclaimed some of its citizens because of their skin colour (for instance, Kenyan Asians), who then had their automatic entry rights to Britain removed by the legislation, except for those born in Britain or with British parents or grandparents.[33] However, the authentication of the discrimination against Black people was not complete until the enactment of the 1971 Immigration Act in 1973. This measure restricted entry rights to "those who, under a kind of contract-labour system, were allowed to come to do a specific job for a limited period: no longer than 12 months in the first instance."[34] Further checks came on the admittance of dependants, coupled with the extended power of police and immigration control to arrest, without a warrant, suspected illegal immigrants. Moreover, immigrant workers could be deported at the home secretary's discretion, if the action contributed to the public good.[35]

All the same, since the 1960s, Britain has also been attempting to combat racism legislatively.[36] For instance, various policies have evolved to serve several purposes, from extensively defining racial discrimination to placing demands on authorities to promote racial equality.[37] Such legislation includes

---

30. Solomos, *Race and Racism*, 51. For further details on the 1948 Nationality Act and its implications see Bevan, *Development of British Immigration*, 112–113; Evans, *Immigration Law*, 59–62.
31. Fryer, *Staying Power*, 387–388.
32. Mustad, Huseby, and Lambine-Christensen, "Post-War Immigration."
33. BBC, "Post-war British Laws."
34. Fryer, *Staying Power*, 391.
35. Fryer, 391.
36. Whether the measures have been productive with the persistent pervasiveness of racism in the UK remains an issue for contemplation.
37. BBC, "Migration's Effect."

the Race Relations Acts of 1965, 1967, 1968, and 1976, the Human Rights Act of 1998, and the Race Relations (Amendment) Act of 2000.[38] The 1976 Act notably brought about organizations like the Commission for Racial Equality, established to investigate race-related complaints, ensure racial equality in practice, and improve race relations.[39] Despite these steps, the plague of racism is unrelenting in British societies, as in the majority of the West.

8.2.2.2 Discrimination in Major Societal Sectors

Britain desperately needed all the labour force it could get to rebuild its ruins from the wars. So by 1948 the famous *Empire Windrush* generation of the Black population that significantly boosted Black presence in Britain appeared.[40] However, by this time, colour bar racism was already taking root in response to the increasing Black population.[41] This racism dimension was essentially a system for "*charging the oppressed* [the Blacks] *for the crimes, whether actual or potential of the oppressor* [the whites]."[42] A few sectors where colour bar racism retains its massive impact on the life of Black people in the UK, and thus, on ADCs' development, are highlighted below.

8.2.2.2.1 Employment

The demobilization of servicemen had reached an excess of two million by March 1919 and up to four million by December of that year. The development was particularly challenging for Black veterans who became stuck and helpless in Britain, unemployed, and with dim hopes of securing other employment due to colour bar racism.[43] It was only in the early 1940s when Britain needed them for the Second World War that Black workers could

---

38. Solomos, *Race and Racism*, 78–79; Messina, " Impacts of Post-WWII Migration," 259–285.

39. Crowther, *Oxford Guide to British*, 440.

40. In many standard texts of the history of race relations in Britain, the epochal event of the arrival of the *SS Empire Windrush* ship that docked at Tilbury with 492 Caribbean immigrants is considered the escalation of the immigration of Black people into Britain and the symbol of race problems. For more on this discourse, see Lunn, " British State and Immigration." See also Kushner, *Battle of Britishness*.

41. Fryer, *Staying Power*, 361. About 8,000 Black people inhabited Liverpool by 1948. Unfortunately, only about 40 percent of these people had jobs and these were either seafaring or shore-related employment. Others were critically unemployed, and this was all due to the colour bar racism. See more in Fryer, *Staying Power*, 373.

42. Emphasis in original text. See Memmi, *Racism*, 139.

43. Miles, "When Race Riots Marred."

secure jobs in British factories. Even then, the unwillingness and resistance from white employers and co-employees were evident.[44] More than a few white workers turned down working with Black people. Many also wanted them sacked.[45]

Britain's Black community found the employment market shut against it. In fact, until 1968, discriminatory public advertisements were not uncommon, with "'no coloureds' instructions to state and private employment agencies."[46] Black people were also often restricted to jobs with slim to no chance of promotion, where they could secure jobs.[47] They "tend[ed] to be the last hired and the first fired, as well as being underrepresented in white-collar and skilled jobs."[48]

Career or employment marginalization of Black people persists in the UK as it was in the nineteenth century when local employers created technical means of discriminating against the Black population in Liverpool and the UK at large.[49] The Royal Society of Chemistry (RSC), for instance, in March 2022 published a report attesting to the reality of racism in the academy and industry of chemical sciences in the UK. The publication, which emerged from qualitative research, paints a sharp picture of "how pervasive racial and ethnic inequalities are within the chemical sciences community, how hard this is to challenge, and the way exclusion and marginalization are to a large extent normalized for many Black chemists and others from minoritized ethnic backgrounds."[50]

Robert Mokaya's journey in the academy is one of many that affirms RSC's findings. Mokaya is the only Black chemistry professor of the 575 in the UK. He shares with BBC Science correspondent Pallab Ghosh how against all odds, he has reached the position of pro-vice-chancellor at Nottingham University. Despite this feat, Mokaya reveals that in his fifteen years of being a professor at the university, none of his research grant applications has ever received approval from Britain's major chemistry funding body (now referred

---

44. Fryer, *Staying Power*.
45. Miles, "When Race Riots Marred."
46. Brown, "'Same Difference,'" 47–48.
47. Zack-Williams, "African Diaspora Conditioning," 537.
48. Cousins et al., *Merseyside in Crisis*, 12.
49. Torkington, *Racial Politics of Health*, 13.
50. Royal Society of Chemistry, "Missing Elements," 1–59.

to as the UK Research and Innovation agency).[51] Jazmin Scarlett, a Black doctoral student, in 2021 shared with Ghosh how she had received over thirty rejections for a postdoctoral research position while her white colleagues were getting hired.[52]

Data released in 2020 by the UK Office for National Statistics also show that between 2016 and 2018, while the median total wealth for the white British population was £314,000, that of the Black African group was £34,000.[53] In all, racial discrimination against Black people in the employment sector cannot but continue to tell on the fortunes of ADCs as their membership remains homogenous primarily along racial lines. One can easily imagine a sustained weakness in the financial capacity of the African congregations as a race-conscious employment market continues to screen the adherents to low-rate jobs. With low-income employment comes the likely need for multiple jobs. This affects availability and commitment in the church, since some jobs require physical presence even on Sundays or other worship days. In the end, ADCs' growth is affected. As one participant reflected, "People want to serve God, but they are caught between family responsibilities, workload, financial burden, and God."

8.2.2.2.2 Education

Since the evil of colour bar racism evolved in British society, the UK's education system has not been free of its influence either. For instance, The League of Coloured Peoples, a prominent Black community civil-rights organization of the 1930s and 1940s, once published a booklet containing a survey report of the textbooks of the times.[54] The report revealed that "the subject of Coloured people [the Black population] is virtually disregarded in most of the History books."[55] Sociologist Kenneth Little similarly noticed that the widespread knowledge and culture of the day were:

---

51. Ghosh, "Royal Society of Chemistry."
52. Ghosh, "Black Scientists Say."
53. Office for National Statistics, "Household Wealth by Ethnicity."
54. A London-based private doctor of Jamaican origin, Harold Moody, established The League of Coloured Peoples in 1931. The organization made representations to several government agencies in its days on behalf of Black people in Britain. See more in The Open University, "League of Coloured Peoples."
55. League of Coloured Peoples, *Race Relations*, 10.

pseudo-anthropological, and concern the "mental inferiority" of Coloured People; the biological "ill-effects" of racial crossing and a variety of other superstitions . . . It is in this cultural "atmosphere" that most children in English society grow up. It is not surprising, therefore, that many of them absorb prejudicial ideas and notions concerning Coloured People.[56]

In 1985, a report of the Select Committee on Race Relations and Immigrations that enquired into the education of children from ethnic minority groups condemned Liverpool's educational system for letting Black children down both in and outside school. Following its findings, the committee declared: "Liverpool . . . left us with a profound sense of uneasiness."[57] The implication of the unsupportive educational system for Black children was that they were less skilled to take advantage of opportunities provided by computing, robotics, and employment in other new industries springing up at the time.[58]

Unfortunately, the lack of support for Black school children in the UK continues. For instance, the 2022 RSC's report on racial and ethnic inequalities in chemical science notes that some Black students had mentioned that "they had noticed lecturers being reluctant to push Black students to succeed."[59] One of the student's comments further exposes the systemic racism in the UK education sector: "There is definitely a double glass ceiling if you are Black and a woman or a girl. You get told to be quiet, speak more softly. That starts early in school too."[60]

Without adequate support to learn and acquire the right skills, the UK education system is already sealing the fate of Black students in low-income jobs apart from the denial of opportunities to optimally explore their potential. ADCs suffer the hit financially. Among the many implications is that they cannot carry out significant charity works even if they want to do so. Plus, sustaining daily church administration is challenging. Indeed, as one participant noted, "When a church doesn't have the financial capacity, a church

---

56. Little, "Some Aspects," 51.
57. Swann, *Education for All*, 735.
58. Zack-Williams, "African Diaspora Conditioning," 538.
59. Royal Society of Chemistry, "Missing Elements," 30.
60. Royal Society of Chemistry, 30.

can fold up. To run a church is capital intensive. And when you don't have that financial capacity, unconsciously, you will just discover that the church is running down."

8.2.2.2.3 Housing

In housing, post-war implications of colour bar racism include accommodation refusal, service decline in cafes, and rejection of dancehall admittance for Black people.[61] Landlords of both public and private shelters also turned down property rentals to the Black community.[62] The refusals and hostility were sometimes indirect and expressed in negative body language of shrugs and nods, besides whispers and comments in public places, buses, and streets.[63] In other cases, colour bar racism also meant landlords "not showing all the available units [to Black home-seekers], steering minorities and Whites into certain neighbourhoods, quoting higher rents or prices to minority applicants, or not advertising units at all."[64] This form of racism, Bonilla-Silva observes, seems to mirror the housing conditions of Black people in 1911.[65] Then, over 50 percent of the approximately three thousand Blacks population who resided at the port, spread over the central and southern slums in the city. Lodgings were often in poor condition and more than one hundred years old.[66]

Sadly, in 2021, the UK Commission on Race and Ethnic Disparities still reported that "Black ethnic groups were . . . disproportionately likely to live in the most deprived neighbourhoods" and "people in the most deprived neighbourhoods tend to be disadvantaged across multiple aspects of life."[67] Moreover, according to the data released by the UK government in 2020, Black Africans and Arab ethnic groups had the lowest homeownership rates in the country with 20 and 17 percent, respectively, compared with their white

---

61. Brown, "'Same Difference,'" 48.
62. Brown, 48.
63. Little, "Colour Prejudice in Britain," 28.
64. Bonilla-Silva, *Racism without Racists*, 3.
65. Bonilla-Silva, 3.
66. Law, *History of Race*, 23.
67. Commission on Race and Ethnic Disparities, "Commission on Race," 40–41.

British counterparts at 68 percent.[68] Understandably, "Race determines . . . economic prospects"[69] as it mediates all spheres of life.

Having a permanent building where regular meetings can be held remains a significant factor in attracting people to church in the UK, as the research findings have suggested. One participant added that "people would be more trusting" of a pastor and the congregation with a permanent location. Yet, where racism continues unabated in the property market, ADCs can only have their church growth challenges multiplied. It is harder to have a stable membership when the church constantly changes its location owning to racial discrimination in the housing sector. A participant rightly concludes as he speaks about church growth in his context that the inability to secure a church property or regular place of worship only "brings limits, and it scatters the people."

8.2.2.3 The Culpability of the Church

The church is not free from the perpetuation of racism, whether in subtle forms of "racial micro-aggression" or more conspicuous verbal and non-verbal expressions.[70] The indictment of the British church is incredibly vivid in a social media post by Welby in 2020. The clergyman observes that "The racism that [Black] people in this country [UK] experience is horrifying. The church has failed here and still does, and it's clear what Jesus commands us to do: repent and take action."[71] Similarly, the Equality, Diversity and Inclusion Committee (EDI) of the Methodist Church in the UK reported in 2017 that while "work has been undertaken over the past fifty years to remove it [racism] from the life of the Methodist Church, it is with a deep sense of sorrow and shame that it is still evident today."[72]

The racial discrimination directed towards Black Christians from British mainline churches through unfriendly reception was a primary rationale for instituting African (including Afro-Caribbean) diaspora congregations

---

68. UK Government, "Home Ownership."
69. Lopez, *Social Construction of Race*, 965.
70. Lindsay, *We Need to Talk*, xxv.
71. Archbishop of Canterbury (Justin Welby): "The racism that people in this country experience is horrifying. The Church has failed here, and still does, and it's clear what Jesus commands us to do: repent and take action." Twitter, 8 June 2020.
72. Poxon, *Unfinished Agenda - Racial Justice*, 2.

in the latter half of the twentieth century in the UK.[73] Elizabeth Henry, the national adviser for the Committee for Minority Ethnic Anglican Concerns (CMEAC), speaking about the hostility towards Black Christians notes that the action resulted in "the loss of not just one generation of churchgoers, but subsequent generations," especially in the Church of England.[74] She adds that African congregations, on the other hand, have evolved to be "the strongest in the country."[75]

An historical hindsight of the era and horror of the transatlantic slave trade[76] similarly exposes the strong bond between racism and the British church. The passive and active involvement of the church was glaring within a trading system that prevented the clergy from liberating enslaved Black people. At the same time, the bishops and abbots could possess slaves for ministry endeavours.[77] On top of that, some Church of England clergy held that enslaved people were so savage that the possibility of their conversion was remote.[78] By implication, the British church became silent spectators, assenting to the perpetuation of racism by enslavement.

Racism through slavery may sometimes appear as belonging to the distant past. Yet the evil remains a relic that informs the structure of the present world's heavily racialized societies.[79] Racism prevails as a perennial challenge undermining the relationship between ADCs and their white hosts. The nature of the death of the Black man George Floyd in Minneapolis is a depictive image of the indignities, discrimination, and unattractive treatment still accorded Black people in most Western societies today.[80] ADCs are, indeed, struggling to breathe under the knees of white supremacy and racial discrimination in their attempts to evangelize their Western hosts.

---

73. Haar, *Halfway to Paradise*, 3.
74. See Davies, "'We Failed '60s immigrants.'"
75. Davies, "'We Failed '60s immigrants.'"
76. I have expanded on the subject of racism and slavery later in this chapter.
77. Hood, *Begrimed and Black*, 118.
78. Dayfoot, *Shaping of the West Indian*, 88.
79. Andrews, *New Age of Empire*, 57.
80. George Floyd died in May 2020 in the hands of Derek Chauvin, a White American police officer, who knelt on his neck for over eight minutes in an excessive show of force. A short video clip is available at "George Floyd: Video Shows Minneapolis Police Officer Kneeling on Neck of Black Man who Died | ABC7," https://www.youtube.com/watch?v=CcsIU9ozt6I&bpctr=1601384175.

The British church must do better in challenging this anomaly. As with the Methodist Conference president, Barbara Glasson, an honest evaluation is a wise and helpful start-point for the British church. Glasson had reflected on the Methodist church's abetment of racism and apologized:

> I am sorry. Sorry for being silent when we [the Methodist church] should have spoken out against the everyday injustices that affect BAME communities. I am sorry that, despite our efforts, we have not done enough for those who feel excluded and we need to do better . . . I am sorry when we have not listened carefully enough and not challenged the assumptions of white privilege and bias.[81]

The UK church would do well with a "serious heart-searching [and the discarding of] superficial platitudes and excuses in accommodating the whole of humanity."[82] The church must publicly and constantly call out the sin of racism in society more frequently and boldly as consistent with the *akínkanjú* quality of an *omolúàbí* in the OSE framework. Perhaps with this extra effort from the church, the war against racism in the UK would be won more quickly, giving way to greater productivity in cross-cultural missions. The result would be the strengthening of the British church with the growth of ADCs.

8.3 Reflecting on the Awkward Idea of Race

Since the seventeenth century, when people began to talk about race as a means for social classification and a type of human identity, societal structures and the understanding of humanity have not been the same.[83] Indeed, the West has continued to connect physical features and variations with human identity and has "been socialised to an ideology about the meaning of these differences based on a notion of heredity and permanence that was unknown in the ancient world and in the Middle Ages."[84] Yet before its modern application to the variation in people's physical qualities or hereditary characteristics,

---

81. Glasson, "Personal Message."
82. Lynn Green, "George Floyd - 'I can't Breathe.'"
83. Smedley, "'Race' and the Construction," 1.
84. Smedley, 4.

race described people with common ties, kinship, breed, or type.[85] Moreover, most writers explained the biological differences in people as rising from environmental factors like the intensity of the sun, which resulted in the dark skin of some persons.[86]

Though Europeans seldom used the terms *race*, *White*, and *slave* in the 1500s, race began to attract social meanings in the seventeenth century as European Enlightenment philosophers[87] developed new ideas about the world, thoughts grounded in secular reasoning, rationality, and science rather than religious understandings.[88] These fresh concepts about the world that thrived into the eighteenth century also applied to human beings. It placed them into hierarchies where White people occupy the topmost level and are supposedly more intelligent and human than other people groups.[89] Unfortunately, this socially constructed racial classification system has remained a mechanism for differentiating various human groups based on their biological variations.[90] As such, the world now has Black, White, "yellow" and other human groups.

8.3.1 Race as a Social Creation

That race is a social construction simply implies that it is whatever people deem it to be. Race is a human invention. While some divergence may still exist in contemplating race either as a social construct or real biological distinctions in people, sociologist Audrey Smedley opines that viewing race as a cultural and social invention is increasingly gaining credence among scholars in various fields.[91] It is becoming harder to correlate race to any fundamental biological difference in people. Even research indicates that the common notion of five races – African, European, Asian, Oceania, and

---

85. Roediger, "Historical Foundations of Race."

86. Smedley, "'Race' and the Construction," 3.

87. The Enlightenment was a European intellectual movement of the seventeenth and eighteenth centuries in which ideas concerning God, reason, nature, and humanity were synthesized into a worldview that gained wide assent in the West and that instigated revolutionary developments in art, philosophy, and politics. Some of the major figures are Jean-Jacques Rousseau (Voltaire), François-Marie Arouet, Adam Smith, Denis Diderot, Charles-Louis de Secondat (Montesquieu), and Immanuel Kant. See more in Duignan, "Enlightenment," in *Encyclopedia Britannica*.

88. Roediger, "Historical Foundations of Race."

89. Roediger, "Historical Foundations of Race."

90. Hearn, "Color-Blind Racism," 275.

91. Smedley, "'Race' and the Construction," 1.

Native American – is more reflective of human distribution across the continents than any actual biological attribute of people.[92] Of the various reasons to imagine race as a social construct instead of genetic variance in people, I find the following explanations advanced in *Sociology: Understanding and Changing the Social World*, an online textbook published by the University of Minnesota, very illuminating.[93]

8.3.1.1 Vague Classification Criteria

The first reason to suggest race as a social construction rather than biological distinctions in humans is that racial categorization measures appear unclear, inconsistent, and unjustifiable.[94] While it is true that many people differ in physical traits (for instance, skin tone, hair colour, or height), which usually form the basis for racial classes, sociologists, biologists, and anthropologists question the essence of this classification mechanism and hence, the biological idea of race.[95] Indeed, the arbitrariness and fluidity of the racial system are easily noticeable, for instance, in the case of non-Anglo-Saxons: Italians, Irish, and Jews, who, over one hundred years ago, did not belong to the white race but are now considered white.[96] Or in 1821 when Mexicans gained their independence as a nation, they did not constitute a race as they have emerged today.[97]

Another phenomenon that reflects the plasticity and blurriness of racial categorization is interracial marriage, where one parent is Black and the other White, as in the genealogy of Meghan Markle, Duchess of Sussex. Society may indeed be quick to classify a child from this union as either Black British or African American. Yet one cannot but wonder what logic is behind this categorization, knowing that such a person could comfortably claim either of parent's ancestry. Indeed, the child is genealogically as Black as they are

---

92. Chou, "How Science and Genetics."

93. This material is adapted from a work produced and distributed under a Creative Commons license (CC BY-NC-SA) in 2010 by a publisher who has requested that they and the original author not receive attribution. It is produced and made available by the University of Minnesota Libraries Publishing through the eLearning Support Initiative. Refer to University of Minnesota, "Meaning of Race and Ethnicity."

94. University of Minnesota, "Meaning of Race and Ethnicity."

95. Yang and Koshy, "'Becoming White Thesis' Revisited," 1, 4.

96. Yang and Koshy, 4.

97. Lopez, *Social Construction of Race*, 971.

White according to the *one-drop* or *hypodescent* rule. Both concepts imply that "anyone with a known Black ancestor is considered Black."[98] In other words, "one drop of Black blood makes a person Black."[99]

8.3.1.2 More Intra-Racial Variations than Inter-Racial

Second, race is a social construct because, within a racial class, there usually are more physical distinctions than between races.[100] For instance, within the so-called White race are lighter-skinned northern Europeans, and darker-skinned Eastern Europeans. One can also notice eye colour and hair length variation within this race. The reality is that, in today's world, where interracial marriages are increasingly common, physical attributes that have served as the basis for classifying people into races are fast disappearing, if they ever existed at all.

8.3.1.3 Human Genetic Similarity

The third explanation for the social construction of race comes from genetics. Research by the National Human Genome Research Institute (NIH) has revealed that "All human beings are 99.9 percent identical in their genetic makeup."[101] The implication is that people of different races are 99.9 percent more alike than they vary. Additionally, the physical differences that account for racial categories are only traceable to 0.1 percent of human genetic composition. Even if people differ in the visible qualities connected to race, modern evolutionary theory suggests that all humans have a shared ancestry. More specifically, "Modern humans originated in Africa within the past 200,000 years and evolved from their most likely recent common ancestor, *Homo erectus*, which means 'upright man' in Latin."[102]

8.3.1.4 Relational Existence

In addition to the explanations available in *Sociology: Understanding and Changing the Social World*, race is a human invention as opposed to a natural

---

98. Hypodescent is a more formal sociological construct of the one-drop rule. See more in Hickman, " Devil and the One Drop," 4.

99. Hickman, 4.

100. University of Minnesota, " Meaning of Race and Ethnicity."

101. National Human Genome Research Institute, "Genetics Vs. Genomics."

102. Wilgar, "Evolution of Modern Humans."

distinction in people because "races are relationally constructed . . . they make sense only in relationship to other racial categories."[103] For instance, there is the so-called Black race because of the creation of a White race. In other words, without the stereotyping of Black people as inferior humans, the White race could not have existed as superior people at the top of the racial hierarchy. So, a bid to describe discriminated against, colonized, and enslaved Black people became an attempt to define the oppressors and subjugators. In essence, imagining the independent existence of one race without the others is simply fruitless. Therefore, races are only meaningful in relation to other racial classes. Again, race is a social invention. Racial stratification is essentially a superficial natural distinction and not an actual genetic variance in humans. In fact, psychologically, it is a concept that springs from fear and ignorance about *the other*.[104]

8.3.2 Differentiating Race and Ethnicity

With the lingering contention about the basis of race (as a social construction or natural variance in people) and its mediation in all spheres of life,[105] conversations about race cannot but present some complexities. So, in navigating this hurdle, an alternative concept that appears less problematic in contemplating human diversity has developed in the literature: ethnicity. Ethnicity refers to "the shared social, cultural, and historical experiences, stemming from common national or regional backgrounds, that make subgroups of a population different from one another."[106]

From the above description, ethnicity tries to avoid the idea of the biological distinctions in humans that race suggests. Instead, it emphasizes and maintains cultural boundaries rather than implying arbitrary innate differences between people.[107] Ethnicity is "the outcome of *the articulation of cultural distinctiveness in situations of political and/or economic competition.*"[108] However, despite the considerable significance attached to ethnicity and

---

103. Lopez, *Social Construction of Race*, 971.
104. Fryer, *Staying Power*, 135.
105. Lopez, *Social Construction of Race*, 965.
106. University of Minnesota, " Meaning of Race and Ethnicity."
107. Mason, *Race and Ethnicity*, 12–13.
108. Emphasis in the original text. Ballard, "Race, Ethnicity and Culture," 28.

ethnic identities, the term, as with race, is also a social creation. Other scholars have made this observation as well.[109]

8.3.3 Racism and Slavery

Considering the relentlessly rising racial biases and prejudice among Europeans since the 1500s, it was only a matter of time before the dual problems of racism and slavery would emerge.[110] The connection between racism and slavery is so inextricable that the two phenomena played out as cause and effect.[111] On the one hand, the precursor of racial mythologies served as foundations for validating the superiority-inferiority relationship within the colonial empire.[112] On the other hand, military prowess, and the realization of administrative control over the colonized, coupled with technological advancements, reverberated in Europe as false notions and stereotypes about other races, aiding the supposed superiority of the White race.[113]

Europeans soon developed economic justification for their prejudice as much profit came from the colonial endeavour that was actively progressing through slave-trade in the seventeenth century.[114] The financial excuse and benefit of slavery to its perpetrators immediately led to the formulation of a rational and consistent ideology of European racism.[115] This racism quickly gained popularity in the seventeenth century as an oral tradition and ideology of a class of slave merchants and sugar planters from Barbados who controlled

---

109. See for instance University of Minnesota, " Meaning of Race and Ethnicity"; Ballard, "Race, Ethnicity and Culture."

110. White, " History of Blacks in Britain."

111. Jordan, *White over Black*, 80.

112. In the Nigerian colony, for instance, Professor of African Studies and Political Science James Coleman observes how the blossoming of imperial rule and colonial administration rested upon the conviction of White supremacy and the idea of Africans' inferiority based on white people's exaggeration of the faults of learned Africans. See Coleman, *Nigeria: Background to Nationalism*, 152.

113. May and Cohen, " Interaction between Race," 112.

114. Of course, there are additional justifications for racial prejudice and racism that found expression in slavery. Such is the nature of religious and pseudo-scientific explanations. For further details, see Rogers and Bowman, "History: The Construction."

115. Rogers and Bowman, "History: The Construction."

the English Caribbean colonies.[116] By the eighteenth century, print media was actively spreading European racism.[117]

In the same era (the eighteenth century), Britain had become one of the most prosperous slave trading nations in Europe. As a front-liner slave transporter, Britain witnessed the great affluence of its seaports at this time. For instance, about £210 million (adjusted for inflation) worth of tobacco, sugar, and cotton cargo in 175 ships docked at British ports in July 1757 alone.[118] The enormous profit enjoyed by Liverpool, one of the seaports and the context of this study, is well captured by British historian Ramsay Muir, as he asserts how the slave-trade

> had flooded Liverpool with wealth, which invigorated every industry, provided the capital for docks, enriched and employed the mills of Lancashire, and afforded the means for opening out new and ever new lines of trade. Beyond a doubt it was the slave trade which raised Liverpool from a struggling port to be one of the richest and most prosperous trading centres of the world.[119]

Following the popularization of racism in the eighteenth century, primarily through print media, by the nineteenth century, especially from the 1840s, Britain was more intentional in promulgating its racist ideology.[120] This conscious propagation of racism happened through all possible channels, including the education system, popular culture, churches, missionaries, and voices from all walks of life.[121] Today, racism continues to reflect in most Western structures and spheres of life, as the research data has shown.

---

116. Fryer, *Staying Power*, 136.

117. Fryer, 136.

118. White, " History of Blacks." Money from the transatlantic slavery was so critical to the British economy that the abolition of the slave trade had to bring reparation payments to slave owners in a manner unparalleled in British history. The £20 million payment amounted to 40 percent of the national budget of British government in 1833 and was only paid off in 2015. For more, see Andrews, *New Age of Empire*, 55–56.

119. Muir, *History of Liverpool*, 195.

120. Sherwood, "White Myths, Black Omissions," 2.

121. Sherwood, 2; see also MacKenzie, ed. *Imperialism and Popular Culture*.

8.3.4 Remembering the Epochal Racial Riots of 1919

Race creation is not without real consequences.[122] Racism, a product of race, not only breeds violence, it is one of the expressions of aggression.[123] This submission by sociological researcher Albert Memmi aptly captures the series of racial tumults that occurred in the port cities of Britain between January and August 1919. With these events forming a vital part of a long history of the Black population in Liverpool and broader Britain, one would expect to find the discourse at the heart of literature exploring race-related issues in Britain.[124] Yet it is seldom the case that scholars focus on race relations in Britain before 1945, when the unprecedented surge in the British Black population from Commonwealth countries began.[125] Notwithstanding, I believe that to understand the racialization of British society today, insight into the numerous violent unrests of 1919 is vital for the following reasons:

First, the pandemonium was extensive, sprouting in many cities ranging from London to Liverpool, Cardiff, Hull, South Shields, Glasgow, Salford, Barry, and Newport.[126] Second, while other large-scale race riots also occurred later in the century, including the escalated conflicts of Liverpool in 1948, Nottingham and Notting Hill in 1958, and several others at different times and locations,[127] the 1919 mayhem was accompanied by severe consequences that are difficult to ignore. For instance, the riots in the nine cities mentioned above produced scores of serious injuries, two hundred and fifty arrests and five murders.[128] One killing that came to the limelight was the murder of Charles Wotten in Liverpool.[129]

8.3.4.1 *The Case of Liverpool*

The Liverpool race conflicts were only a fraction of the many riots of 1919 across Britain. I have focused on them here because Liverpool is not just the context of this study, but its uproars were the most intense and sustained of

---

122. Bonilla-Silva, *Racism without Racists*, 9.
123. Memmi, *Racism*, 139.
124. May and Cohen, "Interaction between Race," 112.
125. May and Cohen, 111.
126. Jenkinson, "Black 1919: Riots, Racism," 905.
127. Historic England, "Racism and Resistance."
128. Jenkinson, "Black Sailors on Red Clydeside," 1.
129. Historic England, "Racism and Resistance."

the unrest in Britain that year.[130] Plus, the events appear to link the gradual crystallization of racism in Britain and the city's contributions to the British colonial empire. As such, the happenings are not without contemporary implications, as is the increase in transnational Black consciousness.[131]

The unrest in Liverpool, and other British cities, grew from the discontent of the indigenous White population with the employment, housing, and pension situations in Britain after the war.[132] Unemployment was high, as were poverty and racial strain, as fallout from the war. Britain had brought in Black soldiers to fight in the wars, and the increase in the Black population was becoming concerning after the war. Soon, the Black community received the blame for the unpalatable living conditions in the land.[133] The result was a street invasion and violent protest from the British working class and ex-service personnel.[134] In the end, Black people had become the scapegoats of the irritations and frustrations of their hosts, who felt the war was a futile exercise, considering the consequent socio-economic woes.[135]

It was only a matter of time before the rising tension and unhealthy race relations between the host community and the Black population would escalate into a more severe phenomenon. Thus, by June 1919, chains of riots sprouted in Liverpool as fragments of several racial unrests occurring in British port towns that year. The disturbances began on 5 June with the murder of fireman Charles Wotten, a twenty-four-year-old Bermudan.[136] The previous day, John Johnston, a West Indian man, had been stabbed in the face for refusing to give two Scandinavian seamen a cigarette.[137] Reprisals ensued, and by the next day (5 June) on Great George Square, there was a severe altercation between some Scandinavian men and Black people, which resulted in police being call. However, the atmosphere became tenser with the arrival of the police, and four officers sustained injuries.

---

130. Jenkinson, "1919 Race Riots," 156.
131. May and Cohen, " Interaction between Race and Colonialism," 112.
132. Sherwood, *African Churches Mission*, 10.
133. May and Cohen, " Interaction between Race and Colonialism," 113–114.
134. Jenkinson, "Black Sailors on Red Clydeside," 1.
135. Jenkinson, "1919 Race Riots," 3, 159.
136. Rand, " Neglected Story."
137. Miles, "When Race Riots Marred."

Consequently, police raided Black residences in the vicinity. Wotten had jumped out of the rear window of his apartment at Upper Pitt Street to escape the arrest. Nonetheless, the police and a mob pursued him to the Queens Dock, where he must have either fallen into the water or been pushed by the crowd that jostled him. He quickly drowned due to a rock thrown at his head by the angry mob.[138]

The uproars of the next few days were more involved with an organized mob of about ten thousand young white men fiercely attacking any Black person they encountered. Black people had their homes raided and razed, and many had to seek shelter in public halls and local prisons.[139] Police reports put the initial figure of the Black population's lodgings destroyed on the nights of 8, 9, and 10 June at fifteen, plus a café for Black men.[140] Sadly, whenever the victims fought back, the press and police tagged them as the aggressors. In fact, many Black people were arrested while others found themselves in court with bandages around their heads in connection with the unrest that trailed Wotten's murder.[141]

8.4 Conclusion

Continuous contemplation of the role of race in church growth realization cannot be stated strongly enough. The complexity of church growth undoubtedly multiplies in a race-conscious context like the UK. Indeed, covert and explicit acts of racism are hard to ignore in Western systems. Racial discrimination shapes all life experiences of Black people in the diaspora, including church growth. Hence, if ADCs are to be successful in their missional engagements in the UK, conversations about race must occupy the fore of their considerations. Then, the opportunity of drawing from helpful resources like the *omolúàbí*-shaped ecclesiology can arise. *Omolúàbí*-shaped ecclesiology can improve cross-cultural relations and foster missions between ADCs and their Western host while also addressing the social relationship dynamics within the church. I have discussed this theological resource and African ecclesiology in the previous chapter.

---

138. Rand, " Neglected Story."
139. Miles, "When Race Riots Marred."
140. Jenkinson, "1919 Race Riots," 166.
141. Rand, "Neglected Story."

CHAPTER 9

Church Growth and Adaptive Leadership

9.1 Introduction

The research findings brought leadership to the fore of the elements impacting ADCs' development in Liverpool. Leadership and organizational development specialist Sebastian Salicru affirms that leadership is key to all establishments and human survival.[1] Thus, I consider the subject of leadership more intensely in this chapter, especially in response to the leadership-related church growth challenges of the research population. I propose the adaptive leadership (AL) strategy, nested in OSE, as a more appropriate leadership technique for ADCs to address the unfamiliar church growth problems confronting them in the UK. These challenges often require new learning and adaptation. The conversation begins by attempting to situate AL within the twenty-first century contemplations of leadership. In the subsequent discourse, I highlight the need for AL. Then I reflect on AL's structure, identifying how the research population can engage with the leadership practice. A brief conclusion ends the chapter.

---

1. Salicru, *Leadership Results*, xxiii.

9.2 Defining Adaptive Leadership

Global influences and generational differences will continue to alter leadership perceptions.[2] As such, a uniform definition of leadership for all ages may be impossible. Nevertheless, twenty-first century leadership contemplations broadly reflect four standard components: process, influence, groups, and shared goals.[3] These elements shape the working definition of leadership in this thesis as a process of collective participation through which a person inspires or influences a group towards achieving a shared goal.

Defining leadership as a process implies that it is not a quality, characteristic, or trait inherent in the leader. Instead, it is a two-way activity where a leader affects the followers while also experiencing changes through interaction with the people. The leadership activity is, thus, characterized by collective participation, reflecting leadership transformation from authority or the leader's dominance to "social engagement."[4] Influence or inspiration is also critical in the process of leadership. Indeed, the leadership *sine qua non* reflects how the leader encourages, changes, or impacts the followers and their interaction.[5] In the definition, the third element (group) reveals the context of the leadership process, that it proceeds among a group of people, however large or small.[6] The goal is vital as another component of the leadership definition because leaders must provide clarity of direction, concrete targets, or abstract visions of a promising future state.[7] Everyone must buy into the goal so that it is not simply enforced and easy is to attain.[8]

I have situated the definition of AL within the above description of leadership, which reflects the general leadership components of the twenty-first century. Although Heifetz's *Leadership without Easy Answers* was the foremost work to express the fundamental idea of AL, it was in *The Practice of Adaptive*

---

2. Uhl-Bien, Marion, and McKelvey, "Complexity Leadership Theory," 300; Northouse, *Leadership Theory and Practice*, 4.
3. Northouse, 5.
4. Sandling, *Leading with Style*, 2.
5. Ruben and Gigliotti, "Communication: Sine Qua Non," 12–30.
6. Northouse, *Leadership Theory and Practice*, 6.
7. Kesting et al., "Impact of Leadership Styles," 24.
8. Sandling, *Leading with Style*, 2.

Leadership[9] that the scholar and his colleagues developed a framework for the concept. They defined AL as the "practice of mobilising people to tackle tough challenges and thrive."[10] Thriving derives from evolutionary biology. Here, an effective adaptation implies three processes: preservation of essential DNA for a species' survival, doing away with non-essential DNA for the current needs of the species, and development of DNA arrangements that best serve the species' present realities. Successful adaptation, thriving, summarily connotes taking the best from history (whether of living systems or organizations) into the future.[11]

The above definition aptly reflects the twenty-first century concerns of leadership in three ways. First, it suggests an evolving (complex and interactive) process of mobilising persons to achieve adaptive changes instead of portraying leadership as traits, persons, or specific acts.[12] Second, the activity of mobilization or motivation points to the influence that comes from the adaptive leader. Third, there is an end to the leadership process: thriving, capturing the idea of a goal in the twenty-first century leadership focus.[13]

9.3 The Need for Adaptive Leadership Style

The research findings have placed the subject of leadership at the fore of church growth determinants for ADCs in Liverpool. The 109 references to leadership issues from twenty-five of the twenty-six research participants have exposed the need for ADC leaders to evaluate their leadership strategy and find a more suitable approach for their new setting. This alternative leadership technique must be able to address the unfamiliar church growth challenges they face. While I acknowledge the scores of leadership styles[14] in existence, I propose the AL style developed by the co-founder of Cambridge

---

9. Heifetz, Grashow, and Linsky, *Practice of Adaptive Leadership*, 9. Some of the works that which evolved as immediate build-up on the subject are Heifetz and Linsky, *Leadership on the Line*; Williams, *Real Leadership*; and Parks, *Leadership Can Be Taught*.
10. Heifetz, Grashow, and Linsky, 14.
11. Roberto, "Becoming an Adaptive Leader," 26.
12. Uhl-Bien, Marion, and McKelvey, "Complexity Leadership Theory," 299.
13. Northouse, *Leadership Theory and Practice*, 258.
14. Leadership styles connote the approaches for motivating or influencing followers. See more in Amanchukwu, Stanley, and Ololube, "Review of Leadership Theories," 9.

Leadership Associates, Ronald Heifetz, in this chapter and present the rationale for advancing this leadership strategy.

First, popular leadership ideas and styles, as with the hierarchical strategy of many ADC leaders, appear to be crashing under the pressure of newly evolving challenges defying extant solutions, such as church growth endeavour in the UK. Leadership and Business expert Julia Varney aptly observes that the conventional, common leadership styles are "no longer effective."[15] ADC leaders in Liverpool are also fast discovering that the leadership model they have brought from Africa is proving unfit for church life in the UK. Their autocratic and centralized leadership strategy often dissuades collaborative efforts and contributions that may advance the church, among other implications. Moreover, as the research data have shown, the task of church growth in the diaspora presents various shades of challenges that ADC leaders did not have to deal with back home in Africa (An instance is the unfamiliar work patterns that sometimes imply members' absence from church on Sundays, as a participant observed). Therefore, their current skillset is insufficient. AL emerges to tackle such complex and strange problems.

Second, globalization and related developments continue to generate an increased awareness of the advanced skills and actions a contemporary leader requires.[16] ADC leaders must also evolve in their clerical functions to lead effectively and experience growth in the UK. The research findings have revealed how ADC pastors must transform into multiple roles to lead their congregations successfully in the UK – responsibilities they did not have to take up before migrating to the UK. Scholar and pastor Titre Ande was precise with his submission, having observed the twenty-first century church. Ande declares that "The inherited roles of the ordained ministers no longer fit the needs of our present situation, so some rethinking is needed to equip clergy with the new skills they require."[17] AL's approach is helpful in this regard. It ensures that leaders demonstrate certain behaviours that aid the organization's sustenance and growth in the face of new realities, as with church growth activities in the UK.

---

15. Varney, " Changing Nature of Leadership," 22.
16. Partida, "Using Dynamic Leadership," 54.
17. Ande, "Introduction: The Leadership Challenge," 2.

Third, the ministry operational models that many church leaders inherited and practise today are unproductive.[18] The emergence of the COVID-19 pandemic particularly magnified the outdated ways many clerics lead their churches. With the immediate need to start doing church online in the first wave of the pandemic, most church leaders were confused and apprehensive over the congregations' growth. Indeed, several of these ministers struggled to engage with the only available channel of sustaining the church. The old pattern of ministry had become inadequate for twenty-first century development. As far back as 2005, Gibbs had confessed: the "ministry training I received over forty years ago was for a world that now no longer exists, and even at the time, it was undergoing radical change."[19] The church must cease to relish a false sense of security in the misguided notion that its existing ministerial training and leadership models are unchangeable, firmly rooted and validated by the Bible.[20] Any church leader who hopes for relevance and church growth today must embrace a leadership approach that permits constant adaptation. Hence the need for the AL style.

9.4 Adaptive Leadership Structure

Here, I explore the AL framework. The conversation progresses in three parts. The first aspect discusses the four knowledge areas that inform the design and process of AL. In the second, I examine the primary ideas or paradigms within the AL framework. Part three unfolds the adaptive leader behaviours and how ADC leaders in Liverpool can exhibit them for intended church growth.

9.4.1 Adaptive Leadership Foundational Orientations

The interplay of academic fields from which AL draws is evident in the fundamental biases undergirding the concept. It is upon these core assumptions that the structure and practice of AL lean. The first is that AL approaches problems from the viewpoint of systems or machines. AL sees problems as convoluted and consistently evolving. They have multiple features linked together in a web of interactions. In other words, AL approaches challenges

---

18. Ande, 4.
19. Gibbs, *Leadership Next*, 9.
20. Gibbs, 11.

as dynamic, complex, and interactive systems.[21] Management consultant Margaret Wheatley contributed massively to this conversation in her book *Leadership and the New Science*.[22] She perceived problems as living systems with a flexible, open, and participatory nature rather than the common hierarchical and mechanical ideas. Second, AL derives from the field of biology. This orientation recognizes that much of an organism's behaviour and stress responses result from adaptation to circumstances. In other words, living organisms develop, change, and thrive in new conditions because of their ability to adjust to internal and external signals and their environments.[23] So, organizations must also find ways of coping with the complexities of their dynamic environments for survival and growth.

AL's third foundational perspective is of service. The clarity of this viewpoint comes from the imagery of a doctor who diagnoses people's discomforts and assists them in finding a viable solution. This activity is similar to the task of adaptive leaders, who support others with their expertise or service-rendering authority to address their problems.[24] Psychiatry is the fourth orientation underlining AL, explaining how adaptive work happens. As in psychotherapy, adaptive leaders know that people need a supportive environment as they confront painful circumstances directly.[25] They are also aware of the cruciality of the journey of addressing the problematic issue because it improves people's adaptive capacity for future challenges. In the process, the people evolve with new attitudes and behaviours, distinguish fantasies from realities, resolve internal conflicts, and put extreme events into perspective.[26]

9.4.2 Key Concepts in Adaptive Leadership

Besides AL's fundamental assumptions, the leadership style also consists of certain constructs pertinent to its practice. I unpack these below.

---

21. Uhl-Bien, Marion, and McKelvey, "Complexity Leadership Theory," 299.
22. See Wheatley, *Leadership and the New Science*.
23. Johnson-Kanda and Yawson, "Complex Adaptive Leadership," 3; Heifetz, *Leadership without Easy Answers*, 3.
24. Northouse, *Leadership Theory and Practice*, 258.
25. Heifetz, *Leadership without Easy Answers*, 5.
26. Heifetz, 5.

9.4.2.1 Technical Problems

Heifetz and other proponents of AL have conceptually identified and grouped the various issues organizations confront into technical and adaptive challenges.[27] By nature, technical problems are complex but solvable with knowledge and procedures already in hand. In other words, the leader's authoritative expertise or the organization's routine operating procedures can handle technical difficulties.[28] Usually, the leader effortlessly defines the problem and provides the solution through an existing management system. The required knowledge to tackle technical issues is already digested and has formed policies in the organization, explaining what to do and who should do it. The existing solutions to technical problems develop from previously accomplished adaptive work.[29]

The following scenario is a typical instance of a technical problem. Some ADC members complain to their pastor that they find it difficult to connect to the church's dedicated social media channel. To the pastor, the problem is quick to diagnose. There is also an existing line of action for tackling such issues. The church's technical department handles any technological concerns, and the pastor does not hesitate to direct people to it. In another instance, a church building gets too small to accommodate all congregants whenever all age groups meet on the last Sunday of the month. The church may decide to rearrange the seats or erect temporary structures to create more room when needed. In this case, the challenge is clear, and the solution is already in place as a routine practice. This hurdle is a technical problem.

9.4.2.2 Adaptive Challenges

Addressing adaptive challenges is a principal rationale behind the development of the AL framework. Adaptive challenges are problems without clear-cut definitions, easy identification, and straightforward solutions based on the current organizational structure, procedure, or resources.[30] In fact, dealing with such issues lies beyond the leader and includes the people. Challenges that are adaptive in nature require new learnings from both the leader and the

---

27. Parks, *Leadership Can Be Taught*, 10.
28. Heifetz, Grashow, and Linsky, *Practice of Adaptive Leadership*, 19.
29. I have explained adaptive work later in this part of the thesis. It is the goal of the AL process. Heifetz, *Leadership without Easy Answers*, 71–72.
30. Northouse, *Leadership Theory and Practice*, 262.

people. As such, resistance often arises due to the sacrifices, trade-offs, and changes in people's beliefs, values, priorities, and roles that these challenges require.[31] Adaptive challenges are indeed demanding to take on.

In alignment with the research data, Kwiyani evinces that, "second generation African immigrants are not staying in their parents' churches."[32] This difficulty of keeping the 2GMs in ADCs presents an adaptive challenge. However, ADC leaders are approaching the problem as technical, addressing it the same way they have done in their home countries. The idea of establishing separate children's and teenagers' worship centres, for instance, does not seem to solve it. 2GMs still feel alienated in most ADCs. The necessary solution will more than likely require new learning altogether. An alternative way of being the church, as with the OSE, may just be the much-needed answer as support to AL. Both structures allow various stakeholders in the church (church leaders, 1GMs, and 2GMs) to dialogue and review their values, habits, and practices to create a more inclusive church.

Treating adaptive challenges as technical problems remains the most common cause of failure in leadership.[33] In other words, "nothing fails like success," for when organizations leverage past successes, failing to sustain invention and creativity in responding to new challenges of a different nature, their doom is almost certain.[34] Hence, an adaptive leader is meticulous enough to differentiate between technical problems and adaptive challenges when addressing tough situations. There may also be situations where the two kinds of challenges blend. In this case, the problem definition is clear, but no immediate solution is available from the existing repertoire of resources and skills.[35]

9.4.2.3 The Form of Adaptive Changes

As opposed to other leadership approaches, which are usually hierarchical and leader-centred when it comes to solving problems, dealing with adaptive challenges is never the leader's sole responsibility, but a concerted effort with

---

31. Northouse, 262.
32. Kwiyani, *Our Children Need Roots*, 29.
33. Heifetz, Grashow, and Linsky, *Practice of Adaptive Leadership*, 19.
34. Patterson et al., *Crucial Conversations*, ix.
35. Campbell-Evans, Gray, and Leggett, "Adaptive Leadership," 546.

the people. The leader simply mobilizes the people to deal with the difficulty in a process that sees them making critical but uneasy adjustments that are often "value-laden, and stir up people's emotions."[36] For instance, the changes may imply preserving some organizational heritage while trading-off certain legacy practices, traditional values, or professional identities. As such, adaptive changes are tricky and require sacrifices.[37]

9.4.2.4 Adaptive Work

Adaptive work is the final fundamental element of AL. It is the goal toward which an adaptive leader focuses and directs the entire leadership practice. Adaptive work develops essentially from the interactive processes occurring between the leader and the people, even though it remains chiefly the followers' duty. As a sort of psychotherapist, the leader's responsibility is to assist or support the people through the process of carrying out task-relevant adaptive work by exhibiting specific behaviours, which I discuss below.[38] Adaptive work evaluates the gap between people's values and clarifies reality. It requires significant effort to bridge the gulf between values and the current situation.[39] The holding environment facilitates adaptive work. This platform is a physical or virtual relationship and space where people can freely voice their concerns and address the adaptive challenges confronting them.[40] The leader expends significant effort in creating and maintaining the holding environment.[41]

9.4.3 Adaptive Leader Behaviours: A Model for ADC Leaders

The awareness of the difficulty of change and its resistance drives the adaptive leader to exhibit certain behaviours throughout the AL process. Through six activities Heifetz and Laurie identify,[42] an adaptive leader mobilizes the people to define the problem and implement a solution. While the leadership

---

36. Northouse, *Leadership Theory and Practice*, 264.
37. Ka and Chan, "Adaptive Leadership," 108.
38. Castillo, " Importance of Adaptive Leadership," 101–102.
39. Heifetz, *Leadership without Easy Answers*, 30–31.
40. I elaborate the holding environment among the behaviours of the adaptive leader later in this chapter. Northouse, *Leadership Theory and Practice*, 271.
41. Northouse, 271.
42. See Heifetz and Laurie, "Best of HBR," 36–48.

behaviours appear in a particular order in this conversation, the arrangement is only a general recipe for being an adaptive leader, owing to the iterative and overlapping nature of the AL model.[43]

9.4.3.1 Getting on the Balcony

The adaptive leader taking a position on a balcony is a metaphor for the preliminary adaptive leader behaviour. It derives from the imagery of a dance floor where, to understand the activities, contacts, and the ongoing chaos on the floor, one must be above it, on the balcony. This mental act of withdrawing from the dance floor gives an adaptive leader a bird's eye view of the complex situation. Stepping back from the field of activity requires reflective thinking from the adaptive leader to uncover evolving patterns within the organization.[44] The leader then has a clearer perspective of actions' context and connections between interactive forces in the system or organization.[45]

For ADC leaders, getting on the balcony may imply consciously evaluating how they do church from an outsider's perspective. This step will, of course, require objectivity and truthfulness to expose beliefs, activities, traditions, or habits hindering growth. Without the *omolúàbí* virtue of *òtító*, "getting on the balcony" may just be a fruitless wondering of the mind, observation, or meditation. However, where the assessment is honest, the root cause of 2GMs' dissatisfaction with ADCs, in this case, may just be on the trajectory of being identified and resolved more quickly.

9.4.3.2 Spotting the Adaptive Challenge

Another vital behaviour of an adaptive leader that derives from getting on the balcony is assessing the situation to identify the adaptive challenges. The leader must interpret emerging patterns and spot value-based, dysfunctional conflicts underlying surface tensions and impairing collaboration within the organization.[46] Carrying out this task will certainly require the leader to be calm and perceptive. Hence the need for the leader to be strong in *omolúàbí*'s quality of *ìwàpèlé*. Leaders must distinguish between technical and adaptive

---

43. Northouse, *Leadership Theory and Practice*, 262.
44. Hazy, "Parsing the 'Influential Increment,'" 181.
45. Ka and Chan, "Adaptive Leadership."
46. Heifetz and Laurie, "Work of Leadership," 36.

challenges because approaching adaptive challenges as technical problems is the most common cause of leadership failure. It is a maladaptive behaviour to use "a response appropriate to one situation in another where it does not apply."[47] As a helpful guide for leaders, Heifetz, Grashow, and Linsky suggest the following indices of adaptive challenges to aid their recognition:[48]

9.4.3.2.1 Contrast between Advocated Values and Behaviour

This adaptive challenge archetype builds on the awareness that people's conduct can sometimes disagree with their professed convictions, values, and beliefs about themselves. An adaptive challenge may occur where an organization's proclaimed values and beliefs are not visible in its actions. For instance, an adaptive challenge develops whenever an ADC alleges to be multi-ethnic, while its language, leadership face, and general church activities are skewed in favour of a specific ethnic group. The implication is that the Western host community, 2GMs, and minority ethnic groups may never feel drawn to the church. Church growth is then affected. Hence, ADC leaders must watch out for this adaptive challenge. Living by the *omolúàbí* principle of *òtító* will go a long way to minimize this expression of adaptive challenge, since truth and integrity negate variation in profession and action.

9.4.3.2.2 Competing Commitments

Like individuals, organizations occasionally have conflicting duties. Resolving this kind of challenge is never straightforward. Leaders must often make painful decisions benefiting one sector of the organization over another. Consequently, some leaders practice avoidance.[49] This sort of situation constitutes another model of adaptive challenge. A notable example from the research data is 1GMs' desire to see their 2GMs demonstrate greater allegiance to ADCs. Nonetheless, it appears to be difficult for the same group of people (1GMs) to adjust or let go of unhelpful stereotypes and cultural practices for multi-ethnicity, more so in a multicultural society like the UK. ADC leaders must always be courageous, demonstrating the quality of *akínkanjú* in *omolúàbí*, to challenge competing commitments within their churches rather than avoid dealing with the problem and risk growth possibilities. Of course,

---

47. Heifetz, *Leadership without Easy Answers*, 73.
48. See Heifetz, Grashow, and Linsky, *Practice of Adaptive Leadership*, 77–87.
49. Heifetz, Grashow, and Linsky, 80–81.

addressing conflicting responsibilities or services may require making tough calls. Hence, the need for the bravery that *akínkanjú* advocates.

9.4.3.2.3 Speaking the Unspeakable

An adaptive challenge can also develop when there are radical ideas, sensitive issues, and painful interpretations of controversial matters that everyone shies away from raising publicly.[50] For instance, an adaptive challenge ensues if there are sacred cows in an ADC, and these persons project ideas inconsistent with the church's values, yet no one can challenge them. The adaptive leader cannot afford to be hesitant in speaking the unspeakable, even if others are. The leader must be able to demonstrate *akínkanjú*. He or she is obligated to speak the truth (*òtító*) as an *omolúàbí*, although the communication must be with love that emanates from *inú rere* for it to be productive. Indeed, if allowed to linger, the scenario above will most likely heighten discontent and conflicts within the church. People will feel undervalued and unappreciated. Before long, the church will start to be depleted or experience a decline.

9.4.3.2.4 Work Avoidance

The fourth index of an adaptive challenge is work avoidance. It occurs where, in response to uncomfortable tension and stress levels occasioned by change prospects in the organization, people develop diversionary methods to escape the need for adjustments or remain in their comfort zone.[51] Such a situation could arise when an ADC decides to replace the coordinators of its children's and teenagers' churches to avoid the need to overhaul the monocultural way of doing church at these centres. The leaders of the ADC in question are simply demonstrating work avoidance here, perhaps due to the fear of disequilibrium or the nature and volume of work that adapting to the new church approach may require. *Omolúàbí* embraces work and not otherwise. Hence, where adaptive leaders live by the principles of *isé* and *akínkanjú*, they would be less likely to practice work avoidance, no matter the tasks associated with the change process. They would find satisfaction in tackling problems rather than evading them.

In all, ADC leaders must pay close attention to every problem to distinguish adaptive challenges from technical ones. This practice will help to avoid

---

50. Northouse, *Leadership Theory and Practice*, 264.
51. Heifetz, Grashow, and Linsky, *Practice of Adaptive Leadership*, 84–85.

maladaptive behaviour. For instance, the evangelism strategy of distributing tracts (small paper leaflets) or door-to-door visitation will more than likely need to stop. These approaches constitute applying technical solutions to an adaptive challenge. Indeed, as one of the research participants reflected, these mission techniques may have worked in Africa but not in the individualistic and secular Western culture like the UK. ADC leaders must learn new solutions and fresh ways of carrying out evangelism in the UK for productivity. Only then can they address the adaptive challenge of developing appropriate evangelistic strategies for successful missions in the UK.

9.4.3.3 Regulating Distress

The third activity of an adaptive leader is to manage distress. This behaviour is crucial because psychologically, people desire consistency. They tend to display more comfort when situations around them and the way they execute their daily activities are predictable.[52] Yet "fluctuation and change are part of the very process by which order is created"[53] and "growth is found in disequilibrium, not in balance."[54] The concern, then, is for an adaptive leader to avoid making change repugnant and overwhelming to the people by introducing just the right amount of stress and regulating the uneasiness within the organization. ADC pastors must be aware of the volume of change they can inject into their congregations and church life at a time as they strive to grow churches fit for their environment. Managing the discomfort occasioned by change calls for the following three-step activity from an adaptive leader:

9.4.3.3.1 Establishing a Holding Environment

The adaptive leader must create a *holding environment*. The holding environment is a "psychological space uncomfortable enough that a person cannot avoid the problem, but safe enough that the person can experiment with a new way of being."[55] It is like toddlers learning to walk and their parents cheering them on, allowing the children to make the moves by themselves. The parents avoid doing the work by holding the children's hands, yet the toddlers are confident that the parents are present even if they fall.

---

52. Northouse, *Leadership Theory and Practice*, 265.
53. Heifetz, *Leadership without Easy Answers*, 18.
54. Heifetz, 20.
55. Cormode, "Adaptive Change Requires."

The holding environment may translate to a physical or virtual structure or space, like a shared language or history that creates deep trust in an institution and its authority and simultaneously permits the people to find support and protection as they share thoughts and frustrations, and understand failures.[56] ADC leaders can create a regular informal chat forum as a holding environment, where mutual respect (captured in *ìwàpèlé* and *ìteríba* characters of *omolúàbí*) will allow contributions from all stakeholders in the church without judgement, disdain, or marginalization of any party. Deliberations in such an atmosphere will also proceed in the shared language of all groups in the church and will not be overwhelmed by the dominant culture's rhetoric. Indeed, the *omolúàbí* virtue of *inú rere* insists on friendliness and making the stranger feel welcome. Sustaining such an open and loving climate will help expose stress overload and discomfort engendered by the possibilities of fast-paced changes happening within the church.

9.4.3.3.2 Providing Direction, Protection, Orientation, Conflict Management, and Shaping Norms

The second behaviour of an adaptive leader in regulating uneasiness is the provision of direction, protection, orientation, conflict management, and the shaping of norms. Providing guidance concerns recognising the adaptive challenges the people or organization is facing and then raising important questions to capture the problems so that the people can confront them more clearly. Protection deals with the proper management of change frequency. The orientation task is to clarify realities and key values to acquaint the people with their new roles and responsibilities resulting from adaptive changes. Conflict management involves leveraging frictions to create opportunities for creativity and learning. Finally, by shaping norms, the adaptive leader maintains productive rules of behaviour shared by the organization while also challenging those that require change.[57] As ADC leaders embrace the AL style for church growth, they must carry out the above activities since people will likely find themselves in new roles or departments due to the necessary adaptive changes happening in the church. People need to be sure of the leader's total support as the way they do church undergoes significant

---

56. Ka and Chan, "Adaptive Leadership," 4.
57. Heifetz and Laurie, "Work of Leadership," 40.

adaptations on the journey towards church growth. *Omolúàbí* leaders would be there for their congregants as they all go through change processes in the church. That is *ìwà rere*.

9.4.3.3.3 Handling Personal Distress

In regulating distress, adaptive leaders additionally learn to manage personal discomfort and despair. They develop the "emotional capacity to tolerate uncertainty, frustration and pain."[58] Adaptive leaders remain sturdy, forbearing the pushbacks of those who resist confronting the problem. They master the art of withholding their perspective until the right moment to intervene.[59] When they eventually act, they allow their proposition, including feedback, to filter through the system or organization without interruption or early interference. They know that interference could be as subtle as interjecting with follow-ups, such as "you are not getting the point" or "no, allow me to say that again." What a way to model the *omolúàbí*'s attribute of *ìwàpèlé*!

Adaptive leaders permit feedback because they know that "if there is no contradictory impression, there is nothing to awaken reflection."[60] So, their silent presence may linger for a while, possibly for weeks. This restraint from speaking enables the people's attention to remain on the idea they have proposed, exposing its benefits and areas of improvement.[61] Managing personal distress may be tricky for ADC leaders, who come from a hierarchical leadership model that discourages critiquing the leader or elder, whether biological or spiritual. Yet, mastering the art of holding steady in the face of heat, criticisms, discouragements, and resistance is an essential practice of an adaptive leader. An adaptive leader would do well to embrace the *omolúàbí* ethos of *ìwàpèlé* to become more effective – an *omolúàbí* who "consciously exercises self-control and moderates his [or her] natural drives, impulses and inclinations."[62]

---

58. Heifetz and Laurie, 40.
59. Heifetz, Grashow, and Linsky, *Practice of Adaptive Leadership*, 305.
60. Lovegrove, *Mosaic Principle*, 232.
61. Heifetz, Grashow, and Linsky, *Practice of Adaptive Leadership*, 129.
62. Olatunji, " Postmodernist Critique of Omoluwabi," 66.

9.4.3.4 Sustaining Disciplined Action

The fourth behaviour of adaptive leaders is maintaining disciplined action. The organization consists of people from different backgrounds, experiences, assumptions, values, beliefs, and habits valuable for learning and creativity.[63] However, when adaptive changes challenge individual beliefs, people commonly resist the adjustments due to fear of loss and the accompanying grief. Consequently, they work towards regaining equilibrium.[64] Some of the ways people try to avoid the changes are by blaming the situation on the leaders or team members, attacking those attempting to address the issue, working hard in task-irrelevant areas, or pretending the challenge is non-existent.

Therefore, the adaptive leader's task is to help people focus on the problem at hand, letting their guard down to confront the challenging situation directly.[65] ADC leaders may secure more participation from their members for the required changes toward church growth when they interpret opposition or work avoidance through the lens of threats and losses rather than rigidity or cowardice on the part of the resistant groups or persons. This way, the pastors can multiply their allies (those who have come to share the importance of sustaining the adaptive work), making achieving the adaptive work of church growth easier and quicker.[66]

9.4.3.5 Returning the Work to the People

With the orientation and direction that authority or leadership provides, people are often quick to run to leaders at the emergence of stress or problems. However, this practice only encourages work avoidance and denies the organization the individual creativities and resources that various persons could offer towards problem resolution.[67] Of course, some leaders also find it difficult to resist the temptation of swinging into action at the slightest perception of disequilibrium within the organization. However, while the leader must not allow conflicts to linger and remain divisive or superficial, overly directive leadership is equally unhealthy for adaptive work.[68]

---

63. Heifetz and Laurie, "Work of Leadership," 41.
64. Cormode, "Constructing a Holding Environment."
65. Northouse, *Leadership Theory and Practice*, 268.
66. Heifetz, Grashow, and Linsky, *Practice of Adaptive Leadership*, 130–131.
67. Heifetz, *Leadership without Easy Answers*, 73.
68. Heifetz and Laurie, "Work of Leadership," 42.

The implication for ADC leaders is to be aware of their influence on the people and support them instead of either controlling or indulging them. ADC leadership would do well by learning to give tasks back to the people to accomplish adaptive work. Growth would be slow or unachievable where leaders do not allow their congregations to value and demonstrate the characters of *isé* and *akínkanjú* in *omolúàbí*. Hence, ADC leaders cannot continue with a central form of leadership, where they spearhead the resolution of all challenges. Some helpful tips in this regard include "empowering people to decide what to do in circumstances where they feel uncertain, expressing belief in their ability to solve their own problem, and encouraging them to think for themselves rather than doing that thinking for them."[69] These steps will help ADC members to feel more included in church administration. They may then be better inclined to increase their devotion or allegiance to their churches.

9.4.3.6 Protecting Leadership Voices from Below

Leadership voices from below represent dissenting views from people who usually must speak to authorities above them as they challenge ideas and initiatives. However, these outliers occasionally pick the wrong times while bypassing communication procedures and command lines in airing their opinions. Therefore, they often come across as mere naysayers and sceptics who the leader should neutralize. Yet these dissenters dare to name the elephants in the room and pose unsettling questions that others (including the leader) are unwilling to ask.[70]

Suppose someone raises a disturbing question within the holding environment of an ADC ministers' meeting. People will observe the leader's attitude to decide how they should react. If the leader resists the urge to silence the seemingly eccentric individual's voice – who, for instance, exposes contradictions within the church – others will see the leader as open to criticisms and unconventional ideas. Then, they will also freely air their concerns and thoughts about any issue. The implications will be improved church programs and projects, and easier identification and deliberate conversation about potential loopholes in church activities before execution. By leveraging

---

69. Northouse, *Leadership Theory and Practice*, 269–270.
70. Heifetz and Laurie, "Work of Leadership," 43.

the ethos of *omolúàbí*, an adaptive leader will be more adept to take "warning or rebuke with an open heart and words of gratitude since such admonition is necessarily to make him [or the organization] a better person [or establishment]."[71] In the end, the church becomes more attractive to outsiders with well-delivered programs.

9.5 Conclusion

Adaptive leadership design attends to complex problems that are difficult to define and require new skills or learning to tackle. Such are the church growth challenges of ADCs in Liverpool. Indeed, the way of being church in Africa continues to prove inadequate for missions or church administration in the UK. Church life demands a fresh approach to be meaningful to the 2GM population of ADCs and their Western host. Therefore, nesting AL within OSE is a productive effort for the research population as AL provides a structure for engaging with unfamiliar problems defying quick fixes and existing solutions, procedures, or skillset.

AL requires ADC leaders to pay close attention to their congregations' challenges to distinguish between technical and adaptive challenges. Then, through specific behaviours, adaptive leaders mobilize the people to confront the tricky situation and thrive. Adaptive work is the goal of AL. Achieving adaptive work ultimately results from the joint efforts of the leader and people, who both undergo critical changes in the leadership process. For the research population, the broad adaptive work is church growth, which will demand sacrifices and value-based changes from both the people and their leaders.

---

71. Olatunji, "Postmodernist Critique of Omoluwabi," 75.

CHAPTER 10

Summary and Conclusions

This dissertation investigated church growth experience amidst African diaspora congregations (ADCs) in Liverpool. It pursued a primary question: What factors significantly impact church growth among the research population? The study aimed at exploring issues shaping ADCs' survival and expansion in Liverpool. It also sought to develop a grounded theory response to the emerging growth challenges of the congregations. Examining church growth phenomenon in the research context is crucial for two reasons. First, of the multidimensional life experiences of the UK ADCs that scholars have explored, church growth has not been a matter of deliberate focus, as a brief consideration of some scholarly literature and leading voices in the UK African Christian diaspora space and a search through selected library catalogues revealed.

Second, growth remains imperative for the church. If Christ, the head of the church, is alive, the body must demonstrate life by growing. With the strong connection between Christ and the church, this work has drawn from the four developmental aspects of Jesus's maturity in Luke 2:52 to define church growth. A growing church must reflect excellence in leadership and administration (wisdom), numerical increase (years), spiritual maturity (divine favour), and social impact (human favour). However, church growth does not happen by chance. Many varying factors across contexts condition it. African diaspora Christians striving to establish churches in the UK soon come to this reality. Moreover, other adaptive challenges confronting immigrants in a new environment magnify church growth difficulties. Hence, for Liverpool ADCs, interesting development patterns are noticeable, making the church growth phenomenon a fascinating research subject.

It is migration that makes the ADC communities in Liverpool possible in the first place. The Bible also projects the alliance between migration and *missio Dei*. Migration has facilitated the spread of Christianity since its emergence until today, when African agents are actively transporting Christianity to Europe. Through the mushrooming of ADCs, Liverpool, the UK, and other Western nations are witnessing the impact of the explosion of (Pentecostal) Christianity in Africa. African Christians are not merely moving to the West and other parts of the world, they are carrying their faith with them and establishing their own congregations.

However, a wide range of elements attends to the survival and growth of predominantly African congregations. Exploring these issues through a qualitative research approach has been the primary concern of this study. The investigation employed ethnographic instruments (primarily semi-structured interviews) for data collection. Having studied three deliberately selected ADCs in Liverpool, the inquiry produced rich research data which was then analysed through the grounded theory approach. The findings suggested that issues associated with leadership, finance, 2GMs' allegiance, ecclesiology, demographics, opportunities and benefits, contextual realities of the UK, negative image, and metaphysical drivers have bearing on ADCs' growth in Liverpool. While all these factors had significant implications, three themes were overarching: ecclesiology, contextual realities of the UK, and leadership.

10.1 Leadership in ADCs

The investigation revealed that leadership issues, such as vision, synergy, church administration, charisma, homiletics, and others, have undeniable imprints on the research population's growth. Through these concerns, the inappropriateness of ADCs' leadership strategy in the UK came to light. The common hierarchical form of leadership in most African churches is unfit for leading enduring congregations in the UK. Thus, the inquiry suggested a reconsideration of ADCs' leadership approach.

The dissertation presented the adaptive leadership style (AL), embedded in OSE, as an alternative and effective leadership technique for ADCs in Liverpool. AL engages both the leader and people in the leadership process, unlike the hierarchical or centralized leadership model, where everyone looks up to the leader for answers. In AL, the leader motivates, mobilizes, encourages, and supports the people in confronting their problems directly and thus thriving. AL is very suitable for new situations and challenges for which adaptations are necessary, such as growing ADCs in the UK.

AL not only prepares ADCs for change, but also provides a design for identifying and tackling current, complex, and unfamiliar challenges. It prevents maladaptive behaviour (the activity of approaching adaptive challenges as technical problems), a common cause of leadership failure. Through its necessitation of collaboration between the leader and the people, for instance, AL ensures that there is collective clarification and evaluation of the church's vision. Its structure also averts needless frictions within the church since the holding environment allows matters that could generate potential conflicts to emerge naturally to be addressed. Indeed, AL's structure allows the airing and handling of dissenting views in a productive manner. In the end, ADCs can benefit from voices and ideas (such as fresh mission strategies) that otherwise would have remained unheard without a leadership framework that permits expression.

10.2 Beyond Homogenous Congregations

The reality of racism in the West may continue to tilt ADCs towards homogeneity. However, while it may be easier for ADCs to begin as homogenous assemblies, remaining so, especially racially and culturally, is harmful to church growth as advanced in this thesis. Hence, this study has proposed transforming from the homogenous church life most ADCs currently present to multi-ethnic churches. Multi-ethnicity represents a more efficient and sustainable way of fulfilling God's global mission (Rev 7:9) and expressing church growth. The benefits of multi-ethnicity to ADCs are numerous. These include making the West more open to embracing the contributions African Christians have brought to Western Christianity, increasing partnership in missions, and enjoying the blessings of cultural diversity in ADC congregations.

While transitioning from homogeneity to a multi-ethnic community is never easy due to required value-laden changes, the benefits trump the difficulties of adapting. There is no escaping multi-ethnicity, even in a culturally plural society like the UK. Indeed, human migrations continue to alter the cultural landscape of the UK, and this is not slowing. Migration is intrinsic to human history and development. By implication, any church that will endure and grow cannot afford to be homogenous, culturally or otherwise. Instead, such a congregation must celebrate and embrace the goodness of diversity in its leadership and entire church life.

10.3 Engaging *Omolúàbí*-shaped Ecclesiology

A critical task in achieving multi-ethnicity, which this work has advanced, is contextualization. OSE is not only a grounded theory solution to the church growth challenges of the research population; it is also a contextualized way ADCs can conveniently and productively be the church in the UK. It derives from an African (Yoruba) model of moral identity, the *omolúàbí*. The *omolúàbí* concept emphasizes the principles of truth and integrity, goodwill, strong character, hard work, and courage, without which there can be no affirmation of personhood among the Yorubas.

OSE has vast implications. For instance, by promoting the social relationship principles of *àjobí* and *àjogbé*, OSE encourages harmony in all relationships. It engenders conflict reduction and smoother interactions between church leadership and the congregation, between 1GMs and 2GMs, and across various divides, including culturally diverse Western hosts. OSE's support for amicability in relationships also extends to the spiritual realm. It promotes the Holy Spirit's recognition in the church's life and seeks to maintain peace with him. By approaching social relationships through the mindset of *àjobí* and *àjogbé*, OSE presents a manner of doing church that acknowledges African sensibilities while listening to other cultures within its context of deployment. In essence, OSE fosters multi-ethnicity, providing a structure for tapping into the merits of cultural diversity in the church.

OSE similarly addresses the persistent problem of racism in the UK and the West. It does this, first, by acknowledging the shared humanity of everyone regardless of their socially constructed racial class. Second, OSE draws from *omolúàbí*'s virtue of goodwill to ensure an open and forgiving church, especially for Africans who are constantly adjusting to the perpetuation of racism in the West. Both attitudes of shared humanity and goodwill also appreciate every culture's contribution to the church, thereby aiding church growth.

In all, OSE provides a framework for experiencing the four dimensions of church growth this thesis proposes. It attests to spiritual maturity by stressing the recognition and harmony with the Holy Spirit, which is the power behind church growth principles. OSE also advocates the social growth of the church. It instructs ADCs to improve engagements with their congregants and society. This way, tendencies for internal conflicts will diminish, and the churches' social interaction and impact in their communities will make them more endearing to outsiders. There is, similarly, an influence on leadership when OSE is in place. OSE demands holistic salvation, whereby the affirmation of Christian identity (whether of the leader or people) is from a moral as well as spiritual standpoint. ADC leaders must walk in truth and integrity and show excellent leadership through diligence and courage. These qualities have several implications, including accountability, valuing training and retraining, and skill in communicating the gospel to minimize offence.

10.4 What More?

Several positives came out of the investigation. First, which is admirable, is the warm reception from the three congregations that participated in the research. Their availability and the support they granted a young African researcher to investigate their communities are indeed commendable and helpful. This was despite the awareness of the vulnerability and risk associated with such gestures. The minister in charge of each congregation was highly resourceful, permitting the researcher to interact with whomever the study required, which provided rich research data. These pastors were similarly significant in securing the willingness and trust of the participants towards the researcher and the investigation. Such a partnership between the church and the academy is appreciated and certainly beneficial for both sides. An increase in collaboration could enhance the church's theology and missions. Moreover, each side will have a richer understanding of their roles and significance in discerning God's activities in the world in which everyone can participate.

Besides the church leaders, congregants (youths and adults), who bared their lives for the investigation without being ashamed to be unguarded, are worthy of thanks, even though some may disagree with my submissions and conclusions. The cooperation of these 1GMs and 2GMs was instrumental in unearthing a theological resource for the global church, *omolúàbí*-shaped ecclesiology. Their openness was equally helpful in richly exploring the church growth experiences of Liverpool ADCs in general. However, both 1GMs and 2GMs must listen to each other more closely to make multi-ethnic congregations work. New, effective, and context-relevant mission strategies will also more likely emerge through such recognition and attention. Moreover, as their voices and concerns receive affirmation, the tendency for 2GMs to sustain their membership at ADCs, even when they become adults, will increase.

Africans must also find ways to properly plant the Christian faith within their cultures. Every culture can bring something to the theological table to enhance current revelations about God, and Africa is no exception. When the Africanization of Christianity happens, resulting in a reflexive Christianization of the African cultures, Africa will be able to contribute more of its own quota to the global church. Africans must celebrate the validity and uniqueness of their diverse cultures and be proud to draw from them in their theological reflections. They cannot continue to solely theologize from a Western frame of mind as though it were the only authentic approach to access God's revelations to humanity. Western dominance in literature and many other spheres of life should not make non-Western cultures look down on themselves as if they have nothing to offer. The only way the universal church can enjoy wholesome growth is to recognize that God is at work in every culture, and each has a revelation of Him they can share with the world.

The UK and Western Christianity have a lot to benefit from the expansion of African Christianity in the region. The hesitation in receiving it as a blessing is unnecessary. The unabating spread of secularism in the West immediately exposes an urgent need for spiritual renewal. African Christianity comes along with the spiritual consciousness and emphasis that the West needs. This "strange" (to Westerners) Christianity could be the spiritual revival resource that the West urgently requires. Indeed, with most world Christians now residing in the global South, the preservation of Western Christianity may just be dependent on fast-exploding African Christianity.

Therefore, it would be productive for more theological institutions in the West to introduce and support the study of African Christianity. This will help in understanding and engaging with the faith more productively. Increased representation of African scholars in these citadels of learning will equally help interact more deeply and deliberately with immigrant Christians. In the end, cross-cultural studies will happen more effortlessly, as will crossbreeding of theological ideas, without necessarily having to travel around the world. Along with earlier scholars of African diaspora Christianity, I declare that the *blessed reflex* is here, and it should be celebrated as a move of the God of missions rather than an undesirable invasion of a racial group.

Regarding the suggested harmony with the Holy Spirit in OSE, this unity will be more sustainable when individual church members retain the mindset that they are "temples of the Holy Spirit" (1 Cor 6:19). The thought that other congregants are also bearers of the Holy Spirit will help members value and love one another regardless of their differences. A church like this will appreciate the contributions of every culture, race, group, class, or age group. Communications will flow from a place of mutual respect, affirmation, and celebration. Thus, friction will bow out to peace. Such an atmosphere is a perfect host for the Holy Spirit. In fact, peace is evidence of his presence, for it is a "fruit of the Spirit" (Gal 5:22).

The church's continuous bond with the Spirit is crucial. No congregation should take the spiritual formation of its members lightly. By implication, every local assembly should capture Bible narratives, explore worship, church histories, and traditions, accept God's forgiveness, be prayerful, attend to God's voice, and act according to God's grace.[1] Nevertheless, the body of Christ must also not forget that "All our friendships, groups, arguments, bonds, births and deaths are embedded in a church relational life."[2] Therefore, the church must be concerned about its social engagement and constantly improve on it. It must be conscious that all its activities are motivated by love, driving it to identify the marginalized, whether in the church or in society, and attend to their needs, as Jesus did (Luke 4:18). Affection for those at the edges will help the church guard against importing assumptions and societal prejudices into its life. As the church provides a crucible for reconciling people to God, it will also become a place for social reconciliation.

The church must equally not forget its central mission of reaching out to the unsaved (Matt 28:18–20). It is the way it "participates in God's love for the world,"[3] for God so loved the world that he reached out to it by sending his son for its salvation (John 3:16). The church must renew its drive for

---

1. Branson and Martinez, *Churches, Cultures and Leadership*, 62.
2. Branson and Martinez, 63.
3. Branson and Martinez, 63.

evangelism and missions. These endeavours must begin to occupy the centre of its agenda to experience the sort of growth this dissertation puts forward. While organized good deeds and social action have their place and beautiful buildings and programs are appealing, the gospel still needs a bearer or preacher. Without a messenger or a sent one, where the church is not actively spreading the good news, many more cannot be converted and join the church (Rom 10:14). The church can also do more to make its budget for missional activities reflect its passion for the unsaved. Additionally, it can sponsor missionaries, missions-related training, and similar organizations. The church must also explore and fund contextually appropriate means of reaching out to the unevangelized in its locality.

Donald McGavran was not out of line to have advocated for church growth. God himself desires the expansion of the church, and Jesus says, "I will build my church, and the gates of hell shall not prevail against it" (Matt 16:18 ESV). However, any increase or advancement of the church must not appear to emphasize one aspect of growth over another. Just as the church matures spiritually, it must put similar efforts into increasing numerically, socially, and in leadership. Jesus's developmental pattern, as recorded in Luke 2:52, presents a good template for the church, his body. Total church growth is possible, and the church must believe in and pursue holistic development in biblical ways.

Moreover, the church needs to remember that every congregation exists within a locality. Contexts shape the life of the church, including its ecclesiology and leadership, as this study has shown. Yet the church also must influence its community and society generally. The church as a body, and individual members, must not keep its gifts of love, grace, peace, truth, justice, mercy, and healing from the world. In the mutual shaping of the church and its community, church leaders must recognize their central role. They can either facilitate or discourage church growth through their practices and approaches to leadership. Pastors must guide their churches to demonstrate concern and care for people, both members of their congregations and outsiders, bringing about social and numerical growth. Church leaders must also encourage activities that help the church pay closer attention to God. This way, the church continues to experience spiritual maturity.

In all of this, leadership intelligence is critical. For instance, leaders must not deny their cultural heritage. Yet they must be careful that their frames of reference, languages and the relational or leadership patterns inherited from their cultures must not overshadow the way they do church. Otherwise, there will be defects in the congregation's corporate spiritual and social formation. But where church leaders can strike a balance, leveraging their cultural strengths and discarding their weaknesses, the church of God would grow more wholesomely, quickly, and numerically. For this reason, the church cannot afford a naive, underdeveloped, or stagnant leadership. Growth needs to characterize this aspect of the church as well.

Ultimately, I believe there is a future for African diaspora congregations and for Christianity in the diaspora. However, their sustenance and growth will largely hinge upon the retention of the offspring of 1GMs. These 2GMs are closer to the host community in many ways as they mature in a land their parents still struggle to adapt to. So, they are likely to be more effective cross-cultural mission agents since they better understand the culture they are growing up in. The implication is that they are more able to develop robust and relevant mission strategies to reach the host community. ADCs would, therefore, do well to be more intentional in nurturing, mentoring, engaging with, and retaining the interest of their 2GMs in church life to preserve their presence and consolidate the relative growth they may be enjoying now.

I hope that this work begins a much-needed conversation and study of the church growth experience of African diaspora congregations to the end that God's mission, especially in the hands of migrants, would be more effective. A further study into this multi-layered phenomenon of church growth among migrant congregations even beyond the UK, which is the context of this research, would certainly be beneficial to the body of Christ as a whole, and more importantly, to every individual, agency, organization, and church concerned about engaging in cross-cultural mission.

Bibliography

Abimbola, Wande. "Iwapele: The Concept of Good Character in Ifa Literary Corpus." In *Yoruba Oral Tradition: Poetry in Music Dance and Drama*, edited by Wande Abimbola, 389. Ibadan: University of Ibadan Press, 1975.

Abiodun, Rowland. "Verbal and Visual Metaphors: Mythical Allusions in Yoruba Ritualistic Art of Orí." *Word and Image* 3, no. 3 (1987): 252–270.

Adebowale, Bosede Adefiola. "Aristotle's Human Virtue and Yorùbá Worldview of Ọmọlúàbí: An Ethical-Cultural Interpretation." (2019). https://www.researchgate.net/publication/331382642_omoluabi/link/5c76a4e3a6fdcc4715a11dd3/download.

Adedayo, Muyiwa Samuel. "The Concept of Omoluabi and Political Development in Nigeria: The Missing Gap." *IOSR Journal of Humanities and Social Science* 23, no. 3 (2018): 1–7. www.iosrjournals.org.

Adedibu, Babatunde. "African-Led Pentecostal Churches in London: Sacralizing Urban Space, Politics of Religious Networking and Creativity." In *African Voices: Towards African British Theologies*, edited by Israel Oluwole Olofinjana, 83–108. Carlisle: Langham Global Library, 2017.

Adedibu, Babatunde Aderemi. "The Changing Faces of African Independent Churches as Development Actors across Borders." *HTS Teologiese Studies/Theological Studies* 74, no. 1 (2018): 1–9. https://www.ajol.info/index.php/hts/article/download/177915/167286.

Adedibu, Babatunde Aderemi. *Coat of Many Colours*. UK: Wisdom Summit, 2012.

Adedibu, Babatunde Aderemi. "Faith without Borders: Maximising the Missionary Potential of Britain's Black-Majority Churches." *Journal of Missional Practice* (2013). https://journalofmissionalpractice.com/faith-without-borders-maximising-the-missionary-potential-of-britains-black-majority-churches/?print=pdf.

Adedibu, Babatunde Aderemi. "Mission from Africa: A Call to Re-imagine Mission within African-Led Pentecostal Churches in Britain." *Missio Africanus Journal of African Missiology* 1, no. 1 (2015): 39–51.

Adedibu, Babatunde Aderemi. "Origin, Migration, Globalisation and the Missionary Encounter of Britain's Black Majority Churches." *Studies in World Christianity* 19, no. 1 (2013): 93–113.

Adedibu, Babatunde Aderemi. "The Urban Explosion of Black Majority Churches: Their Origin, Growth, Distinctives and Contribution to British Christianity." PhD diss., North-West University, South Africa, 2010.

Adefala, Dupe. ""How Rich the Kingdom of God Is!" – An Interview with Dupe Adefala." *ANVIL: Journal of Theology and Mission* 36, no. 3 (2020): 59–64.

Adekanye, Esther. "A Critical Analysis of the Yorùbá Conception of a Person." 2020. https://www.doria.fi/bitstream/handle/10024/176231/adekanye_esther.pdf?sequence=2&isAllowed=y.

Adeniji-Neill, Dolapo, and Ruth Ammon. "Omoluabi: The Way of Human Being: An African Philosophy's Impact on Nigerian Voluntary Immigrants' Educational and Other Life Aspirations." https://fliphtml5.com/ugrj/lxqi/ www.africamigration.com/#google_vignette

Adi, Hakim. "Pan-Africanism and West African Nationalism in Britain." *African Studies Review* 43, no. 1 (2000): 69–82.

Adogame, Afeosemime U. *The African Christian Diaspora: New Currents and Emerging Trends in World Christianity*. London: Bloomsbury, 2013.

Adogame, Afeosemime U. "Celestial Church of Christ: The Politics of Cultural Identity in a West African Prophetic Charismatic Movement." *Studien zur interkulturellen Geschichte des Christentums* 115 (1999): 221–251.

Adogame, Afeosemime U. "A Home Away from Home: The Proliferation of the Celestial Church of Christ (CCC) in Diaspora-Europe." *Exchange* 27, no. 2 (1998): 141–160.

Adogame, Afeosemime U. *Indigeneity in African Religions: Oza Worldviews, Cosmologies and Religious Cultures*. New York: Bloomsbury Academic, 2021.

Adogame, Afeosemime U. *Who Is Afraid of the Holy Ghost?: Pentecostalism and Globalization in Africa and Beyond*. Trenton: Africa World Press, 2011.

Adogame, Afeosemime U., and Cordula Weisskóppel, eds. *Religion in the Context of African Migration*. Bayreuth African Studies Series. Bayreuth: Breitinger, 2005.

Adogame, Afeosemime U., Olufunke Adeboye, and Corey L. Williams. *Fighting in God's Name: Religion and Conflict in Local-Global Perspectives*. Lanham: Lexington Books, 2020.

Adogame, Afeosemime U., Roswith I. Gerloff, and Klaus Hock. *Christianity in Africa and the African Diaspora: The Appropriation of a Scattered Heritage*. Continuum Religious Studies. New York: Continuum, 2008.

Afrane-Twum, Johnson. "The Mission of the African Immigrant Churches in the Multicultural Context of the UK." PhD diss., North-West University, South Africa, 2018.

African Studies Centre Leiden. "Gerrie ter Haar." https://www.ascleiden.nl/content/ASC-community/members/gerrie-ter-haar.

Agee, Jane. "Developing Qualitative Research Questions: A Reflective Process." *International Journal of Qualitative Research Studies in Education* 22, no. 4 (2009): 431–447.

Akanbi, Grace Oluremilekun, and Alice Arinlade Jekayinfa. "Reviving the African Culture of 'Omoluabi' in the Yoruba Race as a Means of Adding Value to Education in Nigeria." *International Journal of Modern Education Research* 3, no. 3 (2016): 13–19.

Akin-John, Francis Bola. *22 Dynamic Laws of Church Growth.* Lagos, Nigeria: Church Growth Services Inc., 2003.

Akin-John, Francis Bola. *The Impact-Driven Church: How to Make Your Church a Force and Not a Figure Today.* Lagos, Nigeria: Church Growth Services Inc., 2008.

Akintoye, Adebanji S. *A History of the Yoruba People.* Dakar: Amalion Publishing, 2014.

Akinwowo, Akinsola. *Ajobi and Ajogbe: Variations on the Theme of Sociation.* Ile-Ife: University of Ife Press, 1983.

Akinyemi, Akintunde. *Orature and Yoruba Riddles.* New York: Palgrave Macmillan, 2015.

Akomiah-Conteh, Sheila. "The Changing Landscape of the Church in Post-Christendom Britain: New Churches in Glasgow, 2000–2016." PhD diss., University of Aberdeen, 2019.

Alajami, Abdulla. "Beyond Originality in Scientific Research: Considering Relations among Originality, Novelty, and Ecological Thinking." *Thinking Skills and Creativity* 38 (2020): 100723. https://www.sciencedirect.com/science/article/pii/S1871187120301978.

Alshenqeeti, Hamza. "Interviewing as a Data Collection Method: A Critical Review." *English Linguistics Research* 3, no. 1 (2014). http://www.sciedu.ca/journal/index.php/elr/article/view/4081/2608.

Alvis, Paul. *The Anglican Understanding of the Church.* London: SPCK, 2000.

Amanchukwu, Rose Ngozi, Gloria Jones Stanley, and Nwanchukwu Prince Ololube. "A Review of Leadership Theories, Principles and Styles and Their Relevance to Educational Management." *Management* 5, no. 1 (2015): 6–14.

Ande, Titre. "Introduction: The Leadership Challenge Today." In *A Guide to Leadership*, edited by Titre Ande, Dave Bookless, Esther Mombo, C. B. Peter and Leaderwell Pohsngap. 1–4. London: SPCK, 2010.

Anderson, Allan. *African Reformation: African Initiated Christianity in the 20th Century.* Trenton: Africa World Press, 2001.

Anderson, Allan. "Evangelism and the Growth of Pentecostalism in Africa." 2000. http://artsweb.bham.ac.uk/aanderson/Publications/evangelism_and_the_growth_of_pen.htm.

Andrews, Kehinde. *The New Age of Empire: How Racism and Colonialism Still Rule the World.* London: Allen Lane, 2021.

Andrews, Tom. "What Is Social Constructivism?" *The Grounded Theory Review* 11, no. 1 (2012): 39–46.

Antwi, Dan J. "Koinonia in African Culture: Community, Communality and African Self-Identity." *Trinity Journal of Church and Theology* VI, no. 2 (1996).

Arain, Mubashir, Michael J. Campbell, Cindy L. Cooper, and Gillian A. Lancaster. "What Is a Pilot or Feasibility Study? A Review of Current Practice and Editorial Policy." *BMC Medical Research Methodology* 10 (2010): 67–73.

Arbuckle, Gerald A. *Culture, Inculturation, and Theologians: A Postmodern Critique.* Collegeville: Liturgical Press, 2010.

Archbishop of Canterbury. "The racism that people in this country experience is horrifying. The Church has failed here, and still does, and it's clear what Jesus commands us to do: repent and take action." Twitter, 8 June 2020. https://twitter.com/justinwelby/status/1270046097357053954.

Archbishop's Council. *Mission-Shaped Church.* Church of England. London: Church House Publishing, 2004.

"Aristotle's Rhetoric." In *The Stanford Encyclopedia of Philosophy*, edited by Edward N. Zalta. Stanford University: Center for the Study of Language and Information, 2002. https://plato.stanford.edu/.

Attia, Mariam, and Julian Edge. "Be(com)ing a Reflexive Researcher: A Developmental Approach to Research Methodology." *Open Review of Educational Research* 4, no. 1 (2017): 33–45.

Awoniyi, Sunday. "African Cultural Values: The Past, Present and Future." *Journal of Sustainable Development in Africa* 17, nos. 1–4 (2015).

Ayegboyin, Deji, and Ademola S. Ishola. *African Indigenous Churches: An Historical Perspective.* Bukuru, Nigeria: African Christian Textbooks, 2013.

Ayokunle, Samson Olasupo A. *Communities of Faith in Diaspora: Elements and Liturgy of Worship.* Ibadan, Nigeria: Baptist Press (Nig.) Ltd., 2021.

Ayokunle, Samson Olasupo A. "Elements Sustaining Public Worship among Diaspora African Christians in Liverpool since 1900." PhD diss., University of Liverpool, 2007.

Babatola, Jadesola. "Literary Inquiry of Social Value Constructs in Tackling Deviance, Delinquency and Decadence: A Review of Selected Yoruba Poems of J.F. Odunjo." 2015. https://www.academia.edu/31128026/LITERARY_INQUIRY_OF_SOCIAL_VALUE_CONSTRUCTS_IN_TACKLING_DEVIANCE_DELINQUENCY_AND_DECADENCE_A_REVIEW_OF_SELECTED_YORUBA_POEMS_OF_J_F_ODUNJO.

Bibliography

Babatunde, Wale. *Great Britain Has Fallen: How to Restore Britain's Greatness as a Nation.* London: New Wine Press, 2002.

Ballano, Vivencio. "Inculturation, Anthropology, and the Empirical Dimension of Evangelization." *Religions* 11, no. 2 (2020): 101.

Ballard, Roger. "Race, Ethnicity and Culture." 2002. 1–44. https://core.ac.uk/download/pdf/33413521.pdf.

Barth, Karl. *Church Dogmatics: The Doctrine of Reconciliation.* Vol. 4.1, Edinburgh: T&T Clark, 1956.

Barth, Karl. *Church Dogmatics.* Edinburgh: T&T Clark, 1957.

BBC. "Post-war British Laws for and against Immigration, 1945–1972." https://www.bbc.co.uk/bitesize/guides/z8sdbk7/revision/4.

BBC. "Reconstructing Britain after World War Two." https://www.bbc.co.uk/bitesize/guides/zx93tyc/revision/1.

Becker, Howard, and Alan Bryman, eds. *Understanding Research for Social Policy and Practice.* Bristol: The Policy Press, 2012.

Bediako, Kwame. *Christianity in Africa: The Renewal of a Non-Western Religion.* Edinburgh: Edinburgh University Press, 1995.

Bell, Judith. *Doing Your Research Project: A Guide for First-Time Researchers in Education, Health and Social Science.* 4th ed. Maidenhead: Open University Press, 2005.

Ben-Rafael, Eliezer. "Diaspora." *Current Sociology* 61, nos. 5–6 (2013): 842–861.

Bendor-Samuel, Paul. "Challenge and Realignment in the Protestant Cross-cultural Mission Movement." *Transformation* 34, no. 4 (2017): 267–281.

Beresh, Nathan. "Contextualize without Compromise: Presenting the Gospel in a Post-Christendom Society." https://www.academia.edu/37660618/CONTEXTUALIZE_WITHOUT_COMPROMISE_PRESENTING_THE_GOSPEL_IN_A_POST-_CHRISTENDOM_SOCIETY.

Berg, Bruce L. *Qualitative Research Methods for the Social Sciences.* Boston: Pearson/Allyn and Bacon, 2007.

Berg, Bruce L. *Qualitative Research Methods for the Social Sciences.* 5th ed. Boston: Pearson, 2004.

Berger, Peter L. *The Desecularization of the World: Resurgent Religion and World Politics.* Washington, DC: Ethics and Public Policy Center, Eerdmans, 1999.

Berger, Roni. "Now I see It, Now I don't: Researcher's Position and Reflexivity in Qualitative Research." *Qualitative Research* 15, no. 2 (2015): 219–34.

Bevan, Vaughan. *The Development of British Immigration Law.* London: Croom Helm, 1986.

Bevans, Stephen B. *Models of Contextual Theology.* Faith and Cultures. Revised and expanded edition. Maryknoll: Orbis Books, 2002.

Bewaji, John Ayotunde. *Beauty and Culture: Perspectives in Black Aesthetics.* Ibadan: Spectrum Books, 2004.

Bewaji, John Ayotunde. "Ethics and Morality in Yoruba Culture." In *Companion to African Philosophy*, edited by Kwasi Wiredu, 396–403. London: Blackwell, 2004.

Birks, Melanie, and Jane Mills. *Grounded Theory: A Practical Guide*. 2nd ed. London: SAGE, 2015.

Blaxter, Loraine, Christina Hughes, and Malcolm Tight. *How to Research*. 4th ed. Maidenhead: Open University Press, 2010.

Bloomberg, Linda Dale, and Marie Volpe. *Completing Your Qualitative Dissertation: A Roadmap from Beginning to End*. London: SAGE, 2008.

Blumer, Hebert George. *Symbolic Interactionalism: Perspective and Method*. Berkeley, California: University of California Press, 1969.

Blunt, Peter, and Merrick Jones. "Exploring the Limits of Western Leadership Theory in East Asia and Africa." *Personnel Review* 26, nos. 1–2 (1997): 6–23.

Boersema, Pieter R. "Contextualization and the Need for Transformation: A Double Etic-Emic-Model." In *Mission und Re-Flexion im Kontext. Perspektiven Evangelikaler Missionswissenschaft im 21. Jahrhundert*, edited by Friedemann Walldorf, 257–263. Nürn-berg/Bonn: VTR/VKM, 2010.

Boff, Leonardo. *Ecclesiogenesis: The Base Communities Reinvent the Church*. Collins Flame. London: Collins, 1986.

Bohning, Wolf Rüdiger. "International Migration and the Western World: Past, Present, Future." *International Migration* 16, no. 1 (1978): 11–22.

Bolden, Richard, and Philip Kirk. "African Leadership: Surfacing New Understandings through Leadership Development." *International Journal of Cross Cultural Management* 9, no. 1 (2009): 69–86.

Bonilla-Silva, Eduardo. *Racism without Racists: Color-Blind Racism and the Persistence of Racial Inequality in the United States*. 2nd ed. Lanham: Rowman and Littlefield Publishers, Inc., 2006.

Bonilla-Silva, Eduardo. *White Supremacy and Racism in the Post-Civil Right Era*. London: Lynne Rienner Publishers, 2001.

Bosch, David. *Spirituality for the Road*. Scottdale,: Herald Press, 1979.

Bowen, John, ed. *The Missionary Letters of Vincent Donovan: 1957–1973*. Eugene: Pickwick, 2011.

Branson, Mark Lau, and Juan Francisco Martinez. *Churches, Cultures and Leadership: A Practical Theology of Congregations and Ethnicities*. Downers Grove: IVP Academic, 2011.

Brenkert, George G., ed. *Corporate Integrity and Accountability*. Thousand Oaks: Sage, 2004.

British Sociological Association. "Statement of Ethical Practice 2017." https://www.britsoc.co.uk/media/24310/bsa_statement_of_ethical_practice.pdf.

Brouwer, Douglas J. *How to Become a Multicultural Church*. Grand Rapids: Eerdmans, 2017.

Brown, Colin. "Same Difference: The Persistence of Racial Disadvantage in the British Employment Market." In *Racism and Antiracism*, edited by Peter Braham, Ali Rattansi and Richard Skellington, 46–63. London: The Open University, 1993.

Bruce, Steve. "The Demise of Christianity in Britain." In *Predicting Religion: Christian, Secular, and Alternative Futures*, edited by Grace Davie, Linda Woodhead and Paul Heelas, 53–63. Burlington, VT: Ashgate, 2003.

Bruce, Steve, ed. *Religion and Modernization*. Oxford: Clarendon Press, 1992.

Bruce, Steve. *Religion in the Modern World: From Cathedrals to Cults*. Oxford: Oxford University Press, 1996.

Bruce, Steve. "Secularization and Church Growth in the United Kingdom." *Journal of Religion in Europe* 6, no. 3 (2013): 273–296.

Bryant, Antony. *Grounded Theory and Grounded Theorizing: Pragmatism in Research Practice*. New York: Oxford University Press, 2017.

Bryman, Alan. *Social Research Methods*. 2nd ed. Oxford: Oxford University Press, 2004.

Bryman, Alan, and Robert G. Burgess. *Analyzing Qualitative Research*. London: Routledge, 1994.

Burke, Johnson, and Larry Christensen. *Educational Research: Quantitative, Qualitative, and Mixed Approaches*. Thousand Oaks: Sage Publications, 2014.

Cacciattolo, Marcelle. "Ethical Considerations in Research." In *The Praxis of English Language Teaching and Learning (PELT)*, 55–73. Leiden, The Netherlands: Brill, 2015.

Caiata-Zufferey, Maria. "The Abductive Art of Discovery: Insights from a Qualitative Study on Unaffected Women Managing Genetic Risk of Breast and Ovarian Cancer." *International Journal of Qualitative Methods* 17, no. 1 (2018). https://doi.org/10.1177/1609406917750973.

Campbell-Evans, Glenda, Jan Gray, and Bridget Leggett. "Adaptive Leadership in School Boards in Australia: An Emergent Model." *School Leadership & Management* 34, no. 5 (2014): 538–552.

Candler School of Theology. "Jehu J. Hanciles." https://candler.emory.edu/faculty/profiles/hanciles-jehu.html.

Carling, Jørgen, Marta Bivand Erdal, and Rojan Ezzati. "Beyond the Insider-Outsider Divide in Migration Research." *Migration Studies* 2, no. 1 (2013): 36–54.

Carr, Eloise C. J., and Allison Worth. "The Use of the Telephone Interview for Research." *NT Research* 6, no. 1 (2001): 511–524.

Castillo, Giselle A. "The Importance of Adaptive Leadership: Management of Change." *International Journal of Novel Research in Education and Learning* 5, no. 2 (2018): 100–106.

Cegielka, Franciszek Antoni. *Handbook of Ecclesiology and Christology: A Concise, Authoritative Review of the Mystery of the Church and the Incarnation in the Light of Vatican II.* Staten Island: Alba House, 1971.

Centre for the Study of Modern Christianity. "Centre for Church Growth Research Staff." https://csmc.webspace.durham.ac.uk/about/people/#:~:text=The%20Centre%20for%20Church%20Growth%20Research%20is%20run%20by%20David,Cooper%20and%20Rob%20Barward%2DSymmons.&text=David%20Goodhew%20is%20Co%2DDirector,Centre%20for%20Church%20Growth%20Research.

Chai, Teresa. "A Look at Contextualization - Historical Background, Definition, Function, Scope and Models." *Asian Journal of Pentecostal Studies* 18, no. 1 (February 2015): 3–19.

Charity Commission for England and Wales. https://register-of-charities.charitycommission.gov.uk/.

Charmaz, Kathy. *Constructing Grounded Theory: Introducing Qualitative Methods.* 2nd ed. London: Sage, 2014.

Chester, Tim, and Steve Timmis. *Total Church: A Radical Reshaping around Gospel and Community.* Nottingham: Inter-Varsity Press, 2007.

Cho, Yong-Gi. *Successful Home Cell Groups.* Seoul: Seoul Logos Co., 1997.

Chou, Vivian. "How Science and Genetics Are Reshaping the Race Debate of the 21st Century." 2017. https://sitn.hms.harvard.edu/flash/2017/science-genetics-reshaping-race-debate-21st-century/.

Christian Enquiry Agency. "Contributions of the Black Majority Church." https://christianity.org.uk/article/contributions-of-the-black-majority-church.

Christine, Leonard. *A Giant in Ghana: 3000 Churches in 50 Years – The Story of James McKeown and the Church of Pentecost.* Chichester: New Wine Press, 1989.

Christopher, David P. *British Culture: An Introduction.* 2nd ed. Abingdon, Oxon: Routledge, 2006.

Chun Tie, Ylona, Melanie Birks, and Karen Francis. "Grounded Theory Research: A Design Framework for Novice Researchers." *SAGE Open Medicine* 7 (2019): 1–8.

Clair, Matthew, and Jeffrey Denis. "Sociology of Racism." https://scholar.harvard.edu/files/matthewclair/files/sociology_of_racism_clairandenis_2015.pdf.

Clarke, Adele. *Situational Analysis: Grounded Theory after the Postmodern Turn.* Thousand Oaks: Sage Publications, 2005.

Coleman, James Smoot. *Nigeria: Background to Nationalism.* Berkeley: University of California Press, 1963.

Collins, Christopher S., and Carrie M. Stockton. "The Central Role of Theory in Qualitative Research." *International Journal of Qualitative Methods* 17, no. 1 (2018). https://journals.sagepub.com/doi/abs/10.1177/1609406918797475.

Comiskey, Joel. *Home Cell Group Explosion.* Houston: Touch Publications, 1998.
Commission on Race and Ethnic Disparities. "Commission on Race and Ethnic Disparities: The Report." 2021. https://assets.publishing.service.gov.uk/government/uploads/system/uploads/attachment_data/file/974507/20210331_-_CRED_Report_-_FINAL_-_Web_Accessible.pdf.
Cope, Diane G. "Methods & Meanings: Conducting Pilot and Feasibility Studies." *Oncology Nursing Forum* 42, no. 2 (2015): 196–197.
Cormode, Scott. "Adaptive Change Requires a Holding Environment." *De Pree Journal.* https://depree.org/adaptive-change-requires-a-holding-environment/.
Cormode, Scott. "Constructing a Holding Environment." https://www.fuller.edu/next-faithful-step/resources/constructing-a-holding-environment/.
Cornell, Stephen E., and Douglas Hartmann. *Ethnicity and Race: Making Identities in a Changing World.* Thousand Oaks, CA: Pine Forge Press, 2006.
Cousins, Liz, Sam Davies, Linda Grant, Nev Kirk, Tony Lane, Martyn Nightingale, Ron Noon, Andy Shallice, and Tony Wailley. *Merseyside in Crisis.* Birkenhead, UK: Merseyside Socialist Research Group, 1980.
Cox, Harvey. *Fire from Heaven: The Rise of Pentecostal Spirituality and the Reshaping of Religion in the Twenty-first Century.* London: Da Capo Press Inc., 1996.
Cray, Graham, ed. *Mission-Shaped Church: Church Planting and Fresh Expressions of Church in a Changing Context.* London: Church House Publishing, 2004.
Creswell, John W. *Research Design: Qualitative and Quantitative Approaches.* Thousand Oaks: SAGE, 1994.
Creswell, John W. *Research Design: Qualitative, Quantitative and Mixed Methods Approaches.* 2nd ed. Thousand Oaks: SAGE, 2003.
Crowther, Jonathan, ed. *Oxford Guide to British and American Culture for Learners of English.* Oxford: Oxford University Press, 1999.
CSW. "Boko Haram Executes Chair of Christian Association of Nigeria in Adamawa State." https://www.csw.org.uk/2020/01/21/press/4530/article.htm.
Dada, Sunday Olaoluwa. "Aristotle and the Ọmọlúwàbí Ethos: Ethical Implications for Public Morality in Nigeria." https://news.clas.ufl.edu/aristotle-and-the-omoluwabi-ethos-ethical-implications-for-public-morality-in-nigeria/.
Damazio, Frank. *Strategic Church: A Life-Changing Church in an Ever-Changing Culture.* Benin, Nigeria: Beulahland Publications, 2015.
Daneel, Marthinus, and Dana Lee Robert. *African Christian Outreach.* African Initiatives in Christian Mission. 1st ed., 2 vols. Menlo Park, South Africa: Southern African Missiological Society, 2001.
David, Matthew, and Carole D. Sutton. *Social Research: The Basics.* London: SAGE, 2004.

Davie, Grace. *Religion in Britain Since 1945: Believing without Belonging.* Cambridge: Blackwell, 1994.

Davies, Charlotte Aull. *Reflexive Ethnography: A Guide to Researching Selves and Others.* Association of Social Anthropologists/ASA Research Methods in Social Anthropology. London: Routledge, 1999.

Davies, Madeleine. "'We Failed '60s immigrants.'" 2013. www.churchtimes.co.uk/articles/2013/25-october/news/uk/we-failed-60s-immigrants.

Davis, Ken. "Multicultural Church Planting Models." *The Journal of Ministry and Theology* (2003): 114–127.

Dayfoot, Arthur Charles. *The Shaping of the West Indian Church 1492–1962.* Barbados: The Press, University of West Indies, 1999.

Denscombe, Martyn. *The Good Research Guide: For Small-Scale Social Research Projects.* Open UP Study Skills. Maidenhead: Open University Press, 2014.

Denzin, Norman K., and Yvonna S. Lincoln. *The Sage Handbook of Qualitative Research.* 3rd ed. Thousand Oaks: Sage Publications, 2005.

Derrida, Jacques. "The Principle of Hospitality." *Parallax* 11, no. 1 (2005): 6–9.

DeYmaz, Mark. *Building a Healthy Multi-ethnic Church: Mandate, Commitments and Practices of a Diverse Congregation.* San Francisco, CA: John Wiley & Sons, 2010.

DeYmaz, Mark, and Harry Li. *Leading a Healthy Multi-Ethnic Church: Seven Common Challenges and How to Overcome Them.* Grand Rapids, MI: Zondervan, 2013.

Dobel, J. Patrick. "Integrity in the Public Service." *Public Administration Review* 50, no. 3 (2016): 354–366.

Dörnyei, Zoltán. *Research Methods in Applied Linguistics: Quantitative, Qualitative, and Mixed Methodologies.* Oxford Applied Linguistics. Oxford: Oxford University Press, 2007.

Duignan, Brian. "Enlightenment." *Encyclopedia Britannica*, 14 October 2021. https://www.britannica.com/event/Enlightenment-European-history.

Dulles, Avery. *Models of the Church.* 1st ed. Garden City: Doubleday, 1974.

Dunlow, Jacob. "Disciples of All Nations: The Challenge of Nurturing Faith in Multi-Ethnic Congregations." *Christian Education Journal* 14, no. 2 (2017): 285–305.

Dwyer, Sonya Corbin, and Jennifer L. Buckle. "The Space Between: On Being an Insider-Outsider in Qualitative Research." *International Journal of Qualitative Methods* 8, no. 1 (2009): 54–63.

Easton, Mark. "The English Question: What is the Nation's Identity?" www.bbc.co.uk/news/uk-44306737.

Elliott, Ralph H. "Dangers of the Church Growth Movement." 1–5. http://www.southernbaptistsermons.org/images/Dangers_of_the_Church_Growth_MovementrrM2.pdf.

Ellis, Stephen, and Gerrie ter Haar. "The Role of Religion in Development: Towards a New Relationship between the European Union and Africa." *European Journal of Development Research* 18, no. 3 (2006): 351–367.

Emerson, Michael O. "The Persistent Problem." 2010. 11–18. https://www.baylor.edu/content/services/document.php/110974.pdf.

Erdman, Charles R. *The Gospel of Luke: An Exposition*. Philadelphia: The Westminster Press, 1936.

Erickson, Frederick. "Qualitative Research Methods for Science Education." In *Second International Handbook of Science Education*, edited by Barry J. Fraser, Kenneth G. Tobin, and Campbell J. McRobbie, 1451–1470. Springer International Handbooks of Education. Heidelberg: Springer, 2012.

Escobar, Samuel. "Mission from Everywhere to Everyone: The Home Base in a New Century." In *Edinburgh 2010: Mission Then and Now*, edited by David A. Kerr and Kenneth R. Ross, 185–198. Oxford: Regnum/Oxford Centre for Mission Studies, 2009.

Escobar, Samuel. *A Time of Mission*. Leicester: Intervarsity Press, 2003.

Evangelical Alliance. "About Us." https://www.eauk.org/about-us.

Evangelical Alliance. "Rev Dr Israel Oluwole Olofinjana." https://www.eauk.org/author/israel-oluwole-olofinjana.

Evans, John Maxwell. *Immigration Law*. London: Sweet & Maxwell, 1983.

Fadipe, Nathaniel Akinremi. *The Sociology of the Yoruba*. Ibadan: Ibadan University Press, 2012.

Fayemi, Ademola Kazeem. "Human Personality and the Yoruba Worldview: An Ethico-Sociological Interpretation." *The Journal of Pan African Studies* 2, no. 9 (2009): 166–176.

Federation of Asian Bishops' Conference (FABC). *Evangelization in Modern Day Asia: The First Plenary Assembly of the Federation of Asian Bishops' Conference*. Hong Kong: Office of the Secretary-General, FABC, 1974.

Finn, John A. *Getting a PHD: An Action Plan to Help Manage Your Research, Your Supervisor and Your Project*. London: Routledge, 2005.

Fleming, Jenny, and Karsten E. Zegwaard. "Methodologies, Methods and Ethical Considerations for Conducting Research in Work-Integrated Learning." *International Journal of Work-Integrated Learning, Special Issue* 19, no. 3 (2018): 205–213.

Flemming, Dean. *Contextualization in the New Testament: Patterns for Theology and Mission*. Downers Grove, IL: InterVarsity Press, 2005.

Flick, Uwe. *An Introduction to Qualitative Research*. 3rd ed. London: Sage, 2006.

Fluegge, Glenn K. "The Dubious History of "Contextualization" and the Cautious Case for Its Continued Use." *Lutheran Mission Matters* XXV, 1, no. 50 (May 2017): 50–69.

Flynn, Rebecca Ann. "Are Strict Churches Really Stronger? A Study of Strictness, Congregational Activity, and Growth in American Protestant Churches." MA thesis, West Virginia University, 2010.

Fontana, Andrea and James H. Frey. "The Interview: From Neutral Stance to Political Involvement." In *The Sage Handbook of Qualitative Research*, 3rd ed., edited by Norman K. Denzin and Yvonna S. Lincoln, 695–728. Thousand Oaks: Sage Publications, 2005.

Forrester, Duncan B. "Review of *Understanding Church Growth*." *Scottish Journal of Theology* 37, no. 3 (1984): 421–423.

Fox, Kate. *Watching the English: The Hidden Rules of English Behaviour*. London: Hodder and Stoughton, 2004.

Fox, Kate. *Watching the English: The Hidden Rules of English Behaviour*. Rev. ed. London: Hodder & Stoughton, 2014.

Frost, Michael, and Alan Hirsch. *The Shaping of Things to Come: Innovation and Mission for the 21st-Century Church*. Peabody: Hendrickson Publishers, 2003.

Fryer, Peter. *Staying Power: The History of Black People in Britain*. London: Pluto Press, 2018.

Fusch, Patricia, Gene Fusch, and Lawrence Ness. "How to Conduct a Mini-ethnographic Case Study: A Guide for Novice Researchers." *The Qualitative Report* 22, no. 3 (2017): 923–941.

Galdas, Paul. "Revisiting Bias in Qualitative Research: Reflections on Its Relationship with Funding and Impact." *International Journal of Qualitative Methods* 16, no. 1 (2017): 1–2.

Garces-Forley, Kathline. *Crossing the Ethnic Divide: The Multiethnic Church on a Mission*. New York: Oxford University Press, 2007.

Garces-Forley, Kathline "New Opportunities and New Values: The Emergence of the Multicultural Church." *The Annals of the American Academy* 612 (2007): 209–224.

The New International Dictionary of the Christian Church. Grand Rapids: Paternoster Press, 1978.

Gbadegesin, Segun. *African Philosophy: Traditional Yoruba Philosophy and Contemporary African Realities*. American University Studies. New York: Peter Lang, 1991.

Gbadegesin, Segun. "In search of *Agbasanko*." *The Nation Newspaper* (Lagos, Nigeria), 28 September 2007.

Gbote, Eric Z.M., and S. Thias Kgatla. "Prosperity Gospel: A Missiological Assessment." *HTS Teologiese Studies/ Theological Studies* 70, no. 1 (2014).

GENUKI. "List of Churches For: Liverpool." https://www.genuki.org.uk/church_list/LANLiverpool.

"George Floyd: Video Shows Minneapolis Police Officer Kneeling on Neck of Black Man who Died | ABC7." https://www.youtube.com/watch?v=CcsIU9ozt6I&bpctr=1601384175.

Gerloff, Roswith. "Black Christian Communities in Birmingham: The Problem of Basic Recognition." In *Religion in the Birmingham Area*. Birmingham, UK: University of Birmingham, 1975.

Gerloff, Roswith. "My Pilgrimage in Mission." *International Bulletin of Missionary Research* 37, no. 1 (2013): 27–30.

Gerloff, Roswith. *Open Space: The African Christian Diaspora in Europe and the Quest for Human Community*. Geneva: World Council of Churches, 2000.

Gerloff, Roswith. *A Plea for British Black Theologies: The Black Church Movement in Britain in Its Transatlantic Cultural and Theological Interaction*. Studies in the Intercultural History of Christianity. Vol. 77, Frankfurt am Main: Peter Lang, 1992.

Gerloff, Roswith. "A Plea for British Black Theologies: The Black Church Movement in Britain in Its Transatlantic Cultural and Theological Interaction with Special Reference to the Pentecostal Oneness (Apostolic) And Sabbatarian Movements." PhD diss., University of Birmingham, 1991.

Gerloff, Roswith. *The Significance of the African Christian Diaspora in Europe (with Special Reference to Britain)*. Society for Caribbean Studies Conference, 1997.

Getz, Gene A. "The Christian Home Part II." *Bibliotheca Sacra* 126, no. 502 (1969): 109–114.

Ghosh, Pallab. "Black Scientists Say UK Research is Institutionally Racist." *Science and Environment*, 11 October 2021. https://www.bbc.co.uk/news/science-environment-58795079.

Ghosh, Pallab. "Royal Society of Chemistry Report Says Racism 'Pervasive.'" *Science and Environment*, 16 March 2022. https://www.bbc.co.uk/news/science-environment-60708712.

Gibbs, Eddie. *Leadership Next: Changing Leaders in a Changing Culture*. Downers Grove: InterVarsity Press, 2005.

Gibbs, Eddie. "The Power Behind the Principles." In *Church Growth: State of the Art*, edited by C. Peter Wagner, ch. 19. Carol Stream: Tyndale House Publishers, 1986.

Gibbs, Eddie, and Ian Coffey. *Church Next: Quantum Changes in Christian Ministry*. Leicester: Inter-Varsity Press, 2001.

Gilbert, G. Nigel. *Researching Social Life*. 3rd ed. London: SAGE, 2008.

Glaser, Barney G., and Anselm L. Strauss. *The Discovery of Grounded Theory: Strategies for Qualitative Research*. Chicago: Aldine Publications, 1967.

Gläser, Jochen, and Grit Laudel. "Life with and without Coding: Two Methods for Early-Stage Data Analysis in Qualitative Research Aiming at Causal

Explanations." *Forum Qualitative Social Research* 14, Article 5, no. 2 (2013): 1–37.

Glasson, Barbara. "A Personal Message from the President of the Methodist Conference, the Revd Dr Barbara Glasson." 2 June 2020. https://www.methodist.org.uk/about-us/news/latest-news/all-news/a-personal-message-from-the-president-of-the-methodist-conference-the-revd-dr-barbara-glasson/.

Global Connections. "Staff Team." https://www.globalconnections.org.uk/about-us/staff.

Goodhew, David, ed. *Church Growth in Britain: 1980 to the Present*. Ashgate Contemporary Ecclesiology. Farnham, Surrey, England: Ashgate, 2012.

Goodhew, David, ed. *Growth and Decline in the Anglican Communion: 1980 to the Present*. 1st ed. London: Routledge, 2017.

Goodhew, David, ed. *Towards a Theology of Church Growth*. Ashgate Contemporary Ecclesiology. Farnham, Surrey, England: Ashgate, 2015.

Goodhew, David and Anthony-Paul Cooper, eds. *The Desecularisation of the City: London's Churches, 1980 to the Present*. Routledge Studies in Religion. London: Routledge, 2018.

Gornik, Mark R. *Word Made Global: Stories of African Christianity in New York City*. Grand Rapids: Eerdmans, 2011.

Grace, Howard. *Vision of a Shared Humanity: Being Aware of Shared Human Nature*. 2019.

Green, J.B. *The Gospel of Luke*. Grand Rapids: Eerdmans, 1997.

Green, Lynn. "George Floyd - 'I Can't Breathe.'" https://www.baptist.org.uk/Articles/580106/George_Floyd_our.aspx.

Greene, Melanie J. "On the Inside Looking In: Methodological Insights and Challenges in Conducting Qualitative Insider Research." *The Qualitative Report* 19, no. 29 (2014): 1–13.

Greeson, Kevin. "Comprehensive Contextualization." In *Discovering the Mission of God*, edited by Mike Barnett, 420–436. Downers Grove: IVP, 2012.

Griffith, Alison I. "Insider/Outsider: Epistemological Privilege and Mothering Work." *Human Studies* 21 (1998): 361–76.

Groody, Daniel G. "Crossing the Divide: Foundations of a Theology of Migration and Refuges." *Theological Studies* 70, no. 3 (2009): 638–667.

Gubrium, Jaber F., and James A. Holstein. *Handbook of Interview Research: Context & Method*. Thousand Oaks, CA: Sage Publications, 2002.

Guetterman, Timothy, Wayne Babchuk, Michelle Howell Smith, and Jared Stevens. "Contemporary Approaches to Mixed Methods–Grounded Theory Research: A Field-Based Analysis." *Journal of Mixed Methods Research* 13, no. 2 (2019): 179–195.

Gushiken, Kevin M. "Cultivating Healthy Discipleship Settings in Multi-Ethnic Churches." *Transformation* 32, no. 1 (2015): 17–26.

Haar, Gerrie ter. *African Christians in Europe*. African Religion in Global Contexts. Nairobi, Kenya: Acton Publishers, 2001.

Haar, Gerrie ter. *Halfway to Paradise: African Christians in Europe*. Fairwater, Cardiff: Cardiff Academic Press, 1998.

Haar, Gerrie ter. *How God Became African: African Spirituality and Western Secular Thought*. Philadelphia: University of Pennsylvania Press, 2009.

Haar, Gerrie ter. *Strangers and Sojourners: Religious Communities in the Diaspora*. Leuven: Peeters, 1998.

Hammarberg, Karin, Maggie Kirkman, and Sheryl De Lacey. "Qualitative Research Methods: When to Use Them and How to Judge Them." *Human Reproduction* 31, no. 3 (2016): 498–501.

Hammersley, Martyn. "On the Teacher as Researcher." In *Educational Research: Current Issues*, edited by Martyn Hammersley. London: Paul Chapman/The Open University, 1993.

Hammersley, Martyn, and Paul Atkinson. *Ethnography: Principles in Practice*. 3rd ed. London: Taylor & Francis Group, 2007.

Hanciles, Jehu. ""Africa is our Fatherland": The Black Atlantic, Globalization, and Modern African Christianity." *Theology Today* 71, no. 2 (2014): 207–220.

Hanciles, Jehu. *Beyond Christendom: Globalization, African Migration, and the Transformation of the West*. Maryknoll: Orbis Books, 2008.

Hanciles, Jehu. *Euthanasia of a Mission: African Church Autonomy in a Colonial Context*. Westport: Praeger, 2002.

Hanciles, Jehu. "Keeping the Faith: Immigration, Religion, and the Unmaking of Global Culture." In *Christianity and Religious Plurality: Historical and Global Perspectives*, edited by Wilbert R. Shenk and Richard J. Plantinga. Eugene: Cascade Books, 2016.

Hanciles, Jehu. *Migration and the Making of Global Christianity*. Grand Rapids: Eerdmans, 2021.

Hanciles, Jehu. ""Singing the Song of the Lord on Foreign Soil": What the Early Centuries Tell Us about the Migrant Factor in the Making of Global Christianity." In *Christianities in Migration: The Global Perspective*, edited by Elaine Padilla and Peter Phan. Palgrave Macmillan's Christianities of the World, 37–53. New York: Palgrave Macmillan, 2016.

Hanciles, Jehu, ed. *World Christianity: History, Methodologies, Horizons*. New York: Orbis, 2021.

Haradhan, Mohajan. "Qualitative Research Methodology in Social Sciences and Related Subjects." *Journal of Economic Development, Environment and People* 7, no. 1 (2018): 23–48.

Hardison, Richard Willson. "A Theological Critique of Multi-ethnic Church Movement: 2000-2013." PhD diss., The Southern Baptist Theological Seminary, 2014.

Harris, Joseph E. *Global Dimensions of the African Diaspora*. Washington, DC: Howard University Press, 1982.

Harrison, Patricia. "Bridging Theory and Training." In *Local Theology for the Global Church: Principles for an Evangelical Approach to Contextualization*, edited by Matthew Cook, Rob Haskell, Ruth Julian and Natee Tanchanpongs, 195-213. Pasadena: William Carey Library, 2010.

Hassan, Zailinawati, Peter Schattner, and Danielle Mazza. "Doing a Pilot Study: Why Is It Essential?" *Malaysian Family Physician: The Official Journal of the Academy of Family Physicians of Malaysia* 1, no. 2-3 (2006): 70-73.

Hastings, Adrian. *The Church in Africa: 1450-1950*. Oxford History of the Christian Church. Oxford: Oxford University Press, 1994.

Hawkins, David. "Foreword." In *African Christianity in Britain: Diaspora, Doctrine and Dialogue*, edited by Chigor Chike, ix-xii. Bloomington: AuthorHouse, 2007.

Hayfield, Nikki, and Caroline Huxley. "Insider and Outsider Perspectives: Reflections on Researcher Identities in Research with Lesbian and Bisexual Women." *Qualitative Research in Psychology* 12, no. 2 (2015): 91-106.

Hayward, John. "A Dynamical Model of Church Growth and Global Revival." Annual Meeting for the Scientific Study of Religion, Houston, Texas, USA, 18-21 October 2000.

Hazy, James K. "Parsing the 'Influential Increment' in the Language of Complexity: Uncovering the Systemic Mechanisms of Leadership Influence." *Journal of Complexity in Leadership and Management* 2, no. 1 (2011): 116-132.

Hearn, Mark. "Color-Blind Racism, Color-Blind Theology, and Church Practices." *Religious Education* 104, no. 3 (2009): 272-288.

Heath, Anthony, and Jane Roberts. *British Identity: Its Sources and Possible Implications for Civic Attitudes and Behaviour*. Department of Sociology, University of Oxford. https://webarchive.nationalarchives.gov.uk/+/http:/www.justice.gov.uk/docs/british-identity.pdf.

Heerden, Willie Van. "'The Proverb is the Drum of God': On the Use of African Proverbs in the Interaction between African Culture and the Christian Faith." *Scriptura: Journal for Biblical, Theological and Contextual Hermeneutics* 81 (2002): 462-475.

Heifetz, Ronald A. *Leadership without Easy Answers*. Cambridge: Belknap Press of Harvard University Press, 1994.

Heifetz, Ronald A., Alexander Grashow, and Martin Linsky. *The Practice of Adaptive Leadership: Tools and Tactics for Changing Your Organization and the World*. Boston: Harvard Business Press, 2009.

Heifetz, Ronald A., and Donald L. Laurie. "Best of HBR: The Work of Leadership." *Harvard Business Review*, December 2001 special issue (2002): 36–48.

Heifetz, Ronald A., and Martin Linsky. *Leadership on the Line: Staying Alive through the Dangers of Leading.* Boston: Harvard Business School Press, 2002.

Hellawell, David. "Inside-Out Analysis of the Insider-Outsider Concept as a Heuristic Device to Develop Reflexivity in Students Doing Qualitative Research." *Teaching in Higher Education* 11, no. 4 (2006): 483–494.

Helmond, Van, and Donna Palmer. *Staying Power: Black Presence in Liverpool.* Liverpool: National Museum & Galleries on Merseyside, 1991.

Hennink, Monique, Inge Hutter, and Ajay Bailey. *Qualitative Research Methods.* 2nd ed. Thousand Oaks: SAGE Publications Ltd., 2020.

Herbert, Hoefer. "Rooted or Uprooted: The Challenge of Contextualization in Missions." *International Journal of Frontier Missiology* 24, no. 3 (2007): 131–138.

Hesselgrave, David J. "Contextualization That Is Authentic and Relevant." *International Journal of Frontier Missions* 12, no. 3 (1995): 115–119.

Hesselgrave, David, and Edward Rommen. *Contextualization: Meanings, Methods and Models.* Pasadena, CA: William Carey Library, 1989.

Heuser, Andreas. "Religio-Scapes of the Prosperity Gospel: An Introduction." In *Pastures of Plenty: Tracing Religio-Scapes of the Prosperity Gospel in Africa and Beyond*, edited by Andreas Heuser, 15–30. Frankfurt: Peter Lang, 2015.

Heyck, Thomas William. "The Decline of Christianity in Twentieth-Century Britain." *Albion: A Quarterly Journal Concerned with British Studies* 28, no. 3 (1996): 437–453.

Hibbert, Evelyn, and Richard Hibbert. *Leading Multicultural Teams.* Pasadena, CA: William Carey Library, 2014.

Hickman, Christine B. "The Devil and the One Drop Rule: Racial Categories, African Americans, and the U.S. Census." *Michigan Law Review* 95, no. 5 (1997): 1161–1265.

Hiebert, Paul G. "Critical Contextualization." *International Bulletin of Missionary Research* (1987): 104–112.

Higgins, Thomas Winfield. "Mission Networks and the African Diaspora in Britain." *African Diaspora* 5, no. 2 (2012): 165–186.

Hinds, Dianne. *Research Instruments.* London: Routledge Falmer, 2000.

His Gospel to Our Peoples. Vol. 2. Manila: Cardinal Bea Institute, 1976.

Historic England. "Racism and Resistance." https://historicengland.org.uk/research/inclusive-heritage/another-england/a-brief-history/racism-and-resistance/.

Hock, Klaus. "Catching the Wing: Some Remarks on the Growing Interface of Migration Studies on African Religions." In *European Traditions in the Study* of Religion in Africa, edited by Ludwig Frieder and Afe Adogame, 329–339. Wiesbaden: Harrassowitz Verlag, 2004.

Hock, Klaus. "Religion on the Move: Transcultural Perspectives. Discourses on Diaspora Religion between Category Formation and the Quest for Religious Identity." In *Christianity in Africa and the African Diaspora: The Appropriation of a Scattered Heritage*, edited by Afeosemime U. Adogame, Roswith Gerloff and Klaus Hock, 235–247. London: Continuum International Publishing Group, 2008.

Hocken, Peter. "Review of *A Plea for British Black Theologies: The Black Church Movement in Britain in Its Transatlantic Cultural and Theological Interaction*." *PNEUMA: The Journal of the Society for Pentecostal Studies* 15, no. 1 (1993): 117–119.

Hollenweger, Walter J. "Foreword." In *A Plea for British Black Theologies: The Black Church Movement in Britain in Its Transatlantic Cultural and Theological Interaction*, edited by Roswith Gerloff. Studies in the Intercultural History of Christianity. Frankfurt am Main: Peter Lang, 1992.

Hong, Young-Gi. *Dynamism and Dilemma: The Nature of Charismatic Pastoral Leadership in the Korean Mega-Churches*. Oxford: Oxford Centre for Mission Studies, 2000.

Hong, Young-Gi "Models of Church Growth Movement." *Transformation* 21, no. 2 (2004): 101–113.

Hood, Robert Earl. *Begrimed and Black: Christian Traditions on Blacks and Blackness*. Minneapolis, MN: Fortress Press, 1994.

Hout, Michael, Andrew Greeley, and Melissa J. Wilde. "The Demographic Imperative in Religious Change in the United States." *American Journal of Sociology* 107, no. 2 (2001): 468–500.

Hunt, Stephen. "'Winning Ways': Globalisation and the Impact of the Health and Wealth Gospel." *Journal of Contemporary Religion* 15, no. 3 (2000): 331–347.

Hunter, George G. *The Contagious Congregation: Frontiers in Evangelism and Church Growth*. Nashville: Abingdon, 1979.

Iannaccone, Laurence, Daniel Olsen, and Rodney Stark. "Religious Resources and Church Growth." *Social Forces* 74, no. 2 (1995): 705–731.

Ijaola, Samson O. "Pentecostalism, the Prosperity Gospel, and Poverty in Africa." In *Pentecostalism and Politics in Africa*, edited by Adeshina Afolayan, Olajumoke Yacob-Haliso and Toyin Falola, 137–158. African Histories and Modernity: Palgrave, Macmillan, 2018.

Ikuenobe, Polycarp. "Good and Beautiful: A Moral-Aesthetic View of Personhood in African Communal Traditions." *Essays in Philosophy* 17, no. 1 (2016):125–163.

Inskeep, Kenneth W. "A Short History of Church Growth Research." In *Church and Denomination Growth*, edited by D.A. Roozen and C.K. Hadaway, 135–148, 1993.

Institute for Church Growth. *Church Planting: A Research Report on Korean Church Planting*. Seoul: ICG, 2003.

Jackson, Bob. *Going for Growth: What Works at Local Church Level*. London: Church House Publishing, 2006.

Jackson, Bob. *What Makes Churches Grow*. London: Church House Publishing, 2015.

Jea, John. *The Life, History, and Unparalleled Sufferings of John Jea, the African Preacher*. Chapel Hill: University of North Carolina, 2001.

Jenkins, Daniel. "Review of The Religious and the Secular, David Martin." *The Journal of Religion* 51, no. 4 (1971): 295–300.

Jenkinson, Jacqueline. "Black 1919: Riots, Racism, and Resistance in Imperial Britain." *The Journal of British Studies* 49, no. 4 (2010): 905–907.

Jenkinson, Jacqueline. "The 1919 Race Riots in Britain: Their Background and Consequences." PhD diss., University of Edinburgh, 1987.

Jenkinson, Jacqueline. "Black Sailors on Red Clydeside: Rioting, Reactionary Trade Unionism and Conflicting Notions of 'Britishness' Following the First World War." https://core.ac.uk/download/pdf/9048067.pdf.

John Paul II. "Post Synodal Apostolic Exhortation: Ecclesia in Africa." 1995. https://www.vatican.va/content/john-paul-ii/en/apost_exhortations/documents/hf_jp-ii_exh_14091995_ecclesia-in-africa.html.

Johnson-Kanda, Ivy, and Robert M. Yawson. "Complex Adaptive Leadership for Organization and Human Development." Paper presented at the 55th Annual Eastern Academy of Management, Providence, Rhode Island, 2018.

Jordan, Winthrop Donaldson. *White over Black*. 2nd ed. Chapel Hill: The University of North Carolina Press, 1968.

Kalu, Ogbu. *African Christianity: An African Story*. Perspectives on Christianity Series. Pretoria: Dept. of Church History, University of Pretoria, 2005.

Karnieli-Miller, Orit, Roni Strier, and Liat Pessach. "Power Relations in Qualitative Research." *Qualitative Health Research* 19, no. 2 (2009): 279–289.

Kelley, Dean M. *Why Conservative Churches Are Growing: A Study in Sociology of Religion*. New York: Harper & Row, 1972.

Kerstetter, Katie. "Insider, Outsider, or Somewhere Between: The Impact of Researchers' Identities on the Community-Based Research Process." *Journal of Rural Social Sciences* 27, Article 7, no. 2 (2012): 99–117.

Kesting, Peter, John P. Ulhøi, Lynda Jiwen Song, and Hongyi Niu. "The Impact of Leadership Styles on Innovation Management - A Review and a Synthesis." *Journal of Innovation Management* 3, no. 4 (2015): 22–41.

Killingray, David. "The Black Atlantic Missionary Movement and Africa, 1780s-1920s." *Journal of Religion in Africa* 33, no. 1 (2003): 3–31.

Killingray, David, and Joel Edwards. *Black Voices: The Shaping of our Christian Experience.* Nottingham: Inter-Varsity Press England, 2007.

Kim, Beaumie. "Social Constructivism." http://epltt.coe.uga.edu/index.php?title=Social_Constructivism.

Kollman, Paul. "The History of Christianity in Africa: Foundations." https://think.nd.edu/bq/tgc-2-2/.

Kugbeadjor, William Doe, and Harvey C. Kwiyani. "Exploring Adaptive Challenges Faced by African Mission Missionaries in Britain: The Case of the Church of Pentecost." *Missio Africanus Journal of African Missiology* 1, no. 2 (2016): 4–15.

Kuhn, Wagner. "Adventist Theological-Missiology: Contextualization in Mission and Ministry." *Journal of the Adventist Theological Society* 27, nos. 1–2 (2016): 175–208.

Kumbi, Hirpo. *The Culturally Intelligent Leader: Developing Multi-ethnic Communities in a Multicultural Age.* Watford: Instant Apostle, 2017.

Küng, Hans. *The Church.* London: Burns & Oates, 1967.

Kushner, Tony. *The Battle of Britishness: Migrant Journeys, 1685 to the Present.* Manchester: Manchester University Press, 2012.

Kvale, Steinar. *Interviews: An Introduction to Qualitative Research Interviewing.* Thousand Oaks: Sage Publications, 1996.

Kwiyani, Harvey C. *Black Light: An Introduction to African Christianity.* Liverpool: Missio Africanus, forthcoming.

Kwiyani, Harvey C. "Can the West Really Be Converted?" *Missio Africanus Journal of African Missiology* 4.1 (2019): 77–96.

Kwiyani, Harvey C. "Mission after George Floyd: On White Supremacy, Colonialism and World Christianity." *ANVIL: Journal of Theology and Mission* 36, no. 3 (2020). https://churchmissionsociety.org/wp-content/uploads/2020/10/Anvil-Volume-36_Issue-3-FINAL-VERSION-2.pdf.

Kwiyani, Harvey C. *Mission-Shaped Church in a Multicultural World.* Grove Mission and Evangelism Series. Cambridge: Grove Books, 2017.

Kwiyani, Harvey C. *Mission-Shaped Church in A Multicultural World.* Oxford, UK: Grove Books Ltd., 2017.

Kwiyani, Harvey C. *Multicultural Kingdom: Ethnic Diversity, Mission and the Church.* London: SCM Press, 2020.

Kwiyani, Harvey C. *Our Children Need Roots and Wings: Equipping and Empowering Young Diaspora Africans for Life and Mission.* 2nd ed. Liverpool, UK: Missio Africanus, 2019.

Kwiyani, Harvey C. *Sent Forth: African Missionary Work in the West.* American Society of Missiology, No. 51. Maryknoll,: Orbis Books, 2014.

Kwiyani, Harvey C., and Paul A. Ayokunle. "African Congregations Adapting to COVID-19: Conversations with African Christian Nurses in Britain." *ANVIL: Journal of Theology and Mission* 37, no. 3 (2021): 32–39.

Lancaster, Gillian A. "Pilot and Feasibility Studies Come of Age." *Pilot and Feasibility Studies* 1, no. 1 (2015): 1–4.

Lancaster, Gillian A., Susanna Dodd, and Paula R. Williamson. "Design and Analysis of Pilot Studies: Recommendations for Good Practice." *Journal of Evaluation in Clinical Practice* 10, no. 2 (2004): 307–312.

Lane, Sherree Vernet. "Multiethnic Worship Representative of Heaven: A Mixed Methods Study." *Ethnomusicology Masters Theses* 7 (2009). https://digitalcommons.liberty.edu/ethno_master/7.

Langham Publishing. "Anderson Moyo." https://langhamliterature.org/author-bio?author_id=9125.

Langham Publishing. "Israel Oluwole Olofinjana." https://langhamliterature.org/author-bio?author_id=7678.

Law, Ian and June Henfrey. *A History of Race and Racism in Liverpool 1660–1950.* Liverpool: Merseyside Community Relations Council, 1981.

Law, Ian. "White Racism and Black Settlement in Liverpool." PhD diss., University of Liverpool, 1985.

League of Coloured Peoples. *Race Relations and the Schools.* London: LCP, 1944.

Levy, Jacob T. "Citizenship and National Identity." *American Political Science Review* 96, no. 1 (2002): 191–192.

Lewis, David. *The Churches of Liverpool.* Liverpool: Bluecoat, 2001.

Liamputtong, Pranee, Erica James, and Virginia Dickson-Swift. *Undertaking Sensitive Research in the Health and Social Sciences.* Cambridge: Cambridge University Press, 2010.

Lim, David S. "Cho Yonggi's Charismatic Leadership and Church Growth." Youngsan International Church Growth Conference, Hansei University, Korea, August 2003.

Lindsay, Ben. *We Need to Talk about Race.* London: Society for Promoting Christian Knowledge, 2019.

Little, Kenneth Lindsay. "Colour Prejudice in Britain." *Wasu* X/$_1$ (May 1943).

Little, Kenneth Lindsay. "Some Aspects of the "Colour Bar" in Britain." In *Race Relations and the Schools*, edited by League of Coloured Peoples. London: LCP, 1944.

Liverpool City Council. "Demographics Headline Indicators." https://liverpool.gov.uk/council/key-statistics-and-data/headline-indicators/demographics/.

Locke, Russell, and Veda Locke. *Evangelism and Church Growth.* Ibadan: The Publishing Board, Nigerian Baptist Convention, 1990.

Lopez, Ian F. Haney. "The Social Construction of Race." *Literary Theory: An Anthology*. Edited by Julie Rivkin and Michael Ryan. 2nd ed. Oxford, UK: Blackwell Publishing, 2004.

Lovegrove, Nick. *The Mosaic Principle: The Six Dimensions of a Successful Life and Career*. London: Profile Books, 2017.

Luckmann, Thomas. *The Invisible Religion: The Problem of Religion in Modern Society*. New York: Macmillan, 1967.

Ludwig, Frieder, and Johnson Kwabena Asamoah-Gyadu. *African Christian Presence in the West: New Immigrant Congregations and Transnational Networks in North America and Europe*. Trenton, NJ: Africa World Press, 2011.

Lunn, Kenneth. "The British State and Immigration, 1945 - 51: New Light on the Empire Windrush." *Immigrants and Minorities* 8, no. 1–2 (1989): 161–174.

MacKenzie, John M., ed. *Imperialism and Popular Culture*. Manchester: Manchester University Press, 1986.

Madigan, Kevin. "Did Jesus "Progress in Wisdom"? Thomas Aquinas on Luke 2:52 in Ancient and High-Medieval Context." *Traditio* 52 (1997): 179–200.

Magesa, Laurenti. *Anatomy of Inculturation: Transforming the Church in Africa*. Maryknoll, NY: Orbis Books, 2004.

Magnus, Englander. "General Knowledge Claims in Qualitative Research." *The Humanistic Psychologist* 47, no. 1 (2019): 1–14.

Mankin, Jim. *The Four Dimensions of Church Growth*. Podcast audio. Prentice Avery Meador, Jr. Papers, 1953–2008 00:23:36. https://digitalcommons.acu.edu/prentice_meador_papers_audio/285/.

Mann, Chris, and Fiona Stewart. *Internet Communication and Qualitative Research: A Handbook for Researching Online*. London: Sage, 2000.

Marti, Gerardo. "Conceptual Pathways to Ethnic Transcendence in Diverse Churches: Theoretical Reflections on the Achievement of Successfully Integrated Congregations." *Religions* 6, no. 3 (2015): 1048–1066.

Marti, Gerardo. *Worship across the Racial Divide: Religious Music and Multiracial Congregation*. New York: Oxford University Press, 2012.

Martin, George H. "Editorial: Why Another Look at Donald McGravan?" *The Southern Baptist Journal of Missions and Evangelism: Donald McGavran and Church Growth, A Quarter Century after His Death* 2 (2016): 5–7.

Mason, David. *Race and Ethnicity in Modern Britain*. Oxford: Oxford University Press, 1995.

Mathers, Nigel, Nick Fox, and Amanda Hunn. *Trent Focus for Research and Development in Primary Health Care: Using Interviews in a Research Project*. Trent Focus Group, 1998 (updated 2002). http://web.simmons.edu/~tang2/courses/CUAcourses/lsc745/sp06/Interviews.pdf.

May, Roy, and Robin Cohen. "The Interaction between Race and Colonialism: A Case Study of the Liverpool Race Riots of 1919." *Race and Class* XVI, no. 2 (1974): 111–126.

Mbiti, John. *African Religions and Philosophy.* Oxford: Heinemann Educational Books, 1969.

McGavran, Donald A. *The Bridges of God: A Study in the Strategy of Missions.* Eugene, OR: Wipf & Stock, 2005.

McGavran, Donald A. *How Churches Grow.* London: World Dominion Press, 1959.

McGavran, Donald A. "Ten Years of Church Growth Ministry in India." *India Church Growth Quarterly* 11, no. 2 (1989).

McGavran, Donald A. *Understanding Church Growth.* Grand Rapids, MI: Eerdmans, 1970.

McGavran, Donald A. *Understanding Church Growth.* Rev. ed. Grand Rapids, MI: Eerdmans, 1980.

McGavran, Donald A. *Understanding Church Growth.* Rev. ed. Grand Rapids, MI: Eerdmans, 1983.

McGavran, Donald A., and C. Peter Wagner. *Understanding Church Growth.* 3rd ed. Grand Rapids, MI: Eerdmans, 1990.

McIntosh, Gary L. *Biblical Church Growth: How You Can Work with God to Build a Faithful Church.* Grand Rapids, MI: Baker Books, 2003.

McIntosh, Gary L. "Defining a Multi-Ethnic Church." https://www.biola.edu/blogs/good-book-blog/2012/defining-a-multi-ethnic-church.

McIntosh, Gary L. "The Life of Donald McGavran: Founding a School." *Great Commission Research Journal* 9, no. 1 (2017): 39–55.

McNamara, Carter. "Business Development: Growing your For-profit or Nonprofit Organization." https://managementthelp.org/businessdevelopment/index.htm.

Mead, Matthew. "Empire Windrush: The Cultural Memory of an Imaginary Arrival." *Journal of Postcolonial Writing* 45, no. 2 (2009): 137–149.

Memmi, Albert. *Racism.* Minneapolis, MN: University of Minnesota Press, 2000.

Mercer, Justine. "The Challenges of Insider Research in Educational Institutions: Wielding a Double-Edged Sword and Resolving Delicate Dilemmas." *Oxford Review of Education* 33, no. 1 (2007): 1–17.

The Merriam-Webster Dictionary. New ed. Springfield, MA: Merriam-Webster, 2016.

Merton, Robert. "Insiders and Outsiders; A Chapter in the Sociology of Knowledge." *American Journal of Sociology* 78 (July 1972): 9–47.

Messina, Anthony M. "The Impacts of Post-WWII Migration to Britain: Policy Constraints, Political Opportunism and the Alteration of Representational Politics." *The Review of Politics* 63, no. 2 (2001): 259–285.

Mikes, George. *How to Be a Brit.* London: Penguin Books, 1984.

Miles, Laura. "When Race Riots Marred the Streets of Britain." *Socialist Review*, no. 450. (2019). https://socialistreview.org.uk/450/when-race-riots-marred-streets-britain.

Miller, David. "Reflections on British National Identity." *Journal of Ethnic and Migration Studies* 21, no. 2 (1995): 153–166.

Milligan, Lizzi. "Insider-Outsider-Inbetweener? Researcher Positioning, Participative Methods and Cross-cultural Educational Research." *Compare: A Journal of Comparative and International Education* 46, no. 2 (2016): 235–250.

Montefiore, Alan, and David Vines, eds. *Integrity in the Public and Private Domains*. London: Routledge, 1999.

Moore, Charity G., Rickey E. Carter, Paul J. Nietert, and Paul W. Stewart. "Recommendations for Planning Pilot Studies in Clinical and Translational Research." *Clinical and Translational Science* 4, no. 5 (2011): 332–337.

Moreau, A. Scott. *Contextualizing the Faith: A Holistic Approach*. Grand Rapids, MI: Baker Academic, 2018.

Moreau, A. Scott, ed. *Evangelical Dictionary of World Missions*. Grand Rapids, MI: Baker Books, 2000.

Morgan, Jim. "The Ultimate Church Growth Model." 2015. http://meettheneed.org/blog/2015/10/the-ultimate-church-growth-model/.

Morris, John Michael. "McGavran on McGavran: What Did He Really Teach?" *The Southern Baptist Journal of Missions and Evangelism: Donald McGavran and Church Growth, A Quarter Century after His Death* 2 (2016): 9–23.

Morse, Janice, Phyllis Stern, Juliet Corbin, Barbara Bowers, Kathy Charmaz, and Adele Clarke. *Developing Grounded Theory: The Second Generation*. New York: Routledge, 2016.

Moyo, Anderson. *The Audacity of Diaspora Missions: The Antioch Multiethnic Church-Planting Model for African Reverse Missionaries in Post Christendom Britain*. LAMBERT Academic Publishing, 2015.

Moyo, Anderson. "The Audacity of Diaspora Missions: The Antioch Multiethnic Church-Planting Model for African Reverse Missionaries in Post Christendom Britain." DMin diss., Asbury Theological Seminary, Kentucky, 2014.

Mugambi, Jesse Ndwiga. *Christianity and African Culture*. Nairobi, Kenya: Acton, 2002.

Muir, James Ramsay B. *History of Liverpool*. London: Redwood Press, 1907.

Murdock, Mike, ed. *The Law of Recognition*, The Laws of Life Series. Fort Worth, TX: The Wisdom Centre, 2007.

Mustad, Jan Erik, Eli Huseby, and Camilla Lambine-Christensen. "Post-War Immigration to Britain." https://ndla.no/en/subjects/subject:23/topic:1:184811/resource:1:90712.

NatCen. *British Social Attitudes Survey: Religious Affiliation among Adults in Great Britain.* http://www.natcen.ac.uk/media/1469605/BSA-religion.pdf.

NatCen. *British Social Attitudes: Record Number of Brits with no Religion.* http://www.natcen.ac.uk/news-media/press-releases/2017/september/british-social-attitudes-record-number-of-brits-with-no-religion/.

National Archives. "Postwar Immigration." http://www.nationalarchives.gov.uk/pathways/citizenship/brave_new_world/immigration.htm.

National Human Genome Research Institute. "Genetics Vs. Genomics Fact Sheet." 2018. https://www.genome.gov/about-genomics/fact-sheets/Genetics-vs-Genomics#:~:text=All%20human%20beings%20are%2099.9,about%20the%20causes%20of%20diseases.

Nel, Marius. "The African Background of Pentecostal Theology: A Critical Perspective." *In Die Skriflig/In Luce Verbi* 53, no. 4 (2019): 1–18.

Neuman, W. Lawrence. *Social Research Methods: Qualitative and Quantitative Approaches.* 6th ed. Boston: Pearson, 2007.

Newcomer, Kathryn E., Harry P. Hatry, and Joseph S. Wholey. *Handbook of Practical Program Evaluation.* 4th ed. San Francisco: Jossey-Bass & Pfeiffer Imprints, Wiley, 2015.

Niemandt, Cornelius, and Lee Yongsoo. "A Korean Perspective on Megachurches as Missional Churches." *Verbum et Ecclesia* 36, no. 1 (2015). https://verbumetecclesia.org.za/index.php/ve/article/view/1421/2484.

Niemandt, Nelus. "The Prosperity Gospel, the Decolonization of Theology, and the Abduction of Missionary Imagination." *Missionalia* 45, no. 3 (2017): 203–219.

Nijhawan, Lokesh P., Manthan D. Janodia, Badamane S. Muddukrishna, Krishnamurthy. M. Bhat, Kurady L. Bairy, Nayanabhirama Udupa, and Prashant B. Musmade. "Informed Consent: Issues and Challenges." *Journal of Advanced Pharmaceutical Technology & Research* 4, no. 3 (2013): 134–140.

Northouse, Peter G. *Leadership Theory and Practice.* 8th ed. Los Angeles: Sage Publications Inc., 2019.

Novick, Gina. "Is There a Bias against Telephone Interviews in Qualitative Research?" *Research in Nursing & Health* 31, no. 4 (2008): 391–398.

Nussbaum, Barbara "African Culture and Ubuntu Reflections of a South African in America." *World Business Academy: Perspectives* 17, no. 1 (2003): 1–12.

Nzacahayo, Paul. "A Biblical and Historical Theology of Mission: Reflections on the Flip Side of 'Reverse Mission.'" In *African Voices: Towards African British Theologies*, edited by Israel Oluwole Olofinjana. Global Perspective Series, 49–62. Cumbria, UK: Langham Global Library, 2017.

O'Donovan, Wilbur. *Biblical Christianity in African Perspective.* Carlisle: The Paternoster Press, 1996.

Oden, Thomas C. *How Africa Shaped the Christian Mind: Rediscovering the African Seedbed of Western Christianity.* Downers Grove, IL: InterVarsity Press, 2007.

Office for National Statistics. "Household Wealth by Ethnicity, Great Britain: April 2016 to March 2018." https://www.ons.gov.uk/peoplepopulationandcommunity/personalandhouseholdfinances/incomeandwealth/articles/householdwealthbyethnicitygreatbritain/april2016tomarch2018.

Office for National Statistics. "Religion by Local Authority, Great Britain, 2011 to 2018." 5 April 2019. https://www.ons.gov.uk/file?uri=/peoplepopulationandcommunity/culturalidentity/religion/adhocs/009830religionbylocalauthoritygreatbritain2011to2018/religionbylocalauthorityjd11tojd18.xls.

Ola, Joseph. "African Pioneered Churches in the West: Limitations and Possibilities." *Missio Africanus Journal of African Missiology* 4, no. 1 (2019): 53–75.

Ola, Joseph. *Christ as 'Ọ̀rọ̀' ('Word') Among the Yorubas: An Africanisation of Logos Christology.* Liverpool: Hope University, 2020.

Ola, Joseph. "Reverse Mission: Recognising Limiting Factors and Identifying Creative Possibilities." MA thesis, Liverpool Hope University, 2017.

Ola, Joseph. "Strangers' Meat is the Greatest: African Christianity in Europe." 2019. https://www.academia.edu/41993424/_STRANGERS_MEAT_IS_THE_GREATEST_TREAT_AFRICAN_CHRISTIANITY_IN_EUROPE.

Olaleye, Samuel A. *Strategies for Church Growth.* Lagos, Nigeria: Spirit and Life Equipping Ministries, 2012.

Olanipekun, Olusola Victor. "Omoluabi: Re-thinking the Concept of Virtue in Yoruba Culture and Moral System." *Africology: The Journal of Pan African Studies* 10, no. 9 (2017): 217–231.

Olatunji, Adeyinka Oluseye. "A Postmodernist Critique of Omoluwabi in Yoruba Thought." PhD diss., University of Ibadan, 2021.

Olofinjana, Israel Oluwole. *20 Pentecostal Pioneers in Nigeria: Their Lives, Their Legacies.* Vol. 1. Bloomington, Indiana: Xlibris Corporation, 2011.

Olofinjana, Israel Oluwole, ed. *African Voices: Towards African British Theologies*, Global Perspectives Series: Langham Global Library, 2017.

Olofinjana, Israel Oluwole. "Everyday Heroes." 10 October 2014. https://www.eauk.org/culture/friday-night-theology/heroes.cfm.

Olofinjana, Israel Oluwole. *Partnership in Mission: A Black Majority Church Perspective on Mission and Church Unity.* Watford: Instant Apostle, 2015.

Olofinjana, Israel Oluwole. *Reverse in Ministry & Missions: Africans in the Dark Continent of Europe.* Central Milton Keynes, UK: AuthorHouse, 2010.

Olofinjana, Israel Oluwole. "Reverse Missiology: Mission Approaches and Practices of African Christians within the Baptist Union of Great Britain." *Evangelical Review of Theology: A Global Forum, World Evangelical Alliance Theological Commission* 42, no. 4 (2018): 334–345.

Olofinjana, Israel Oluwole. *Turning the Tables on Mission*. Watford: Instant Apostle, 2013.

Oluwole, Sophie. "Who are (We) the Yoruba?" Pre-Word Philosophy Day Conference, National Theatre, Lagos, 12 June 2007.

Omartian, Stormie. "Foreword." In *Power through Prayer*, written by Edward M. Bounds, 7–16. Chicago: Moody Publishers, 2009.

Omideyi, Modupe. *Transformed to Transform: Journey to Bring Change to a Community*. Liverpool: Love and Joy Ministries Ltd., 2017.

Opdenakker, Raymond. "Advantages and Disadvantages of Four Interview Techniques in Qualitative Research." *Forum: Qualitative Social Research* 7, no. 4 (2006): 1–13.

Opefeyitimi, Ayo. "Ayajo as Ifa in Mythical and Sacred Contexts." In *Ifa Divination, Knowledge, Power, and Performance*, edited by Jacob Olupona and Rowland Abiodun, 17–31. Bloomington, IN: Indiana University Press, 2016.

Orobator, Agbon E. *Theology Brewed in an African Pot*. Maryknoll, NY: Orbis Books, 2008.

Ortiz, Manuel. *One New People: Models for Developing a Multiethnic Church*. Downers Grove, IL: InterVarsity Press, 1996.

Osoba, Joseph Babalola. "The Nature, Form and Functions of Yoruba Proverbs: A Socio-Pragmatic Perspective." *IOSR Journal of Humanities and Social Science* 19, no. 2 (2014): 44–56.

Ott, Craig. "Globalization and Contextualization: Reframing the Task of Contextualization in the Twenty-First Century." *Missiology: An International Review* 43, no. 1 (2015): 43–58.

Ott, Craig, Stephen J. Strauss, and Timothy C. Tennent. *Encountering Theology of Mission: Biblical Foundations, Historical Developments, and Contemporary Issues*. Encountering Mission. Grand Rapids, MI: Baker Academic, 2010.

Owomoyela, Oyekan. *Yoruba Proverbs*. Lincoln: University of Nebraska Press, 2005.

Lexico.com. (Online Dictionary). Lexico.com, 2021.

Oyebade, Oyewole, and Godwin Azenabor. "A Discourse on the Fundamental Principles of Character in an African Moral Philosophy." *African Journal of History and Culture* 10, no. 3 (2018): 41–50.

Oyeneye, Yinusa O., and M O. Shoremi. "The Concept of Culture and the Nigerian Society." In *Essentials of General Studies*, edited by Odugbemi Olumakinde O. Ago Iwoye: CESAP, 1997.

Oyerinde, Oyeyemi Aworinde. "'Omoluabi' - The Concept of Good Character in Yoruba Traditional Education: An Appraisal." *Andrian Forum* 4 (1991): 190–203.

Oyeshile, Olatunji Alabi. "Towards an African Conception of a Person: Person in Yorùbá, Akan, and Igbo Thoughts." *Orita: Ibadan Journal of Religious Studies* xxxiv/1–2 (2002).

Oyewale, Philip Bukola. "A Critical Analysis of Marital Instability among Yoruba Christian Couple in the North West of England." PhD diss., Liverpool Hope University, 2016.

Paas, Stefan. "A Case Study of Church Growth by Church Planting in Germany: Are They Connected?" *International Bulletin of Mission Research* 42, no. 1 (2017): 40–54.

Palaganas, Erlinda, Marian Sanchez, Visitacion Molintas, and Ruel Caricativo. "Reflexivity in Qualitative Research: A Journey of Learning." *The Qualitative Report* 22, no. 2 (2017): 426–438.

Palmer, Colin A. "Defining and Studying the Modern African Diaspora." *The Journal of Negro History* 85, no. ½ (Winter-Spring 2000): 27–32.

Paredes, Tito. "Short-Term Missions: What Can Be Rescued, What Can Be Criticized, and the Challenge of Contextualization." *Latin American Theology* 2, no. 2: 249–259.

Parks, Sharon Daloz. *Leadership Can Be Taught: A Bold Approach for a Complex World.* Boston, MA: Harvard Business School Press, 2005.

Parratt, John. *Reinventing Christianity.* Grand Rapids, MI: Eerdmans, 1995.

Partida, Becky. "Using Dynamic Leadership to Prepare for the Future." *Supply Chain Management Review* 19, no. 4 (2015): 54–56.

Patten, Malcolm. *Leading a Multi-Cultural Church.* London: Society for Promoting Christian Knowledge, 2016.

Patterson, Kerry, Joseph Grenny, Ron McMillan, and Al Switzler. *Crucial Conversations: Tools for Talking When Stakes Are High.* 2nd ed. New York: McGraw-Hill, 2012.

Patton, Michael Quinn. *Qualitative Research & Evaluation Methods.* 3rd ed. Thousand Oaks, CA: Sage, 2002.

Payne, M.W. "Akiwowo, Orature and Divination: Approaches to the Construction of an Emic Sociological Paradigm of Society." *Sociological Analysis* 53, no. 2 (1992): 175–187.

Perkins, John. *Beyond Charity: The Call to Christian Community Development.* Grand Rapids, MI: Baker, 1993.

Perry, Samuel L. "Racial Diversity, Religion, and Morality: Examining the Moral Views of Multiracial Church Attendees." *Review of Religious Research* 55, no. 2 (2013): 355–376.

Peters, Maquita. "Bishop Michael Curry's Royal Wedding Sermon: Full Text of 'The Power of Love.'" 2018. www.npr.org/sections/thetwo-way/2018/05/20/612798691/bishop-michael-currys-royal-wedding-sermon-full-text-of-the-power-of-love?t=1613010367390.

Pezalla, Anne E., Jonathan Pettigrew, and Michelle Miller-Day. "Researching the Researcher-As-Instrument: An Exercise in Interviewer Self-Reflexivity." *Qualitative research: QR* 12, no. 2 (2012): 165–185.

Pickett, Mark. "Caste-Sensitive Church Planting: Revisiting the Homogeneous Unit Principle." *Transformation* 32, no. 3 (2015): 177–187.

Piper, John. *Bloodlines: Race, Cross, and the Christian*. Wheaton, IL: Crossway, 2011.

Pitt, Ricard. "Fear of a Black Pulpit? Real Racial Transcendence Versus Cultural Assimilation in Multiracial Churches." *Journal for the Scientific Study of Religion* 49, no. 2 (2010): 218–223.

Powell, Mary Ann, Morag McArthur, Jenny Chalmers, Anne Graham, Tim Moore, Merle Spriggs, and Stephanie Taplin. "Sensitive Topics in Social Research Involving Children." *International Journal of Social Research Methodology* 21, no. 6 (2018): 647–660.

Poxon, Stephen. *The Unfinished Agenda - Racial Justice and Inclusion in the Methodist Church*. Methodist Council, 2017. https://www.methodist.org.uk/media/1097/counc-mc17-53-equality-diversity-inclusion-april-2017.pdf.

Prill, Thorsten. "Migration, Mission and the Multi-ethnic Church." *Evangelical Review of Theology* 33, no. 4 (2009): 332–346.

Princeton Theological Seminary. "Afe Adogame: Maxwell M. Upson Professor of Religion and Society." https://www.ptsem.edu/people/afe-adogame.

Punch, Keith. *Introduction to Social Research: Quantitative and Qualitative Approaches*. 2nd ed. London: Sage, 2005.

Puthussery, Ouseph Thomas "Marriage and Migration: A Social-Theological Analysis." PhD diss., University of Liverpool, 2011.

Råheim, Målfrid, Liv Heide Magnussen, Ragnhild Johanne Tveit Sekse, Åshild Lunde, Torild Jacobsen, and Astrid Blystad. "Researcher-Researched Relationship in Qualitative Research: Shifts in Positions and Researcher Vulnerability." *International Journal of Qualitative Studies on Health and Well-being* 11, no. 1 (2016). https://pubmed.ncbi.nlm.nih.gov/27307132.

Rainer, Thom S. *The Book of Church Growth: History, Theology, and Principles*. Nashville, TN: Broadman Press, 1993.

Rand, Lisa. "The Neglected Story of Liverpool's 'Other' Riots is Finally Being Told." *Liverpool Echo*. 30 September 2019. https://www.liverpoolecho.co.uk/news/liverpool-news/neglected-story-liverpools-other-riots-16973314.

Rea, Louis, and Richard Parker. *Designing and Conducting Survey Research: A Comprehensive Guide*. 3rd ed. San Francisco, CA: Jossey-Bass, 2005.

Reifsnider, Usha. "Lessons from South-Asian Christians." Paper presented at the Centre for Missionaries from the Majority World Conference, Sheffield Community Church, Sheffield, 13 October 2018.

Religious Communities and Sustainable Development. "Adedibu, Babatunde Aderemi." https://in-rcsd.org/en/conference/presenters/presenters/adedibu-babatunde-aderemi.

Richard, Hivner L. "Religious Syncretism as a Syncretistic Concept: The Inadequacy of the "World Religions" Paradigm in Cross-Cultural Encounter." *International Journal of Frontier Missiology* 31, no. 4 (2014): 209–215.

Rink, Dieter, Annegret Haase, Katrin Grossmann, Chris Couch, and Matthew Cocks. "From Long-Term Shrinkage to Re-Growth? The Urban Development Trajectories of Liverpool and Leipzig." *Built Environment* 38, no. 2 (2012). https://www.researchgate.net/publication/263145381_From_Long-Term_Shrinkage_to_Re-Growth_The_Urban_Development_Trajectories_of_Liverpool_and_Leipzig/download.

Roberto, John. "Becoming an Adaptive Leader: Based on the Work of Ronald Heifetz and Marty Linsky." *Lifelong Faith* 5, no. 1 (2011): 26–33.

Roediger, David R. "Historical Foundations of Race." https://nmaahc.si.edu/learn/talking-about-race/topics/historical-foundations-race.

Rogers, Andrew, and Richard Gale. *Faith Groups and the Planning System: Policy Briefing*. London: University of Roehampton, 2015.

Rogers, David, and Moira Bowman. "A History: The Construction of Race and Racism." https://www.racialequitytools.org/resourcefiles/Western%20States%20-%20Construction%20of%20Race.pdf.

Rooms, Nigel. *The Faith of the English: Integrating Christ and Culture*. London: Society for Promoting Christian Knowledge, 2011.

Roozen, David, and Kirk Hadaway. *Church and Denominational Growth*. Nashville: Abingdon Press, 1993.

Ross, Kenneth R. "'Blessed Reflex': Mission as God's Spiral of Renewal." *International Bulletin of Missionary Research* 27, no. 4 (2003): 162–168.

Ross, Kenneth R. "Non-Western Christians in Scotland: Mission in Reverse." 1–11. https://www.ctbiarchive.org/pdf_view.php?id=210.

Ross, Paula T., and Nikki L. Zaidi. "Limited by Our Limitations." *Perspectives on Medical Education* 8, no. 4 (2019): 261–264.

Royal Society of Chemistry. "Missing Elements: Racial and Ethnic Inequalities in the Chemical Sciences." *Perspectives* (2022). https://www.rsc.org/globalassets/22-new-perspectives/talent/racial-and-ethnic-inequalities-in-the-chemical-sciences/missing-elements-report.pdf.

Ruben, Brent D., and Ralph A. Gigliotti. "Communication: Sine Qua Non of Organizational Leadership Theory and Practice." *International Journal of Business Communication* 54, no. 1 (2017): 12–30.

Rubin, Herbert J., and Irene Rubin. *Qualitative Interviewing: The Art of Hearing Data*. 2nd ed. Thousand Oaks, CA: Sage, 2005.

Ryan, Reeves. "What is the Septuagint?" https://www.thegospelcoalition.org/article/what-is-the-septuagint/.

Saidin, Khaliza. "Insider Researchers: Challenges and Opportunities." *Proceedings of the ICECRS* 1, no. 1 (2017). https://dx.doi.org/10.21070/picecrs.v1i1.563.

Salicru, Sebastian. *Leadership Results: How to Create Adaptive Leaders and High Performing Organisations for an Uncertain World*. Milton QLD, Australia: John Wiley & Sons Australia, Ltd., 2017.

Sandberg, Jörgen, and Mats Alvesson. "Ways of Constructing Research Questions: Gap-spotting or Problematization?" *Organization* 18, no. 1 (2011): 23–44.

Sandling, Jonathan. *Leading with Style: The Comprehensive Guide to Leadership Styles*. Scotts Valley, CA: CreateSpace Independent Publishing Platform, 2015.

Schaller, Lyle E. *Effective Church Planting*. Nashville, TN: Abingdon Press, 1979.

Schineller, Peter. *A Handbook on Inculturation*. New York: Paulist Press, 1990.

Schostak, John. *Interviewing and Representation in Qualitative Research Projects*. Open University Press, 2006.

Schwarz, Christian. *Natural Church Development: A Practical Guide to a New Approach*. Beds: British Church Growth Association, 1996.

Seligmann, Linda J., and Brian P. Estes. "Innovations in Ethnographic Methods." *American Behavioral Scientist* 64, no. 2 (2020): 176–197.

Shenk, Wilbert R. "Recasting Theology of Mission: Impulses from the Non-Western World." *International Bulletin of Missionary Research* 25, no. 3 (2001): 98–107.

Shepperson, G. "African Diaspora Concept and Context." In *Global Dimensions of the African Diaspora*, edited by Joseph E. Harris, vii, 532 p. Washington, DC: Howard University Press, 1993.

Sherwood, Marika. *Pastor Daniels Ekarte and the African Churches Mission*. London: The Savannah Press, 1994.

Sherwood, Marika. "White Myths, Black Omissions: The Historical Origins of Racism in Britain." *History Education Research Journal* 3 (2003). https://www.researchgate.net/publication/242158972_White_Myths_Black_Omissions_the_Historical_Origins_of_Racism_in_Britain.

Shiner, Larry. "The Concept of Secularization in Empirical Research." *Journal for the Scientific Study of Religion* 6, no. 2 (1967): 207–220.

Shutte, Augustine. *Philosophy for Africa*. Rondebosch, South Africa: UTC Press, 1993.

Simson, Wolfgang. *Houses That Change the World*. Carlisle: Paternoster, 2001.

Smedley, Audrey. ""Race" and the Construction of Human Identity." *American Anthropologists* 100, no. 3 (1999): 1–13.

Smith, David. "The Church Growth Principles of Donald McGavran." *Transformation* 2, no. 2 (1985): 25–30.

Social Research Association. "Ethics Guidelines." http://the-sra.org.uk/wp-content/uploads/ethics03.pdf.

Solomos, John. *Race and Racism in Britain*. 3rd ed. New York: Palgrave Macmillan, 2003.

Spickard, James V., and Afe Adogame. "Introduction: Africa, the New African Diaspora, and Religious Transnationalism in a Global World." In *Religion Crossing Boundaries*, edited by James V. Spickard and Afe Adogame, 1–28. Leiden: Brill, 2010.

Spickard, James V., and Afeosemime U. Adogame. "Africa, the New African Diaspora, and Religious Transnationalism in a Global World." *Our House Book Chapters and Sections* 45 (2010). https://inspire.redlands.edu/cgi/viewcontent.cgi?article=1045&context=oh_chapters.

Stark, Rodney. *The Rise of Christianity: A Sociologist Reconsiders History*. Princeton, NJ: Princeton University Press, 1996.

Stark, Rodney. *What Americans Really Believe*. Waco: Baylor University Press, 2008.

Stark, Rodney, and William Sims Bainbridge. *The Future of Religion: Secularization, Revival, and Cult Formation*. Berkeley: University of California Press, 1985.

Staylor, Richard. *Dimensions of Church Growth*. Nashville, TN: Broadman & Holman Publishers, 1989.

Stetzer, Edward John. "The Evolution of Church Growth, Church Health, and the Missional Church: An Overview of the Church Growth Movement From, and Back To, Its Missional Roots." *Journal of the American Society of Church Growth* 17, no. 1 (2006): 87–112.

Stott, John. *The Message of Romans*. Leicester: IVP, 1994.

Stuckey, Heather L. "The Second Step in Data Analysis: Coding Qualitative Research Data." *Journal of Social Health and Diabetes* 3, no. 1 (2015): 7–10.

Sturge, Mark. *Look What the Lord Has Done: An Exploration of Black Christian Faith in Britain*. Bletchley, UK: Scripture Union, 2005.

Sue, Derald Wing. *Overcoming Our Racism: The Journey to Liberation*. San Francisco: Jossey Bass, 2003.

Sundiata, Ibrahim K. "Africanity, Identity and Culture." *A Journal of Opinion* 24, no. 2 (1996): 13–17.

Sundkler, Bengt G. *Bantu Prophets in South Africa*. Oxford: Oxford University Press, 1961.

Suri, Harsh. "Purposeful Sampling in Qualitative Research Synthesis." *Qualitative Research Journal* 11, no. 2 (2011): 63–75.

Swann, Michael Meredith. *Education for All: Report of the Select Committee of Inquiry into the Education of Children from Ethnic Minority Group*. London: Her Majesty's Stationery Office, 1985.

Taber, Charles R. "The Limits of Indigenization in Theology." In *Readings in Dynamic Indigeneity*, edited by Charles H. Kraft and Tom N. Wisley, 372–399. Pasadena, CA: William Carey Library, 1979.

Tahaafe-Williams, Katalina "A Multicultural Church? Multicultural Ministry as a Tool for Building the Multicultural Church." PhD diss., University of Birmingham, 2012.

Talman, Harvey. "Comprehensive Contextualization." *International Journal of Frontier Missions* 21, no. 1 (2004): 6.

Tamar, Kushnir, and Melissa A. Koenig. "What I Don't Know Won't Hurt You: The Relation between Professed Ignorance and Later Knowledge Claims." *Developmental Psychology* 53, no. 5 (2017): 826–835.

Tamney, Joseph B. *The Resilience of Conservative Religion*. Cambridge: Cambridge University Press, 2002.

Tamney, Joseph B., Stephen D. Johnson, Kevin McElmurry, and George Saunders. "Strictness and Congregational Growth in Middletown." *Journal for the Scientific Study of Religion* 42, no. 3 (2003): 363–375.

Temple of Praise. "Our Story." http://www.templeofpraise.org.uk/ourstory/.

Tennent, Timothy C. "The Challenge of Churchless Christianity: An Evangelical Assessment." *International Bulletin of Missionary Research* 29, no. 4 (2005): 171–177.

Thabane, Lehana, Jinhui Ma, Rong Chu, Ji Cheng, Afisi Ismaila, Lorena Rios, Reid Robson, et. al. "A Tutorial on Pilot Studies: The What, Why and How." *BMC Medical Research Methodology* 10, no. 1 (2010): 1.

The National Church Leaders' Forum. "NCLF Update News Re Dr Roswith Gerloff." 1 August 2013. https://nclf.org.uk/nclf-update-news-re-dr-roswith-gerloff/.

The Open University. "League of Coloured Peoples." https://www.open.ac.uk/researchprojects/makingbritain/content/league-coloured-peoples.

The Queen's Foundation. "Rev Dr Israel Oluwole Olofinjana." https://www.queens.ac.uk/people/fellows/revd-israel-oluwole-olofinjana.

The Religious Studies Project. "Afe Adogame." https://www.religiousstudiesproject.com/persons/afe-adogame/.

Theological Education Fund. *Ministry in Context: The Third Mandate Programme of the Theological Education Fund (1970–77)*. Bromley, Kent: Theological Education Fund, 1972.

Thomas, Aliki, Anita Menon, Jill Boruff, Ana Maria Rodriguez, and Sara Ahmed. "Applications of Social Constructivist Learning Theories in Knowledge Translation for Healthcare Professionals: A Scoping Review." *Implementation Science* 9, no. 1 (2014): 54.

Thomas, Jeremy N., and Daniel V. Olson. "Testing the Strictness Thesis and Competing Theories of Congregational Growth." *Journal for the Scientific Study of Religion* 49, no. 4 (2010): 619–639.

Thumma, Scott. "Exploring the Megachurch Phenomena: Their Characteristics and Cultural Context." http://hirr.hartsem.edu/bookshelf/thumma_article2.html.

Timonen, Virpi, Geraldine Foley, and Catherine Conlon. "Challenges When Using Grounded Theory: A Pragmatic Introduction to Doing GT Research." *International Journal of Qualitative Methods* 17, no. 1 (2018). https://journals.sagepub.com/doi/abs/10.1177/1609406918758086.

Togarasei, Lovemore. "The Pentecostal Gospel of Prosperity in African Contexts of Poverty: An Appraisal." *Exchange* 40, no. 4 (2011): 336–350.

Tolmie, Francois. "Tendencies in the Interpretation of Galatians 3:28 since 1990." *Acta Theologica* 19 (2014): 105–129.

Torkington, Ntombenhle Protasia. *The Racial Politics of Health: A Liverpool Profile.* Liverpool, UK: Merseyside Area Profile Group, 1983.

Tovey, Philip. *Inculturation of Christian Worship: Exploring the Eucharist.* Milton Park, UK: Routledge Revivals, 2020.

Towns, Elmer L. "The Relationship of Church Growth and Systematic Theology." *Journal of the Evangelical Theological Society* 29, no. 1 (1986): 63–70.

Towns, Elmer L., John N. Vaughan, and David J. Seifert. *The Complete Book of Church Growth.* Illinois: Tyndale House Publishers, 1981.

Trinity Presbyterian Church. *A Service of Worship and Celebration of the Lord's Supper.* El Paso, TX: Trinity Presbyterian Church, 2009.

Trotman, Arlington. "Black, Black-led or What?" In *Let's Praise Him Again: An African Caribbean Perspective on Worship*, edited by Joel Edwards, 12–35. Kingsway, 1992.

Uhl-Bien, Mary, Russ Marion, and Bill McKelvey. "Complexity Leadership Theory: Shifting Leadership from the Industrial Age to the Knowledge Era." *The Leadership Quarterly* 18, no. 4 (2007): 298–318.

UK Government. "Home Ownership." (2020/02/04). https://www.ethnicity-facts-figures.service.gov.uk/housing/owning-and-renting/home-ownership/latest#by-ethnicity.

University of Minnesota. "The Meaning of Race and Ethnicity." In *Sociology: Understanding and Changing the Social World.* Minneapolis, MN: University of Minnesota Libraries Publishing, https://open.lib.umn.edu/sociology/chapter/10-2-the-meaning-of-race-and-ethnicity/.

Unluer, Sema. "Being an Insider Researcher While Conducting Case Study Research." *The Qualitative Report* 17, Article 58 (2012): 1–14.

Utley, Bob. "Luke the Historian: The Gospel of Luke." https://ia800203.us.archive.org/4/items/LukeTheHistorianTheGospelOfLuke/VOL03A.pdf.

Van Engen, Charles E. *The Growth of the True Church*. Amsterdam: Rodopi, 1981.
Van Engen, Chuck. "Is the Church for Everyone? Planting Multi-Ethnic Congregations in North America." *Global Missiology* (2004): 2–39.
Van Gelder, Craig. *The Essence of the Church: A Community Created by the Spirit*. Grand Rapids, MI: Baker Books, 2000.
Varney, Julia. "The Changing Nature of Leadership." *NZ Business*, May 2015, S22+. Gale. https://link.gale.com/apps/doc/A427422985/ITOF?u=livhope&sid=ITOF&xid=f37bd86d.
Vasileiou, Konstantina, Julie Barnett, Susan Thorpe, and Terry Young. "Characterising and Justifying Sample Size Sufficiency in Interview-Based Studies: Systematic Analysis of Qualitative Health Research over a 15-Year Period." *BMC Medical Research Methodology* 18, no. 1 (2018): 1–18.
Wagner, C. Peter. *Strategies for Church Growth*. London: MARC Europe and British Church Growth Association, 1987.
Wagner, C. Peter. *Your Church Can Grow: Seven Vital Signs of a Healthy Church*. Ventura, CA: Regal Books, 1976.
Wagner, Charles Peter. *Our Kind of People: The Ethical Dimensions of Church Growth in America*. Atlanta: J. Knox Press, 1979.
Wagner, Charles Peter. *Strategies for Church Growth: Tools for Effective Mission and Evangelism*. Ventura, CA: Regal, 1987.
Wagner, Charles Peter. *Your Church Can Grow*. Rev. ed. Ventura, CA: Regal Books, 1984.
Walliman, Nicholas. *Research Methods: The Basics*. London: Routledge, 2011.
Walls, Andrew F.; edited by Mark R. Gornik. *Crossing Cultural Frontiers: Studies in the History of World Christianity*. Maryknoll, NY: Orbis Books, 2017.
Walls, Andrew F. "Mission and Migration: The Diaspora Factor in Christian History." *Journal of African Christian Thought* 5, no. 2 (2002): 3–11.
Ward, Peter. *Perspectives on Ecclesiology and Ethnography*. Grand Rapids, 2012.
Warren, Robert. *The Healthy Churches' Handbook*. London: Church House Publishing, 2004.
Webster, Daniel. "Tani Omideyi Becomes First Ethnic Minority Chair of Alliance Board." News release, 21 March 2016. https://www.eauk.org/current-affairs/media/press-releases/tani-omideyi-becomes-first-ethnic-minority-chair-of-alliance-board.cfm.
Wengraf, Tom. *Qualitative Research Interviewing*. London: SAGE, 2004.
Wheatley, Margaret J. *Leadership and the New Science: Learning about Organization from an Orderly Universe*. 1st ed. San Francisco: Berrett-Koehler Publishers, 1994.
White, Lorraine. "The History of Blacks in Britain: From Slavery to Rebellion." https://www.socialistalternative.org/panther-black-rebellion/history-blacks-britain-slavery-rebellion/.

White, Pattrick. *Developing Research Questions.* 2nd ed. London: Palgrave, 2017.

Whitehead, Tony L. "Basic Classical Ethnographic Research Methods." *Ethnographically Informed Community and Cultural Assessment Research Systems (Eiccars) Working Paper Series.* 2005. http://www.cusag.umd.edu/documents/workingpapers/classicalethnomethods.pdf.

Whitehead, Tony L. "What Is Ethnography?" *Ethnographically Informed Community and Cultural Assessment Research Systems (Eiccars) Working Paper Series.* 2004. http://www.cusag.edu/documents/workingpapers/epiontattrib.pdf.

Whiteman, Darrell L. "Contextualization: The Theory, the Gap, the Challenge." *International Bulletin of Missionary Research* (1997): 2–6.

Wilgar, Hannah. "Evolution of Modern Humans." (2016). https://www.yourgenome.org/stories/evolution-of-modern-humans.

Wilkinson, Colin. "Introduction." In *The Churches of Liverpool*, edited by David Lewis, 175: Liverpool: Bluecoat, 2001.

Williams, Dean. *Real Leadership: Helping People and Organizations Face Their Toughest Challenges.* 1st ed. San Francisco, CA: Berrett-Koehler, 2005.

Williams, Jonathan. "Celebrating Multiethnic Churches." https://www.imb.org/2019/04/11/celebrating-multi-ethnic-churches/.

Wilson, Bryan R. *Religion in Secular Society: A Sociological Comment.* New thinker's library. London: Watts, 1966.

Wilson, Carlton E. "Racism and Private Assistance: The Support of West Indian and African Missions in Liverpool, England during the Interwar Years." *African Studies Review* 35, no. 2 (1992): 44–72.

Wolffe, John. *God and Greater Britain: Religion and National Life in Britain and Ireland, 1843–1945.* New York: Routledge, 1994.

Wong Gabrielle Ka, Wai, and Diana L. Chan. "Adaptive Leadership in Academic Libraries." *Library Management* 39, no. 1/2 (2018): 106–115.

Yancey, George A. *One Body. One Spirit: Principles of Successful Multiracial Churches.* Downers Grove, IL: InterVarsity Press, 2003.

Yang, Philip Q., and Kavitha Koshy. "The "Becoming White Thesis" Revisited." *The Journal of Public and Professional Sociology* 8, no. 1 (2016): 1.

Yirenkyi, Kwasi. "The Church and the Quest for Africa's Modernization." *Griot* 10, no. 1 (1991). https://www.proquest.com/docview/1297959222?pq-origsite=gscholar&fromopenview=true#.

Zack-Williams, Alfred B. "African Diaspora Conditioning: The Case of Liverpool." *Journal of Black Studies* 27, no. 4 (1997): 528–542.

Zoom. "About Zoom." https://explore.zoom.us/en/about/.

Zurlo, Gina A., Todd M. Johnson, and Peter F. Crossing. "World Christianity and Mission 2021: Questions about the Future." *International Bulletin of Mission Research* 45, no. 1 (2021): 15–25.

APPENDIX I

Expanded Code List

Name	Files	References
Contextual Realities of the UK	21	56
Catholicism as Church Idea	2	2
Immigration Issues	4	5
Challenges with Place of Worship	7	9
Racism	4	4
Secularism	11	15
Weather	1	1
Work-Family-Life Balance	13	15
Congregation's Demographics	5	6
Ecclesiological Dispositions and Praxis	21	56
Church Growth Understanding		
All-round Development	2	2
Branch Multiplication, Spiritual, and Numerical	1	1
Church Administration	3	3
Communal Impact	2	3
Numerical and Branch Multiplication	3	3
Numerical and Social	1	1
Numerical and Vision Achievement	1	1
Numerical Increase	1	1
Social Growth	1	1
Social, Spiritual, and Numerical	1	1
Spiritual and Numerical	11	11
Spiritual Growth	4	4

Name	Files	References
Vision Achievement	2	2
Fluidity between Churches	1	1
Relationship Dynamics within the Church	12	12
Liturgy	4	5
Music	2	2
Homogeneity	18	25
Cultural Stereotypes and Traditions	11	16
Contextualization	1	1
Finances	4	4
Leadership	25	109
Church Management or Organization	8	12
Accountability and Integrity	3	3
Crisis Management	1	1
Time Management	5	6
Vision	9	12
Education or Training	1	1
Discipleship	4	4
Gender and Age	1	1
Homiletics	6	7
Charisma	12	17
Leadership Style	5	5
Mission Strategy	16	28
Synergy	14	22
Spiritual Enablement	5	9
Church's Poor Image	1	1
Membership Benefits	5	7
2GMs' Allegiance to ADCs	8	13

APPENDIX II

Religious Affiliation Among Adults in Great Britain NATCEN's British Social Attitudes Survey

All respondents were asked: "Do you regard yourself as belonging to any particular religion? IF YES: Which?"

	1983	1984	1985	1986	1987	1989	1990	1991
	%	%	%	%	%	%	%	%
Church of England/Anglican	40	39	36	37	37	37	37	36
Roman Catholic	10	12	11	10	10	11	9	10
Other Christian	17	14	17	16	16	16	14	15
All Christian	67	66	63	63	63	64	60	61
Non-Christian	2	2	2	3	3	2	3	3
No religion	31	32	34	34	34	34	36	35
Base	1,761	1,675	1,804	3,100	2,847	3,029	2,797	2,918

	1993	1994	1995	1996	1997	1998	1999	2000
	%	%	%	%	%	%	%	%
Church of England/Anglican	32	33	32	29	27	27	27	30
Roman Catholic	11	9	9	9	11	9	9	9
Other Christian	16	15	15	15	14	14	16	16
All Christian	*59*	*58*	*56*	*53*	*52*	*51*	*52*	*55*
Non-Christian	3	3	3	4	4	3	3	5
No religion	37	38	40	43	43	45	44	40
Base	*2,945*	*3,469*	*3,633*	*3,620*	*1,355*	*3,146*	*3,143*	*3,426*

	2001	2002	2003	2004	2005	2006	2007	2008
	%	%	%	%	%	%	%	%
Church of England/Anglican	29	31	27	29	26	22	21	23
Roman Catholic	11	9	9	9	9	9	9	9
Other Christian	14	14	15	15	18	16	18	18
All Christian	*54*	*54*	*50*	*53*	*54*	*48*	*48*	*50*
Non-Christian	4	4	6	3	6	6	6	7
No religion	41	41	43	43	40	46	46	43
Base	*3,287*	*3,435*	*4,432*	*3,199*	*4,268*	*4,290*	*4124*	*4,486*

	2009	2010	2011	2012	2013	2014	2015	2016
	%	%	%	%	%	%	%	%
Church of England/Anglican	20	20	21	21	16	17	17	15
Roman Catholic	9	9	9	9	9	8	9	9
Other Christian	15	15	17	17	16	17	17	17
All Christian	*44*	*43*	*47*	*47*	*41*	*42*	*43*	*41*
Non-Christian	5	6	7	6	8	8	8	6
No religion	51	50	46	48	50	49	48	53
Base	*3,421*	*3,297*	*3311*	*3248*	*3244*	*2878*	*4,328*	*2,939*

Percentage not belonging to a religion by age

	1986	Base	1990	Base	2000	Base	2010	Base	2015	Base	2016	Base
18–24	55%	436	54%	336	59%	277	65%	229	62%	290	71%	169
25–34	48%	567	47%	512	53%	614	57%	446	58%	635	61%	425
35–44	34%	615	40%	560	46%	715	60%	637	54%	728	56%	480
45–54	26%	506	32%	456	39%	521	51%	557	51%	764	56%	507
55–64	22%	452	25%	382	27%	501	47%	563	45%	711	50%	494
65–74	18%	324	23%	330	21%	432	31%	497	34%	684	40%	494
75–94	15%	197	19%	207	17%	359	24%	357	24%	509	27%	363

Religious affiliation by age: 2016

	18–24	25–34	35–44	45–54	55–64	65–74	75+
	%	%	%	%	%	%	%
Church of England/Anglican	3	5	8	13	22	26	40
Roman Catholic	5	9	9	10	9	8	7
Other Christian	14	15	15	16	16	22	25
Non-Christian	6	11	12	5	3	3	1
No religion	71	61	56	56	50	40	27
Base	169	425	480	507	494	494	363

APPENDIX III

List of Some ADCs in Liverpool

S/N	Name	Nationality
	Pentecost Baptist Church Int'l	Nigerian
	The Redeemed Christian Church of God (RCCG), Love Assembly	Nigerian
	The Apostolic Church	Nigerian
	Glory Worship Church	Nigerian
	Deeper Christian Life Ministry	Nigerian
	Alive Believers Church & Community Centre	Nigerian
	Love Economy Church	Ghanaian
	Temple of Praise	Nigerian
	RCCG, Divine Revelation Parish	Nigerian
	Christ Authority Baptist Church Int'l	Nigerian
	Pentecost Baptist Church, Norris Green Branch	Nigerian
	The Gospel Faith Mission Int'l (GOFAMINT)	Nigerian
	Christian Gold House Chapel Ministry Int'l	Ghanaian
	Winners' Chapel International	Nigerian
	RCCG, Dominion Assembly	Nigerian
	RCCG, Mount Zion Parish	Nigerian
	RCCG, Garden of Hope	Nigerian
	Christ Apostolic Church, Mountain of Prayer	Nigerian
	The Church of Pentecost, Liverpool Central Assembly	Ghanaian
	The New Life International Mission, Liverpool	Nigerian

	Mountain of Fire and Miracle Ministries Int'l (MFM) Liverpool	Nigerian
	Life Changers Empowering Church	Ugandan
	Ahavah International	Nigerian
	Christian Life Centre	Nigerian
	The Faith Ministry	Nigerian
	Apostolic Faith Mission International Ministries (Vessels of Honour Worship Centre)	Zimbabwean

APPENDIX IV

Interview Questions

The following questions are aimed at exploring the factors influencing church growth among diaspora African churches in Liverpool:

1. Tell a bit about yourself in relation to the church.
2. When you hear the term church growth, what comes to mind? Why?
3. How has your church grown since inception? How have other African churches grown? What do you think are the reasons behind this?
4. What challenges have you faced in your efforts at church growth?
5. What do you think is the future of African churches in Liverpool?
6. How many Africans churches do you reckon currently exist in Liverpool?

APPENDIX V

Research Information Sheet

Outline of the research (a couple of sentences in non-specialist language): The African diaspora churches in Liverpool experience church growth within a different context from their home countries. While some churches have been experiencing positive growth, some others have continued to struggle for sustenance and others are declining. This research therefore tries to examine the factors that are responsible for these various kinds of growth and arrive at a possible viable solution for the same.

Who is the researcher?
Name: Paul Ayokunle
Institution: Liverpool Hope University
Researcher's University email address: 18008430@hope.ac.uk

What will my participation in the research involve?
You will participate in a one-to-one interview session

Will there be any benefits to me to taking part?
Yes, you will help in reducing the challenges of church growth faced by existing African churches in Liverpool. You will also be providing future African churches and missionaries with relevant information for growing their churches in diaspora Liverpool.

Will there be any risks to me in taking part?
Minimal risks.

What happens if I decide that I don't want to take part during the actual research study, or decide that the information given should not be used?
You have the choice whether or not to take part in the research study, and will be asked to state your consent at the start of the interview. If you, after completing the interview, decide that you do not wish your data to be used, please email the researcher and none of your data will be used.

How will you ensure that my contribution is anonymous?
The recording of the interview and any data drawn from it will be assigned an individual code which will be its unique identifier used in analysis of the data. In any reports or publications arising from this research, none of the following will be identified:

>Your name
>The name of your church
>The exact geographical location of your church

All recordings and written transcripts will be held securely in password-protected folders on the researcher's computer which is itself password and firewall-secured. All data will be deleted by the end of September 2022.

Please note that your confidentiality and anonymity cannot be assured if, during the research, it comes to light that you are involved in illegal or harmful behaviours that I may need to disclose to the appropriate authorities.

RESEARCH CONSENT FORM

Title of research project: Factors Influencing Church Growth among Diaspora African Churches in Liverpool
Name of researcher: Paul Ayokunle

1. I confirm that I have read and understand the information sheet for the above research project and have had the opportunity to ask questions.	Yes / No
2. I understand that my participation is voluntary and that I am free to withdraw at any time, without giving any reason.	Yes / No
3. I agree to take part in this research project and for the anonymised data to be used as the researcher sees fit, including publication.	Yes / No

Name of participant:
Signature:
Date:

APPENDIX VI

Sample Interview Transcript

Number of Speakers: Two
Interview Duration: 00:27:41
I: Interviewer
R: Respondent

[Recording starts 00:00:00]

I: I appreciate you for your voluntary participation in this research. But to confirm that, I just need you to give your oral consent to your voluntary participation in this research. So, I will quickly read the content of the consent form to you, and you will confirm if you agree with them or not.
R: OK.
I: So, do you confirm that you have understood the details and you have had the opportunity to ask questions?
R: Mm-mm.
I: Alright.
R: I do.
I: OK. Do you understand that your participation is voluntary and that you are free to withdraw at any time without giving any reason?
R: Yes, I do.
I: Alright, thank you. And, finally, do you agree to take part in this research project and for the anonymized data to be used as the researcher sees fit including publications?
R: Completely.
I: Alright, thank you so much. So, we can kick-start the whole process now.
R: OK.

I: OK. As a way of starting, can I just ask if that you tell a bit about yourself in relation to the church?

R: I am a Nigerian who relocated to the UK in the year 2000. And at the initial stage I had difficulty getting a church to worship, where to worship. I went to an English church first and the culture shock almost derailed my faith.

I: Wow.

R: [Laughs]. Because the way they do things was quite different from the way I have, you know, I am used to worshipping where I come from.

I: Hmm, of course.

R: And fortunately for me I linked with my present pastor, the pastor of my present church.

I: OK.

R: Which is entirely African. Right up . . . you know my early – just exactly what I am used to.

I: Back from home. [Chuckles].

R: And I became a kind of leader in the church; I am a deaconess in the church.

I: Alright.

R: And, you know, I belong to the choir. I am a very active member of the choir and part of the pastoral team. So, I would say, I am quite an active person in the church. Until very recently, I was a member of the board of trustees.

I: OK.

R: But I recently relinquished that post for personal reasons.

I: OK. You're really involved in the life of the church then.

R: Very involved, very involved.

I: Wow. That's lovely. Thank you for sharing that. So, when you hear about the term church growth, what comes to your mind and why?

R: Church growth to me is in two dimensions.

I: Alright?

R: Numerical and spiritual. By numerical what I mean is, using the church where I am now as a template, when we started, I think we started with about six people, and over the years, you know, God was adding to us. We were expanding, expanding, right up to where we are till date that we even have to hold two services. So, to me that is the church growing.

I: Hmm.

R: The other part of church growth for me is the spiritual growth of the members of the church. You see someone comes into the church who you know – I don't want to sound pious, but you know, I am just talking from my level of faith. You see someone come into the church that you know this person is still a bit worldly, what the bible describes as carnal, and over the years you see the person give up this carnality. You know, like maybe the person used to smoke, the person used to drink, the person used to go clubbing and didn't see anything wrong in these, but with teaching over the years the person by the help of the Holy Spirit comes to realize that look there is a way we live in the kingdom where I am now, which is the kingdom of Christ, which does not really go well with the way I have been living. And you can see the change in the person. That to me is a very important part of growth. It means the person has grown. Not, you know. . . . Yes, it has added to the numbers of the church, but the person has personally grown spiritually as well.

I: Hmm.

R: That is important.

I: Alright, thank you. That's a vast understanding of the concept. So, you mentioned something when you were explaining, when you were responding to that question, that the church has multiplied into having two services and all that. So, if I may push that further, how has your church grown since inception or since you joined the church and perhaps how has other African churches around grown?

R: I can only talk about my church. Because, unfortunately, I am tunnel vision when it comes to attending church. I am a one church person. I have always been a one church person from home.

I: OK.

R: And, you know, I have remained a one church person. My mum, of blessed memory, used to call it church prostitution. You don't go from one church to the other. So, since I joined my present church, I can't tell you about any other church, really; because, I have not been involved in any other church.

I: Hmm.

R: But for my church, the way the church has grown, number one: I have to commend the effort of the pastor. The pastor of the church, you know, the senior pastor of the church is an outgoing person. And when we initially started, if he was driving along the street of Liverpool and he saw any Black person, he would back and go and speak to the person. In fact, that is how he met me in the first place. He would go and speak to the Black person, you know, not minding whether the person was Nigerian, Ghanaian or whatever. And, you know, just make friend with the person and all that. And, eventually, some would join the church. And also, I found that members have invited others to join. For instance, I was in work one night and I had an African nurse working with me. And as it is my usual pattern or way, I was just singing as I was doing my work, because I love singing. In fact, sometimes I don't even realise that I am singing until someone says, oh, what song is that? Was I singing?

I: [Laughs].

R: So, I was just singing, and she heard me singing, and she recognized that I was singing choruses. And she said, "Oh, are you a Christian?" I said, "Yes, I am." And we got talking. And I introduced my church to her. And she visited and never left.

I: Wow.

R: Till today she is still a member of that church.

I: Wow.

R: And, you know, other members have done that as well. So, in that area, our church has grown. The more, you know, for people reaching out and pastor being a selfless person. One incident always stands out when I talk about people being attracted to our church to make it grow in number. We had a member who for whatever reason left the church. Then he ran into trouble, not really him, you know, the church he went to another member there ran into problem. I don't know what the nature of the problem is. And then they went to the pastor of that church. And the pastor was like, "What's my business with that?"

I: Hmm.

R: "What do you want me to do?" So, he now told that friend to say, "Look, you know what, I know the pastor of the church where I left, let's go and speak to him; if anybody can help, he will help. But I don't know if he will; because, you know, I left the church." So, they came and spoke to the senior pastor. And, of course, selflessly he helped, not minding that the two of them who came to him were not even members of his church.

I: Wow.

R: He helped and solved the problem for them. And the church member that left and his friend that he met both returned to the church.

I: Wow.

R: Because, you know, according to him, he said, "If not being a member of his church he can put himself out so much for us, how much more would he do for members of the church?" And they returned. And not only did they return, they brought a lot of their friends, because they were students in *uni* back then. They brought a lot of their friends, you know, to church by word of mouth; "Oh, do you know the pastor did this? The pastor. . . ." "Oh, yeah, I would like to be part of that." You know, so, a lot of them came to the church. And that is how, you know, the church grew.

I: Thank you for sharing that and the experience that you also added. Of course, it is obvious that from what you shared that the pastor has a critical role to play in the church growth agenda and the members also as you have shared have their own parts to play as well.

R: Exactly.

I: That's a big one. Thank you. So, what challenges do you think the church has faced in its effort, in its agenda for church growth?

R: For my church, the major challenge has been. . . . It's unfortunate that I have to say this, but it's the truth and I am going to say it. The major challenge for church growth for my church has been defamation of character.

I: Hmm.

R: I will explain this. When people have left the church for whatever reason, then they go out, they start to talk bad about the church. So much so that people who don't even know the pastor would start talking; oh, such and such, you know, did this and, you know. . . . Sometimes they even say it to the presence of the pastor. And you would ask, "Oh, do you know this person?" "No, I don't know him oh." But such a person that has heard that bad report would never – well, don't let me use the word never – would hardly come to join the church.

I: Hmm. [Laughs]. That's logical.

R: Would hardly come to join the church, because the person's mind has already been biased. And only by the grace of God, only by the grace of God would such a person join the church if God is adding that person to the church. You know, there is a place where God plant you. You cannot carry a cheque for HSBC and go and line up at Halifax and expect to cash it. If the place God is planting you is this church that you have heard bad things about and because of the bad things you have heard about the church you are not where God have planted you, you will struggle to make it. That is my own conviction. And I see it in a lot of the people I have had contact with over the years who have left the church. There is a particular brother that anytime I see him it always grieves my heart. And I always tell him, "You are not where God planted you." Because, I know, and he knows. He always . . . Anytime I say it, he goes, "Yes, eh, but. . . ." You know, he would always have an excuse. I will say, "You are not where God planted you." You know where God planted you and you left the place because of animosity, because of what people said and all that. And this is a very, very big problem for my church, for church growth because a lot of things has been said that are not true. That, you know, when people were part of the church, they champion the course of the church; but for whatever reason when they leave, why do they have to deride and bring down the church and prevent others from coming to where God is planting them? That is a very, very big thing with church growth. I don't know if it happens in other churches as it does in mine. But I wouldn't be surprised if it does. And maybe that is why, you know, our churches are not growing the way they should. I don't know. It could be.

I: Hmm. Of course. Of course. So, what other issues do you think are impacting upon the growth of your church?

R: The growth of my church?

I: Yeah, where you worship, in your setting, what other issues are impacting upon the growth of the church in your settings? Yeah, where you worship.

R: Where I worship?

I: Yeah, you have mentioned defamation of character, right? That it is big on the growth of the church. Is there any other issue?

R: The other thing I will point out is members being preoccupied with work and not doing the work of evangelism as we should. For instance, I will be the first one to hold my hand up to say, I hardly, hardly do evangelism. I do pray, but praying, praying for people to become part of the church is different but going out and bringing them. I do nights. I come back from work; I sleep to recover for the next round of night. And the only people I see myself being exposed to are my work colleagues who don't even live within the vicinity of the church. So, getting them to come to church to become members of the church is almost impossible. And they are the only ones I am exposed to.

They are the only ones I am in contact with. So, I find that over the years I personally, I have not been able to bring anybody into the church, because I hardly ... I don't have time to go, you know, to go out and talk to people on the street. And if that happens to me, I guess it will happen to all other members as well. We are all so busy. We are all so busy getting shaped, doing work to pay our bills and do all the things we need money for. Only God will help us. [Laughs].

I: Amen. [Laughs].

R: [Laughs].

I: [Laughs]. Thank you. So, by and large, what do you think is the future of African churches in Liverpool?

R: African churches in Liverpool? One other thing, sorry, maybe I ... You know, sorry to take you back.

I: It's alright.

R: One other thing that I see that is affecting church growth is that our children once they have grown to the level where they leave home or, you know, they ... yeah, when they ... I put it like, oh, they've flown the nest, you know, they have left the nest, they are now on their own, they hardly, hardly, hardly come back to that church. For instance, personally, my own children, I have two children; one lived away in London, the other one live here in Liverpool. But he doesn't see my church as his church.

I: Hmm.

R: If I say, "Oh, won't you come to church?" He will say, "Oh, it's your church, it is not my church."

I: Wow. Do you think.... [Chuckles]. Is there any reason behind that, why they don't want to identify with the African church here?

R: Well, I mean, he grew up in the church. But then, he grew up, got married, had his home. Fair enough, you know, where his home is it's not close to the church. He lives in Crosby; the church is in Liverpool. But I know that if he wants to, he can still attend at least occasionally. But if I say, "Oh, you are not even coming to church." He will say, "Oh, that's your church." He doesn't see it as his church.

I: [Laughs]. Do you think it has to do with the way ...

R: And I know that a lot of our children feels that way; "Oh, that's mum's church, that's dad's church."

I: Hmm. Do you think it has to do with the way we do church?

R: And when they grow, they just go out of the church. If our children are not coming to church, it means they are not bringing their mates, their colleagues to church.

I: Hmm. That's right.

R: And that is one of the things that caused the death of the British churches.

I: Hmm.

R: And except God helps us, I see it happening to our churches as well. I am in my late sixties. And if my children are not coming to church, it means over time as people grow older and God calls us home, who is going to continue the church? Because, our children don't see this church as their church, they see it as their parents church.

I: Hmm. Could it be because the church looks alien to them? Is it because of the way we do church or what?

R: We were brought up in Nigeria; we are used to just that pattern of worship. They are not. A lot of them were brought up here; they don't have the same orientation as we have. Our orientation is purely African. Anything I am thinking of I always first of all think of it in terms of African culture. They don't. Their line of reasoning is very British, not African. We see – I mean, my mum's church was my church. There was no other way to think of it. Until I left Nigeria, anytime I was there, my mum's church was my church. Which other church would you say you have?

I: [Laughs].

R: Your mum's church is your church; you grew up there. But that to them is African way of thinking. And because they were brought up here, the culture they are exposed to is, um, should I say an independent culture? You know, they are very independent of us the parents. And that is a very big issue. It is a very big issue in the growth of the African church. And if we don't address it . . . hmm. I can point to one, two, three members of this our church now that are in the same age range as me whose children don't come to church. So, I am not the only one. We are all in the same age range, in our sixties, and our children don't come to church. As others grow to that age range as well and their children stop coming to church, who is going to carry on the church?

I: That's a huge challenge for the African churches. Hmm. That's a huge one. Thank you. Thank you for laying that on the table. So, finally, do you have an idea of the number of African churches we have in Liverpool now?

R: I don't. I know of a few. I know we have different branches of Redeemed, we have Deeper Life, we have Winners Chapel, which in all the years I have spent in Liverpool I can't even tell you where they worship. That is to tell you how tunnel vision that I am. [Laughs].

I: [Laughs].

R: I know we have, you know, those churches. And I couldn't tell you... I know we have Alive Believers just down the road from us here. But I couldn't tell you how many African churches we have. I know there are quite a few. Because, the populations of Africans in Liverpool in the last, is it twenty years I have been here, has grown tremendously. And, you know, we have quite a few African churches around. But I cannot tell you the population.

I: Alright.

R: I know we have Congolese churches; we have Ghanaian churches; we have Nigerian oriented churches. When I say Nigerian oriented, it is not a purely Nigerian congregation; you have some Ghanaians. Like my church, for instance, we call it a church for all nations; because, we have people from different African countries worshiping there more. But we do have some that are purely Congolese church or Ghanaian church and, you know, things like that. But we are all African churches, and we meet spiritual needs of people. [Laughs].

I: Alright. OK, thank you. Actually, that brings us, that last comment brings us to the end of the interview. But if you have any other comment to pass, any input to add concerning this research, feel free to comment.

R: Yeah, the last point I brought up about our children has been something that I have been worrying about and praying about. It worries me a lot. If myself as a leader in the church, and I don't take that lightly, I don't take it for granted, and I mean, not going to church on a Sunday to me was like my right hand was paralyzed. Most times I come back from work, and I just have a shower, get dressed and go to church. Even my place of work, they know that, oh you have to go to church. I have to go to church. If they have to... It is one of the two 'have to' that I have in my life; I don't have many. I have to go to church, I have to be in tune with my God, and I have to go to work. Those are the only two 'have to'. Any other thing, there is no 'have to'. But if me with that orientation, with that conviction cannot even get my children to come to church, how much more people that are not as committed as me?

I: Hmm...

R: And that . . . In fact, in the last one year that has bothered me a lot. And I have been praying about it. It's you know . . . In fact, this is the first time I am talking about it to anybody. But it is something that has bothered me a lot and which I have been seeking the face of God for. Because, I know that that was what caused the death, and I used the word death in quote, of British churches. Because, it got to a stage where all their children were not going to church. It was just the old ones that were going to church. And they were dying off, dying off. And when they all died, the church became empty and were taken over. The church buildings were taken over. Some were made into restaurants, some were made into hostels, some were taken over by Muslims, some by Buddhist and all that. So, what is going to happen to us if we go down that path? We need to do something about it now.

I: Hmm. That's right. That's right. Thank you for sharing that concern. And I hope that this work in some ways would be able to help the church leaders, missionaries, and all Africans to be able to do missions better and be able to reach out to the younger generations also.

R: Amen.

I: So that the future of the African church in Liverpool and in the UK will be very bright. Thank you for sharing that concern. And that brings us to the end of the interview.

R: You are welcome.

I: Thank you for your voluntary participation.

R: You are welcome.

I: And for engaging with the questions.

R: You are welcome. I wish you all the best in your work.

I: Amen. Amen. Thank you. Thank you so much.

R: Yeah, and your future endeavour.

I: Amen.

R: Thank you.

I: Thank you.

R: Thanks for the privilege of having me.

I: You're welcome. Thank you so much.

R: [Laughs].

[End of Audio 00:27:41]

Langham Literature, with its publishing work, is a ministry of Langham Partnership.

Langham Partnership is a global fellowship working in pursuit of the vision God entrusted to its founder John Stott –

> *to facilitate the growth of the church in maturity and Christ-likeness through raising the standards of biblical preaching and teaching.*

Our vision is to see churches in the Majority World equipped for mission and growing to maturity in Christ through the ministry of pastors and leaders who believe, teach and live by the word of God.

Our mission is to strengthen the ministry of the word of God through:
- nurturing national movements for biblical preaching
- fostering the creation and distribution of evangelical literature
- enhancing evangelical theological education

especially in countries where churches are under-resourced.

Our ministry

Langham Preaching partners with national leaders to nurture indigenous biblical preaching movements for pastors and lay preachers all around the world. With the support of a team of trainers from many countries, a multi-level programme of seminars provides practical training, and is followed by a programme for training local facilitators. Local preachers' groups and national and regional networks ensure continuity and ongoing development, seeking to build vigorous movements committed to Bible exposition.

Langham Literature provides Majority World preachers, scholars and seminary libraries with evangelical books and electronic resources through publishing and distribution, grants and discounts. The programme also fosters the creation of indigenous evangelical books in many languages, through writer's grants, strengthening local evangelical publishing houses, and investment in major regional literature projects, such as one volume Bible commentaries like the Africa Bible Commentary and the South Asia Bible Commentary.

Langham Scholars provides financial support for evangelical doctoral students from the Majority World so that, when they return home, they may train pastors and other Christian leaders with sound, biblical and theological teaching. This programme equips those who equip others. Langham Scholars also works in partnership with Majority World seminaries in strengthening evangelical theological education. A growing number of Langham Scholars study in high quality doctoral programmes in the Majority World itself. As well as teaching the next generation of pastors, graduated Langham Scholars exercise significant influence through their writing and leadership.

To learn more about Langham Partnership and the work we do visit langham.org

www.ingramcontent.com/pod-product-compliance
Lightning Source LLC
Chambersburg PA
CBHW070234240426
43673CB00044B/1790